# TALES OF A WILD DOG

## MEMOIRS OF A ROCK WARRIOR

### CARL CANEDY

#### WITH PHILLIP HARRINGTON

NEW HAVEN PUBLISHING

Published 2024
NEW HAVEN PUBLISHING LTD
www.newhavenpublishingltd.com
newhavenpublishing@gmail.com

All Rights Reserved
The rights of Carl Canedy with Phillip Harrington, as the authors of this work, have been asserted in accordance with the Copyrights, Designs and Patents Act 1988.

All rights reserved. No part of this book may be re-printed or reproduced or utilized in any form or by any electronic, mechanical or other means, now unknown or hereafter invented, including photocopying, and recording, or in any information storage or retrieval system, without the written permission of the Author and Publisher.

Cover Photo© Carl Canedy
Cover Design ©Eric Philippe

Copyright © 2024
All rights reserved © Carl Canedy with Phillip Harrington
ISBN: 978-1-949515-68-8

*To my wife, Dianne, who has been there since day one. For being there through all the craziness, the random tours, the relentless drumming, and the countless bands. For always having my back.*

*To my daughter, Erin Alexandra Canedy-Hunter, for truly grasping the concept of "rock until you drop." For urging me to follow my passion and for convincing me to keep going.*

*To my brother Frank, for his love and kindness.*

*To Hank McBride, for the words of wisdom that led to the accomplishments here within.*

*To David "Rock" Feinstein, for the brotherhood, and for the ongoing voyage.*

*And to the legendary Jonny Zazula: a friend, a mentor, a brother. Who was always kind, positive, and helpful. For being such a great support system and a great friend.*

# Content

Preface by Martin Popoff .................................................. 6
Some Friends .................................................................. 8
Foreword by Erin Canedy-Hunter ...................................... 14

Rough Start ..................................................................... 17
Red Drums and a Tank .................................................... 26
A Charmed Life ............................................................... 29
Jim Nunis ........................................................................ 31
On the Road ................................................................... 37
The Annual Half-A-Beer .................................................. 40
Kelakos ........................................................................... 42
The Brotherhood Begins .................................................. 47
The Music Man ............................................................... 53
Paying Our Dues ............................................................. 56
Two Inches of Hard Rock & Roll ..................................... 59
Bad Advice ..................................................................... 63
Manowar ........................................................................ 66
Getting Higher ................................................................ 69
Arista .............................................................................. 72
Wild Dogs ....................................................................... 75
Elf & Ronnie James Dio .................................................. 84
Wild Dogs Tour ............................................................... 87
In the Raw ...................................................................... 91
Metallica and Jonny Z .................................................... 104
The Rock & Roll Hotel .................................................. 106
Live ............................................................................... 110
Anthrax: Fistful of Metal ............................................... 114
Let Them Eat Metal ...................................................... 122
Exciter: Violence and Force .......................................... 125
Helstar: Burning Star .................................................... 128
Jack Star: Out of the Darkness ..................................... 131
Rhett Forrester: Gone with the Wind ............................ 137
Anthrax: Armed and Dangerous .................................... 142
TT Quick ....................................................................... 146
Overkill: Feel the Fire ................................................... 149
Life in the Mid-80s ....................................................... 152
Blue Cheer: The Beast is Back ...................................... 155

| | |
|---|---|
| Anthrax: Spreading the Disease | 159 |
| Thrasher | 163 |
| Attila: Rolling Thunder | 168 |
| Hollywood | 171 |
| Heavier Than Thou | 176 |
| Possessed: Beyond the Gates | 179 |
| Roxx Gang: Love 'Em And Leave 'Em | 183 |
| E-X-E; Stricken By Might | 192 |
| Apollo Ra: Ra Pariah | 197 |
| Dianne | 202 |
| Becoming Erin's Dad | 209 |
| Neon City | 213 |
| Young Turk | 219 |
| Rockin' N Rollin' Again (Almost) | 241 |
| Vengeance | 246 |
| Canedy: Headbanger | 257 |
| Brotherhood of Metal | 263 |
| Canedy: Warrior | 269 |
| Wild Dogs: 40 Years On | 273 |
| Surprise! | 275 |
| | |
| Epilogue: Dear Diary; 70 Years On | 280 |
| | |
| Photo Gallery | 281 |

# Preface

Welcome one and all to Carl's remarkable, insider, boots-on-the-ground memoir of a metal time long ago, but still burning hot in the force of nature that is Carl "The Sacred One" Canedy.

I can't say I was there for the original *Rock Hard* debut in 1980, but as soon as I saw the front cover of the reissued version of the album in 1981, now re-christened *The Rods*, I snapped it up, only to find that, alas, there was indeed some grinding, churning heavy metal coming out of America in the low '80s. To be sure, the New Wave of British Heavy Metal was ablaze, but outside of Van Halen, Gamma, Sammy Hagar and, more Rods-adjacent, Riot, there wasn't much going on in America or, for that matter, my country of Canada.

As for that cover, man, Carl looked badass, as did Gary and Rock, and the music enclosed did not disappoint, sounding like an upgrade on The Godz from Ohio and The Boyzz from Illinois. Next came the band's near masterpiece *Wild Dogs*, and The Rods were laying the foundation for that whole Shrapnel and Megaforce world, in which Canedy would participate well beyond his core band. To be sure, The Rods would be joined by another upstate New York band in Manowar, and Megaforce and Shrapnel would see kinship in Metal Blade Records, but it is The Rods, and specifically Carl, that would anchor the scene.

And why Carl? Well, as you'll read throughout this book, he was a musicologist of all things metal, a galvanizer on the social scene, as well as on the ground with the likes of Metallica, who picked up a thing or two from the first two Rods albums and the band's take-no-prisoners live shows. And then Carl would serve as one of the US metal scene's consummate early-days producers. He made the classic Rods catalogue sound expensive but still bold and gritty, but he'd also apply his skills to the likes of Exciter, Helstar, Overkill and Possessed. Most historically potent of the lot was Anthrax, with Canedy having produced the *Fistful of Metal* debut as well as the band's 1985 masterwork *Spreading the Disease*. In fact, look for Joey Belladonna, in the pages that follow, to explain that Carl even had important things to say about how to arrange and record vocals.

And you know, back to The Rods, he's writing, he's singing and, like I say, he's producing. He's basically being the mover-and-shaker he still is today into his seventh decade, still flying the flag for metal through The

Rods and myriad side-projects, still with irons in the fire in music and beyond. Now you get to find out, often from first-hand storytelling from most of the golden-era New York metal scene, just how important Carl was to all of these rockers as they jockeyed for positions in bands up and down the state. Carl and his writer buddy Phillip Harrington have far exceeded expectations on painting vividly and with meticulous detail this vibrant scene, and, most boldly, Canedy's pressure point place within it.

Martin Popoff
Toronto, ON
10/05/2023

# Some Friends

**Andy Hilfiger;** *Fashion Executive*
"I was a bit younger than Carl - he was good friends with my brothers, so I have known him from a young age. I always looked up to him. Not only is he an amazing drummer but he is such a great, humble person. He never forgot where he came from. That period (early 1980s) was a great time for music - there were always great bands playing. We were all in bands. There were a lot of great musicians in the area, and Carl was one of the first to make it. I remember Carl when he was in Kelakos, which was before heavy metal became a thing. Everything was categorized as 'rock.' And we were there to witness the transformation - the development of the heavy metal scene. And Carl really helped pioneer that transition. He really led the pack. He was a pioneer. He inspired us to do the same. In fact, in '83, my band was able to open for The Rods. What an experience that was."

**Mark Strigl;** *Founder, Former Producer and Host of the Talking Metal Podcast, Current Host of SiriusXM's Ozzy's Boneyard and HairNation*
"Now The Rods were an important force, but the things Carl touched as a producer - and being in the studio for literally ground zero of extreme metal - are why I feel Carl is so important to the history of heavy metal. Carl was there for not just one release, but many. Like Possessed. Where would heavy metal be without a band like Possessed, right? I consider Possessed to be possibly the first death metal band. When you listen to the album Beyond the Gates that Carl did with them and how extreme that is - that was so revolutionary. And then there is Anthrax. Anthrax's Scott Ian, in his autobiography, wrote about Anthrax going into the studio with Eddie Kramer - and Eddie just didn't get it. He wanted to add reverb because Hysteria (Def Leopard) had just come out and he thought that that's how Anthrax should sound. Carl is the guy that DID get it. When you look at Spreading the Disease, that sound is what we know and love to this day. A sound that expanded the boundaries of heavy metal and became thrash with that opening cut AIR. That's the beginning of Anthrax as we know it right there. That was a new area for the genre. It wasn't what Metallica or Slayer had done at that point. This was a new sound. And then we should talk about Exciter's Violence and Force. It was a great release that was just so powerful and so extreme for those times. When I heard the title track, that was like nothing I'd ever heard. And then there is Overkill's Feel the Fire. That is four bands that truly were important in pushing the genre forward. And it's not a coincidence that Carl was there for all of those. Giving them

*the confidence, giving them the approval to push ahead with this new sound. A lot of producers wouldn't have done this. They would have said, 'No, we got to listen to what's going on in the charts now.' That wasn't what he was about. And I think that just speaks volumes to who he is as a person. He's somebody who was able to help these bands do something that, in my opinion, had never been done before. Fearless in the studio. I think that's really important to remember because so many people are scared of the unknown. And he went to the unknown."*

**Jeff Plate;** *Ex-Savatage, Ex-Metal Church, Trans-Siberian Orchestra, Alta-Reign*

"When I was 17, I hooked up with a local guitarist who was a bit older. He was familiar with the scene and the club circuit - everything that was going on around here (upstate NY). He turned me on to The Rods. He said, 'You got to go check out this band!' This was like 1979 or 1980, somewhere during that time. There was such an active live-music scene around here. I mean, there were cover bands all over the place - there was every kind of band you could think of. There was always something going on. It was a lot of fun. I remember going to see The Rods - and I believe it was at a club in Elmira, New York. And I was completely blown away. Carl was a beast behind the drum kit. The Rods were a hard rock metal band. They had a bunch of original songs, but they were doing a lot of AC/DC and heavier-style rock. They were loud as hell. They were all dressed in black. They all had long hair, cut-off jean jackets and that kind of thing. I mean, I was 17 years old, and drumming was my thing. And I was just really starting to come into my own with this. And when I saw Carl, I was just completely blown away. He was just so good behind the drum kit and then he would do a solo. God knows how long it was, but it was a showstopper every time.

When you're young and you see a band like this, you are kind of almost afraid to approach them because they were like big rock stars - they're gods up there (on the stage). I remember approaching Carl one time and I most likely had a few drinks in me, just to get the courage to go up and talk to him and compliment him. He was the nicest guy. It was exactly the opposite of what I was watching on stage. When Carl was behind the drum kit, he was one thing. And when he came off stage and was talking with people, he was soft-spoken and a super nice guy. He was listening to every word you said, and he was really engaged. He was not just blowing people off. And it just really struck me how he carried himself. The Rods played this area a lot. Back then, I would go see The Rods whenever I could. And then Carl and I talked a bit during those gigs. I used Carl as a template for myself and my drumming. I loved his style, I loved his power, and I loved his aggressive approach. Even to this day, I still think of Carl and the early days. I remember one of the first times I talked to him: I finally got the courage to ask him for drum lessons. And he was like, 'Well, I am really not teaching right now. But if you would like, I could give you a call sometime. And we could talk about technique.' So, I gave him my number.

And sure enough, he called me one night. We just talked on the phone and that made a huge impact on me. Here is this guy that I was looking up to - he was an inspiration. He was my idol. He was like, this drum God. And here is little me. Carl was on the other end of the phone, just answering my questions. This really gave me a cool perspective. It put me in a different place as far as how to conduct myself. I always appreciated that. He did not come off the stage and strut around and act like he was the shit, you know? I mean he really was the shit. But he did not carry himself like that at all. That made such an impact on me. It taught me that you must be humble. When he was off stage, he was Carl Canedy - just one of the one of the nicest, most genuine people you were ever going to meet."

**Bob Aquaviva;** *Recording Professional, Songwriter, Industry Manager*
"Now at that time, there was a lot of competition with the local bands. Fierce competition, but it was friendly. To have Carl in your corner certainly elevated a band. The Rods were local legends. And of course, he had just produced some really big albums. So to get Carl for a project was a big deal. He was very positive in the studio, but he was very demanding. He beat the snot out of some of those guys.

**Alex Perialas;** *Audio Engineer, Mixer, Producer and Associate Professor Emeritus: Music Performance of Ithaca College*
"Pyramid Sound was a studio that was started by my father and two other people. My dad was in the music business from 1959, until basically the late 90s early 2000s. I started working there when I was 16 years old, basically. And I was in high school, and I sort of worked my way through the ranks. I'd known Carl for a long time prior to the recording of Anthrax. I had done some other projects with Carl. I made one of Carl's very first recordings with the band Kelakos. That's how I met Carl - I recorded that project with them. There were a lot of strong personalities in that band, and they were all very musical. They were close friends – almost like brothers, and they would scrap with each other. Not necessarily, but the two guitarists tended to butt heads a bit. They were all really smart. So, you got a bunch of smart people that are musical and there was tension in that project – but it wasn't horrible by any means. I enjoyed it.

"Now, Kill Em' All was recorded at Music America. And Paul Curcio was the producer, and Chris (Bubacz) was the engineer on that project. So, the next band that was slotted to go into the studio for Megaforce was

Anthrax. And they were going to go there (Music America). Carl was going to do the record, and Carl was going to do the record in Rochester. Curcio was supposed to be getting new equipment, because after the Metallica project, he planned on upgrading equipment. So, Anthrax got there, and there was no gear. And the gear was supposed to be there, but didn't arrive on day one, day two, or day three. So, then Carl reached out to me. Scott and Charlie came to Ithaca. I played them some stuff that I had been working on with a band from Binghamton, New York – it had heavy guitars, and vocally, it was very Mercyful Fate-ish. The drums were Rush-like. It was kind of a progressive metal project. They (Anthrax) called Jonny and Jonny said, 'Okay, if you want to do it there, we'll do it there.' And then my dad drove to New York and met Johnny Z. They had a conversation because in that era Jonny didn't have a lot of money. And on a handshake, they made a deal! So, a handshake deal that lasted for our entire career together. With Carl and his crew, there was never a problem. We always got along fine.

We understood each other. The bands? They were all very serious. They were all young, but they had business minds - including Anthrax and Overkill. You know, those guys were all business - always. There were a bunch of smaller bands that we did together. Some didn't necessarily get notoriety, but they made pretty good records. They might not have been quite as prepared. But when it came to the A-listers, they, there was no messing around, you know, they were all, they were there for one reason – and that was to make a great record."

**Joe Van Audenhove;** *Evil Invaders*
"Once I discovered The Rods, those wild dogs made a big impression! The artwork of Wild Dogs, with the 3-headed dog, is still one of my favorite album covers. The raw guitar sound and the badass songs on that album would drive any real hard rock fan batshit crazy. I remember seeing them live in 2009 at the Headbangers Open Air in Germany. I was blown away by their performance. It was rock and roll to the fucking bone! Rock and Gary were playing back-to-back, then they went all the way down to the floor and came back up while still playing. I'm very grateful to have had the chance see them perform back then, and then again a few years later in Belgium at the Graspop Metal Meeting. Their style and attitude have definitely had an influence on me as a musician."

**Billy Sheehan;** *Talas, David Lee Roth Band, Niacin, Winery Dogs, Sons of Apollo*
"The Thrasher record was one of my very first recording experiences – and I'm glad Carl was there. Not only were there rock-solid drum parts for me to lock on to, but he was a joy to work with. I've carried my experience

*from those sessions through the decades and they have served me well. I very much appreciate Carl reaching out to me, to play on that record."*

**Mark Tornillo**; *TT Quick, Accept*
"I've known Carl since 1983 when he produced our TT Quick EP for Megaforce Records. He is a consummate professional, an excellent songwriter, drummer, and producer. I am sure he will be an excellent author as well. I'm proud to call him a friend."

**Joe Bouchard**; *Blue Oyster Cult*
"Overall, I'd say upstate NY bands were better rehearsed and played their parts cleaner, but that's just a random observation, not really a great survey of the scene. I know with Blue Öyster Cult, we strived to keep the musicality on the highest level, and we slowly moved up the ladder. I remember a great gig at the Dome at the Murray Athletic Center in Elmira. I didn't know The Rods before that show, and I missed The Rods' opening set. Years later when I was talking to friends in the area they would often relate about how awesome that gig was. Billy Hilfiger, an Elmira native who played in my band The Cult Brothers for years, told me about Carl many times. Carl was frequently mentioned as a great drummer and a good person to know."

**Giles Lavery;** *Warlord, GLM Artists, Dragonsclaw, BraveWords Records*
"Working with Carl has been a fantastic experience. The amount of rock and metal history that he is associated with is quite remarkable! When you talk to him and put it all together – that here are many bands that he has produced, recorded, worked with and played with, and the people that he is otherwise connected with. He is a bit like a heavy metal Kevin Bacon, everything can seemingly be linked to Carl Canedy! He was even the first drummer with Manowar. To work with him is great. He is a very humble and down to earth guy, who understands how things worked then and how things work now. It's not the same business in 2024 as it was in 1984 - and he fully comprehends that we need to take a different approach these days to get to the finish line, whereas some guys are still stuck in the old, outdated mindset and can't get out of their own way because of that... but not Carl. Truly a pleasure."

**Phillip Harrington;** *Co-author, Fan, Civilian*
"When starting this project, I knew what I was getting into. Because, first and foremost, I was a fan. Carl has done a LOT in the past 50 years. Illustrious, eminent, and acclaimed are all fitting adjectives to describe his vast body of work. He has performed on more than 26 studio albums, and

he is credited with production on more than 59 albums. So, that's a lot to unpack. That's a lot of material to write about. But what I did not expect was to come out of this project as a fan of Carl, for who he is as a person. He has become my role model and has truly affected my life in a positive manner. When soliciting commentary, almost every person had the same thing to say: 'Carl is such a great guy! He is very humble.' Well, they were not bullshitting me. He is the real deal. He is a genuinely great guy who has done so much for the metal genre. And he has an amazing story!"

**Fred Coury;** *Cinderella*
"I would see them (The Rods) perform all the time. I was young - maybe 16 or so. They often played at a club in Binghamton called Popeyes. The Rods were untouchable at the time. I even saw them opening for Blue Oyster Cult, at the Broome County Arena. I remember watching Carl - he had a Fibes kit, and it was chrome. That's the first time I'd seen anything like that. He was like the first rock star that I had ever met. The one thing about Carl is that he has never changed. I was a super fan, and he had given me a pair of sticks back then. And to me at the time, that was the biggest thing. Watching Carl play was definitely a big part of my formative drumming years. I am still a fan. Everything that he does is great. And the first Rods record? Nothing's going to touch it. It was absolutely incredible."

**Ron Wray;** *Rock Historian, Upstate, NY Musicologist*
"Now, Carl is an interesting story because he is a performer, a great songwriter, a producer, and an engineer. But if you watched Carl play, he really has a love and a passion for drumming, I mean, he is just incredible. I remember a few years ago when we put David Feinstein in the Syracuse Hall of Fame and The Rods played. And I took my son Jeff with me. He was in his late 30s at the time. During their performance, he turned around and said to me, 'Dad, who plays like that? That guy's a beast.' And he was talking, of course, about Carl. And he's seen some good people in his time. Carl is, to me, one of the great drummers I have ever seen in my lifetime. You know, forget he's from this area. I'm talking about worldwide great drummers. I really love his passion and watching him perform. When you leave a Rods show, you always get your money's worth."

## Foreword by Erin Canedy Hunter

From an early age, I watched my father practice, perform and work with so many amazing musicians. I grew up around music – it was the world that I was raised in. When I was a toddler, my mother worked full-time. My father's studio was 10 minutes or so from the house, so my dad took care of me while Mom was at work. I was with my dad most of the time. Mom often tells me about these macho, rugged rockers coming into the studio – real tough, intimidating-looking guys. And they would all take turns holding me and feeding me. That was my childhood environment. It was not until I was much older that I realized how unique that was – and eventually how inspirational my father was in the rock world. Initially, I was perplexed when people started telling me how musically influential my dad was to them. To me, he had always been "Dad." And as a father, he was always there for me. He performed that role perfectly. He was the only male homeroom parent at my school. He participated in all of my school events. You really did not see that participation from a lot of the fathers. It was my dad and the mothers at the events. He was always there. He was invested. If someone asked him his title, he always referred to himself as "Erin's Dad" – and he followed up regularly with "It is the best title I have ever had." He has always been very humble and focused on his role as a father. So I never really knew of his accomplishments until I was much older. And I could not be prouder. His ambition has never ceased to amaze me. It is one of the many things I admire most about him. I always knew he was special. As a father he was unique. As teens, my friends always seemed to be embarrassed of their fathers. Most of my peers did not seem to have a good relationship with their fathers. But my father was always cool. As a dad and as a musician. At 32, I can fondly look back and know that he did not miss a moment in my life. He really is a different breed of musician. The type who is humble, kind, and driven – and does it without knocking anyone else down. I have heard many stories about his professional life, but that only skims the surface of his personal life, of his childhood and of his adventures as a father. Now, after many years of playing gigs, writing music, and traveling the road, he is ready to sit down and tell the tales. These are the stories that need to be told. Some have been shared in small circles amongst his family and friends. Some he has never shared before, except with his bandmates or family members. Now he gets to share them with fans from all over the world. My dad has always been my hero, and even more so as I have gotten older and realized what he sacrificed. I hope that everyone can see the man that I see when I look at my father, and I hope you will enjoy reading about the legacy that he has created.

*"In my life, I love you more."*
With all my love and gratitude,
Your Daughter, Erin.

# Rough Start

My earliest memory was at the age of three and a half. It was 1956, and my parents owned a small apartment house located in Elmira, New York. The apartment house held seven rental units. A couple of the rental units were actually single rooms which shared a bathroom. We lived in one of those small rooms situated at the back of the apartment house. My very first memory is of my parents fighting in the hallway that led to the shared bathroom. I was standing in between them, pounding on each of their stomachs. They were screaming at each other, and I was desperately trying to get them to stop. I had no clue what was going on. I was only three and a half and it was absolutely terrifying. Later, when I was in my early 20s, I mentioned it to my mother. She looked shocked when I told her of that memory. She denied it repeatedly. She said, "Carl, there is no way you could remember that." I insisted that I absolutely did remember. We went round and round for a bit, and then she finally admitted that, yes, it actually happened. She confirmed it. I do not recall how I felt about having that memory confirmed, but in my mind, it was very real, and it was very present.

A year or so after the big argument, I recall riding in the car with my parents. I was sitting in between them – with no seatbelt, of course (this was long before child seats were a thing). We were driving towards where my grandparents lived, which was in Waverly, New York. Neither of my parents told me where we were going. I remember my father being incredibly sweet. I don't remember my mother's mood at all, but I do remember my father being very nice. We finally ended up in Sayre, PA. My parents then took me into an unfamiliar house and there I was introduced to the residents, a middle-aged couple, who were also very unfamiliar. I did not say anything – I just stood there, not really sure what was going on. I remember my parents giving the couple a quart of milk and some money. My parents said goodbye, and that was it. Just like that, my parents were gone. And unbeknownst to me, this was to be my primary residence for almost a full year. My first night there, the couple took me to a room which held a bed with a terrifying mattress. The mattress had springs underneath it – it was not a box spring, just a mattress with springs beneath. Laying on the mattress, the slightest movement led to a horrific noise in response. I remember feeling each spring moving against my back, and because of that, I was certain that there was a monster underneath the bed. I was unable to sleep that night. I was scared. I was confused and I was lonely. When I was dropped off that day, I had an overwhelming feeling of abandonment, although I was not yet old enough to put words to those feelings. I do not remember much about the next morning, other than the lady telling me, "Go down the street and there's the school." So I walked down the street by myself. And that's how I started my very first day of kindergarten. To add insult to injury, what felt natural to me was recognized as 'left-handedness'. The teacher insisted I write only right-handed. It was one more piece that made me feel isolated, abandoned and like the "moron" that my cousin Rita repeatedly called me.

I ended up staying with the couple for the entire school year. I did not have any friends in the area, and it was a terribly lonely year. Now, don't get me wrong... the couple were very nice to me, but they certainly were not invested in my upbringing. They did not spank me, and they did not yell at me, but they pretty much left me alone to my own devices. At this point, Mom and Dad had split up, which was the catalyst for me staying in Sayre. Mom lived with Grandma in Waverly, NY, which was about a five-minute cab ride away. I later found out that, in Pennsylvania, you only need to be four and a half to start school – and in New York, you need to be five years old. My parents figured that if I was enrolled in school during the day, then it would be less of a hassle for everyone while they sorted out their separation.

The people I lived with owned a diner in downtown Sayre. They were older – old enough to have a 20-year-old daughter. Sadly, I can't remember their names. That is not surprising, as I had almost no true interaction with them. I was pretty much left on my own. The biggest takeaway from the experience, other than rejection and loneliness, was that the lady loved to clean with bleach. One day while they were cooking cabbage, I was stuck in the house. It seemed as if they had doused the house in bleach. I was afraid to say anything, so I sat there. After a few hours, I threw up because I was so sick from smelling the mixture of bleach and cabbage. To this very day, I still have a problem with the smell of bleach. To some, bleach is the scent of cleanliness. For me, it is the memory of being trapped with the overwhelming stench of cabbage and bleach.

I later discovered that my distant relatives, Uncle Sebastian and Aunt Antoinette, lived around the corner. I did not know this for quite some time. Eventually I would come to visit them on occasion. They were a bright light in my dreary little start on life. I clearly remember they had a wood burning stove that they used to bake and cook on. Sometimes Aunt Antoinette would make these huge sandwiches for Uncle Sebastian. Scrambled eggs on homemade bread. She would send me off to the foundry just down the road, where Uncle Sebastian worked, with several of these huge sandwiches. They both seemed very old at the time, and I believe they both passed away before I was seven.

Each Friday, the couple would put me in a cab and send me to my grandmother's house in South Waverly. Once at Grandma's, Mom would take me downtown and buy me a toy. I stayed with Mom until Sunday evening, and then Mom would put me in a cab and send me back to the couple's house.

Throughout much of my adult life, Sunday would come and I would get very depressed. I would feel very down. It was very sudden. It was always Sunday afternoon or Sunday evening when it would hit, and I never really understood why. One day, I was talking to a therapist, and I came upon the fact that every Sunday night, I was put in a cab and sent home. I spent five days a week with people I did not really know. I wouldn't see my mother for five days, let alone my father - who knew when I would see my father? But for five days I was without my mother, so those Sunday nights were really depressing. I figured it out and it kind of dissipated after I put the two pieces of the puzzle together.

During my weekend visits, Grandma would continuously make nasty comments about my father. For some reason, Grandma really disliked my father, and I really was not sure why. He was always very kind and loving to me. Which was the opposite of how the majority of my extended family members treated me. They tended to treat me as a pariah, as a bastard son, who was a drain on Mom. I could never understand why, but even as a child, it was very evident, and it was an incredibly difficult time. It would take over 60 years for me to find out why they treated me differently.

On weekends, when I would visit Mom at Grandma's house, I found a safe haven with the next-door neighbors – an African-American couple with the last name of Griffin. Each weekend, I would go see Mrs. Griffin and she was so sweet to me. Her husband was a bit of a curmudgeon, and a bit gruff, but he still tolerated me. They had a piano and Mrs. Griffin would let me tap on it a little bit, but it annoyed Mr. Griffin, so I couldn't play it while he was home. Mrs. Griffin was very endearing, and the Griffins' house was a retreat from the chaotic world that I was in at that time. I loved going there. Mrs. Griffin always gave me fresh baked cookies, and to a five-year-old, there was nothing better. Mrs. Griffin was nicer to me to me than my family. She always welcomed me with a big smile. This was in 1958 or 1959 – and back then, in some areas, African-Americans were treated poorly and were often discriminated against. There was never an issue about race with my family. No one in my family ever said anything about "black" or "white". I have to say kudos to my family for being cool back then.

My mother, America Rosalia Marcoccoa, and my father, Lawrence William Canedy, were both natives of Elmira, New York. I do not know how they met or what transpired in their early years as a new couple. By the time I was old enough to understand, neither Mom nor Dad relayed such stories to me. Mom was an incredibly hard worker. She had that old-school toughness that was so necessary in those times. She had been afflicted with polio at a young age. As a youth, she had to have several surgeries to correct the remnants of the wretched disease. She had to have some bones removed from her ankle, and as a result, she walked with a slight limp. It was quite apparent that she was often in pain. Often, walking caused her great discomfort. But Mom was not one to complain. She went to work every day. She had a great work ethic, which she had inherited from her mother and father. Her parents, my grandparents, had come here straight from Italy.

They adjusted quickly and before long they purchased a small market, which my grandmother ran. My grandfather became the chief of police for Horseheads, NY. My grandparents valued hard work and family, and fully embraced the American dream. But for some reason, my grandfather wanted the children Americanized as much as possible. Hence my mother's name: America. He also asked my grandma to prepare meat-and-potato-based dishes for the kids (American food), in place of their beloved traditional Italian fare. I always thought that was strange. As a result, my mother, who was 100% Italian, could not make a proper red sauce. Do not get me wrong, she was a great cook, but she excelled only at standard American fare. Not that we had many options. We were poor. But as a kid, I really was not aware of how poor we were until I was a bit older, when some of the other kids teased me for it.

By the time I was seven, I was living with Mom in Elmira. By then she had secured a place of her own. I had also gained a friend. Karen Hannon lived next door and quickly became my best friend. Whenever her family went somewhere, her parents took pity on me and allowed me to tag along. I spent a lot of time with them. Some resemblance of a family was extremely comforting. Karen seemed to enjoy my company and her parents were good to me. Thank God for them. Karen and I are still good friends to this day. I hung out with Karen and her sister, Cheryl, frequently. In the summer we did everything together - I was always with them. I remember one day going to Karen's house and asking her mother, "Can we girls go to the park?" And I think she was with some other neighbors - all ladies. They all thought that was hysterical. Of course, I was embarrassed, but then I thought, "Eh, what the hell. We're all friends." From then on, I was considered "one of the girls" by Karen's family.

Often, when the weather was pleasant, the other kids and I would go over the large riverbanks and try our luck fishing in the Chemung River. I often carried a kitchen ladle, so that I could scoop up minnows, which made for the best bait. On one occasion, the other kids had just left and only I remained by the river. I was using the ladle to scoop up a school of minnows, when from out of nowhere, a large man quickly ran up and grabbed me. He picked me up and started to carry me off. Apparently, he had been watching us for some time, and when the others left, he went straight for me. When this guy grabbed me, of all things, I fought him off with the ceramic ladle. He was desperately trying to carry me off, and I punched, kicked, and whacked him with the ladle and with everything I had.

He was very close to taking me into the darkness under the bridge, but he finally gave up. He decided it was not worth another smack in the face with the ladle. I ran home as fast as I could and told Mom. Now, my mom was a sweetheart, but I felt she often neglected to have my back. Well, when I told her, she quickly blew me off. Maybe she did not believe me. Maybe she thought the police would not do much. I do not know why, but I was in shock, and it hurt that my mother was not as upset as I was. My mother was dating a guy named Bill at that time. I never saw Bill spend the night, but he would visit on weekends. He was a nice enough guy. The following night, when Bill was at our house, I was sleeping in my room, and I began to have terrible nightmares and call out in my sleep. Bill came to my room and asked what was wrong. I explained to Bill about the incident by the river. Bill wasted no time, and he went right to the police. They caught the guy! I guess this was not the first time he had been in trouble for something like that, because he ended up going to prison. Years later when the would-be abductor was out of jail, I saw him walking on the street. It gave me the biggest, creepiest chill to see him again. That really was a traumatic moment.

I still was able to see my father on weekends. Dad decided he wanted to build a go-kart for me. For a kid in 1960, there was nothing cooler than a go-kart. And my dad was going to build me one from scratch! My memories of him are very clear. One time, he took me to the hardware store to get some parts for the go-kart. While at the counter, I must have had chapped lips, because my dad took out a tube of Chapstick and put it on my lips while smiling at me and looking at me in the eye. I will never forget that or the taste of the original Chapstick and my father at that moment. To this day, the original Chapstick brings back a flood of emotions. Every year my daughter buys me Chapstick because of this story. Something so small and simple - but when you are young and lonely, those small moments are the world. So, my dad built this go-kart for me, and he journaled the entire thing. It was great and I still have that journal. It is mostly drawings and lists of parts needed; but it recounts what a great guy my father really was. He lived close to Mom at this time, and when possible, I would also go see him in the mornings and he would cook breakfast for me. He was dating a woman named Emma, who clearly was not a big fan of kids, and she clearly did not like me intruding. But that was not going to stop me from coming over. There was this one moment that has stuck with me forever: I got mad at him for something - I cannot recall what exactly - but I told him "You are not my father!" And my father sat there calmly. He made me sit on the couch until I cooled down. When I finally cooled off, I apologized. It was such a different approach than my mother, who went right for the broom or belt when I said something out of anger. I used to hide the belts so Mom could not use them on me. Mom used to find her belts hidden in the strangest places - she told me once they found her favorite belt hidden under the oven. I must have done something bad to hide it that well!

My father had quite a high degree of patience. And he really seemed to understand me. One instance remains vivid. I had read the book *The K-House Mystery* by Grace Trobaugh Hay, and I thought it was fantastic. I was just a child and K-House was geared towards kids. It was the first book that hooked me. I was really excited about this book, and I recommended it to my father. Most adults would never read a kid's book, especially based on a child's recommendation, but my father read it. I know because he returned my copy extremely dog-eared. It was a library book, and seeing the many obviously dog-eared pages, I panicked, because I knew the librarian was going to yell at me. So, after seeing the dog-ears, I chastised my father. I think many adults would have been pissed, to get scolded by a kid. But my father just laughed it off and, being the cool dad he was, he apologized. Fast forward to around 2015, when I had been thinking about that moment frequently. One day while talking to my cousin Joe on the phone (he lived in Elmira at the time), I asked him to check out the local library for that particular book. The following week, he went to the library and then called me with the results. Not only did they have that book, but they had one issued in 1958. It was also excessively dog-eared - it was the same exact copy! I now have that book; I just had to keep it. If anyone who works for the Elmira Library is reading this, I am very sorry I kept the book. I owe you a copy.

Just as I was making friends, Mom and I moved yet again, this time to California. We had some family out there who told Mom that there was "plenty of work in the factories out here." So off we went. We took the bus there, which I recall rather well. A bus ride across the country is long and tedious, especially for a child. I especially remember stopping in New Mexico at bus stops and seeing the Native Americans at the bus stop. They looked incredibly sad and downtrodden. This was depressing for a sensitive kid such as myself. The only Natives I had seen previously were on TV. That stuck with me for some time. In case you did not assume it by now, I was a highly sensitive kid; I believe the term now is "empath". I always had the ability to sense things that were not implied or were not visible. Empath was not a known term back then - anything of the sort was labeled as "psychic." My mother used to tell me a story about how, on a warm and sunny day, I came inside, and as all the other kids were playing outside, she was a bit perplexed. "Carl, why are you inside? It is such a nice day. Why are you not playing outside?" And I said, "Mom, it is going to rain." She asked, "Who told you it is going to rain?" To which I quickly answered, "God told me." And sure enough, torrential downpours occurred within the next 15 minutes.

Once in California, we quickly settled into an apartment in Culver City. And before you know it, I am back in the same position as before: going to a new school, not knowing anyone, and having no friends. Mom quickly landed a job but was instantly so busy with work that I barely saw her. She would come and make dinner and go right to sleep. I was pretty much on my own at that time. However, there were some benefits to California. *The Many Loves of Dobie Gillis* and *Dr. Kildare* were filmed close to our apartment in Culver City, and I was able to watch them filming, which was a huge thing for an East Coast kid in the early '60s. Whenever I had some money, I would go to the movie theater. I recall watching a double bill of *A Hard Day's Night* and *Lord of the Flies*. *Lord of the Flies* absolutely terrified me. To see Piggy succumb to violence was terrifying - at that age, we had a lot of similarities. We both were chubby (called "husky" back then), we both wore glasses, and we shared personality traits. I saw myself in that character. And I really identified with him. *Lord of the Flies* stayed with me for years. Seeing The Beatles in *A Hard Day's Night* brought out the opposite emotions. I was euphoric watching them. By then, I had witnessed The Beatles on *Ed Sullivan* - that was a game changer. That event influenced an entire generation of soon-to-be musicians, myself included. Seeing Ringo playing and the adoration from the audience was mind-blowing. I always knew I wanted to play the drums but seeing that really validated that desire. More on that later.

Once we moved to Culver City, I really did not have much contact with my father. Things were very different back then: not everyone had a phone and when they did, long-distance calls were outrageously expensive. After coming home from school one day, Mom told me that she and Dad were going to get back together! I was absolutely thrilled. We were to go back east to live with my father! We quickly packed our meager possessions. We were going to leave the following afternoon. I was so excited I could barely sleep. Now, my mother had a habit of keeping things from me. I am sure she meant well - she was most likely trying to protect me. I was a sensitive child, and she was aware of this. Or maybe she thought that I would not understand? I am not sure why, but what happened next was devastating. The morning we were to leave, she received a phone call at 5 AM. She burst into tears immediately. My father had passed away in the middle of the night. He had been sick for some time, but Mom had never told me that he was sick. Apparently, Dad's illness helped spur Mom to come back home. It is the absolute worst thing a child can hear - that one of your parents is dead. That you will never see them again. That they are gone forever. At that age, nothing compares to that. My father was the one person who went out of his way to treat me respectfully. And now he was gone. After delivering the news, my mother sent me (by myself) to school to pick up my transcripts. That was a tough walk. There was no time to process emotions. When you are that young, you really do not know what "death" is, you only know that you will never see that person again. That they are not coming back. The loneliness I had felt over the past couple of years was amplified immensely. When I returned, we left immediately for the airport.

At the airport, my mother was crying – she was in rough shape. But she had suddenly forgotten about me. I was running behind her trying to keep up. I felt as if she did not even know I was there. And perhaps she thought I was too young to understand death or understand loss, or her own grief was so immense that she had not considered mine. On the flight, the flight attendants were rushing to console my mom as she was devastated - rightfully so. But Mom acted like I was not even there. Well, at least I would be comforted by my old friends and family members when we got home, right? That is what I had hoped and thought. But instead, Mom dropped me off at my grandma's house. The one who deeply hated my father. I stayed there for a week while my mother cleaned out my father's apartment house and made funeral arrangements. I remember my cousin Mike taking me to get a suit. It was to be my first funeral. It was a blur for the most part, but I remember standing in the funeral home, and they handed me a folded-up flag. It was then that I broke down. The realization that I would never see my father again hit. It was a very rough time.

Thank God for music. It was around this time that I discovered music - and it became a sanctuary. I gradually evolved beyond my first 45 single, which was "Purple People Eater", to full albums. And while The Beatles' appearance on *Ed Sullivan* was extremely motivating, the radio played a very important role in starting me off. I recall slowly turning the radio dial one day, mostly out of boredom. A Perry Como-type song was playing. Next. I kept going - and it was another Perry Como-type song. I turned once again and… BAM! There it was. Whatever was playing on the radio at that moment really spoke to me. It was a very powerful moment. I do not recall the song, but I recall 'getting it.' It all made sense. From then on, my musical exploration went wild. I always had the radio on. I was always listening to music.

**Karen Hannon;** *Childhood Friend*
*"It was a tough time. It was rough for all of us, but Carl especially. My parents welcomed Carl into our home with open arms. But as for what Carl was going through, my parents really tried to shield us (my siblings and I) from that. We were young and most likely we would not have understood. Carl was always part of our life, and we did not discuss the circumstances of his situation. Not even by Carl. Maybe he chose to bury it? Carl kept it inside. I really had no idea at the time. But despite everything, we had so many good experiences - just being kids. It was a rough neighborhood also and there was always fighting, but Carl was considered the peacemaker. He was non-confrontational and always had a smile on his face. I really missed him when he went to California. He was my best friend at that time."*

# Red Drums and a Tank

My first recollection of wanting to play the drums was at the age of four. My mother had taken me to a wedding reception at The American Legion in Waverly, NY. There was an inert Sherman tank parked in the front of the Legion, a leftover from World War 2. Legions and VFWs throughout the States would often use nonfunctioning tanks, planes, and artillery pieces as lawn decorations. For the government, it was probably cheaper to deliver it to a VFW hall as opposed to scrapping it. I will never forget that massive tank sitting on the Legion's front lawn. When you are four and a half, a big, beastly tank is quite impressive. What could be cooler than a tank? Well, I was about to find out. Upon entering the Legion, something abruptly called out to me. The wedding band was on break, their instruments resting on the stage. I noticed it immediately, right then and there - it was as if the heavens opened, an angelic chorus emitted, and a holy white light radiated upon the one and only thing cooler than an Army tank: a bright red drum set! I really did not know what it was about those drums, but I knew that was what I wanted - I wanted my very own set of red drums. I wanted to play the drums. That was a huge moment in my life. I cannot explain it - I certainly was not knowledgeable about drums or music at that age. But there was something about that drum set: it called out to me. I will never forget that day. From that day on, I was obsessed.

Despite my early adoration, I was to remain drumless for quite some time. I made an honest effort to play the drums when I was in the 6$^{th}$ grade - I signed up for band class. I desperately wanted to drum but there was one problem: since Mom had moved me late in the school year, all of the drum slots were full. I had to settle for the only open instrument available - the clarinet. I played clarinet for a year. Though not my first instrument of choice, I kind of enjoyed the clarinet. But it was not the drums, and I was not going to settle. After growing bored with the clarinet, and with the drum chair still full, I eventually purchased a practice pad and some cheap sticks. It was no drum set, but it was a start. The practice pad was simply slanted hardwood with a hard rubber pad, nothing like the comfy flat pads of today. I was constantly tapping on my practice pad. It was loud, clunky, and had no rebound. But since it was drumming, I was fine with it.

Around that time, I really started getting into music. It was bands like Vanilla Fudge, Blue Cheer, and The Rascals that really took hold. When I saw Carmine Appice with Vanilla Fudge on *The Ed Sullivan Show*, that was it. That was life changing. Those bands really helped influence my style once I started drumming. And of course, like most musicians that came from the same era, The Beatles' appearance on *The Ed Sullivan Show* was highly influential. It was such a fantastic time for music, but for me, it was the drummers that really made an impression.

My luck with securing a drum set was about to change. A friend from school purchased a three-piece drum set from a shop called Hamlin's Music in Elmira. If he was able to get a new drum set, then it certainly was not out of reach for me. I was envious, and I marched right over to Hamlin's after seeing his new set. Hamlin's was a family-run outfit, very by the book, and retails were set to match the MSRP in the catalogs. They *never* discounted items. And without a discount (a large one), I was never going to get a drum set. Hamlin's was way out of my league, and they certainly let me know. They made it very clear they were not willing to barter. Heavily discouraged, I was walking home when I stumbled upon a very small shop close to Hamlin's. It was called Gabel's Music Service, and it was a very unassuming shop. It did not look like the type of shop that would sell drums and electric guitars. It did, however, look like a great place to buy a wind instrument or a new piano. Which is not a place I could brag to my friends about hanging out in. So I walked in there out of desperation. It was clearly for the older, more traditional musician. Well, I happened to be there on the right day. In the far corner, all by its lonesome, sat a drum set. It was the only one and I wanted it. The shopkeeper almost never carried drum sets, or so he told me. He had ordered it for a customer who never picked it up. It was a Gracie drum set. I had no idea what a Gracie set was at the time (turns out it was junk), but it was a 4-piece kit with cymbals. It was priced at $360. That was a lot of money back then. So I mustered the courage and asked him if he could cut me a deal and finance it. Surprisingly, he told me, "Yeah, we can do that!"

He and I went to the post office where my mother was working. She was working as a window clerk, and we marched right up to the window. We probably embarrassed her, but I begged her to sign the installment agreement right then and there. She finally relented and signed the document. And that was it. I finally had my drums! Thank God he allowed us to purchase the set on an installment plan. Mom's salary as a post office clerk was not much at the time, definitely not enough to purchase a drum set outright. From that moment on, all I did was practice, practice and practice. I played every day, only putting the sticks down at night to prevent annoying my neighbors and family. I practiced six or seven days a week. I felt right at home behind that kit. Unfortunately, it was not long before the Gracie set began to break down. The chrome plating began to come off, the cymbal stands began to break, and the thumb screws came out. Now, a slowly dying drum set is a bad thing for someone on a limited budget, but looking back, it taught me some valuable lessons. I had to learn to modify, adapt and improvise to make that kit work - all very important skills that came in handy later in my touring years. I might have been cursing the set at the time, but I am grateful for it now. That kit taught me a lot.

# A Charmed Life

By the time I was 13, financially, life was looking better for Mom and me. By then, we were living in the apartment house that Dad once had. I was lucky enough to have my own room, which was almost like a one-bedroom apartment. It was a fantastic room for a teenager. That was where my drums were set up. It was a massive room, and the sound was fantastic. I practiced constantly, sometimes for four or five hours a day. Most kids with a drum set and a house full of tenants would not be able to practice as much, but as the title of this chapter states, I was getting glimpses of a charmed life. If any of the tenants complained, my mother would say, "I'm sorry, you'll have to move." That was extremely cool. I do not think most parents would have done that. I am sure it was unpleasant for the other tenants - and if any happen to be alive and are reading this, I deeply apologize. I think only one tenant moved over the years due to my drumming. A few even seemed to enjoy it. One tenant told me, "I can tell when you are mad by the way you drum!" She was very complimentary and extremely patient, and I do not know how she tolerated it, but she did. She died in that house - I really hope it was not from my drumming. But I practiced constantly, every day after school and on the weekends as much as possible. I was improving. But looking back, I was still quite terrible, and the next move was a bit impetuous.

    I had been drumming for six or seven months when I was able to advance beyond solitary practice. At that time, you would dial 411 to speak with an operator who would give you the number of the person you wanted to call. The operator was usually a local person. In this instance, the operator who answered was extremely friendly, and somehow, we just struck up a conversation. We began talking about music and then she told me that her boyfriend was in a band. They were looking for a drummer. Now, I really had no clue how to play, but I do not think I knew that at the time. She said, "Let me talk to him and see if they could use you." That led to me showing up for a jam session. As a result, I wound up in the band. My very first band. God bless them for giving me a chance. They were a few years older and why they gave me a shot is beyond me. Maybe they were desperate? I really did not know what I was doing. I would just tap along; I was just learning to play drums. I was learning from records at home. I was practicing and evolving, but I was not good enough to be in a band. It did not help that the Gracie drum kit was very weak sounding. I did not know how to tune it either. But God bless them for that opportunity, because it was my first band - and it was a lot of fun. It was truly a great experience. We even played a couple of private parties and made some money. At one gig, I took home $50, and I thought that was incredible. That was a lot of money for a young teenager in the late 1960s. It was then that I realized I could make money doing this full-time. To discover that it is possible to make money doing something that you truly loved (and would do for free) was a miraculous revelation.

I moved my drum set in front of the mirror - that is how I learned. I used the mirror to watch myself and adjust my technique. And there was a record player. I would listen to records and try to play along with them. I was not good in the early years, but I was still playing in bands. After high school, I took some time off from bands to work on my style. At that point, I was practicing six hours a day. I had an acoustic and electric guitar by then, and there was a piano in the house, so if it was too late to play the drums, I would play the guitar or piano. I was obsessed.

**Greg Bubacz;** *Longtime Friend*:
*"I remember the first time I saw Carl play. There was a high school dance, and the lights came on in the auditorium - people were starting to leave. And that is when he started his drum solo. He was not very good. Everyone is leaving and this guy is still trying to drum. But we were in rival high school bands, so there was always a bit of trash talk. Well, a few years later I was in a band, and we lost our drummer (who was very accomplished). The other guys in the band all said, 'We need to have Carl Canedy in the band.' My response was 'That hack? You guys are insane. There is no way.' It took them a while to convince me to give him a shot. So that weekend we went to watch Carl's band play. Let's just say, it took the entire band to pick my jaw up off the floor. In just a few years he became an AMAZING drummer! To this day, it was one of the best drum performances I have ever seen. It is clear how he got so good - he was devoted. Carl used to live with his mother in an apartment house. I remember his room. It was massive. But the only thing in the room was a mattress and a drum set. That shows you what he was all about - eat, sleep and drums. He was very, very dedicated."*

# Jim Nunis

Early in high school, I met a kid named Jim Nunis. Jim was a year or so older than me. We were into the same music: Cream, Mountain, Led Zeppelin, Jeff Beck and Hendrix. Jim also played guitar, after giving up the drums. So naturally, we hit it off immediately. We became fast friends. We would spend our days and nights listening to music and jamming at his house on Foster Ave in Elmira, NY. It was just the two of us - drums and a guitar. We were playing our hearts out every day. After a few months, we felt it was time to escalate our jam sessions and bring in some other players. We found a singer: a kid from school named Mark Banfield. Classmate Rich Terpolilli joined us on bass and another classmate by the name of Gary Cozad became our keyboard player. We would practice in Jim's garage and eventually we evolved into playing school dances and small parties. After a few gigs, Mark left, and Gary took over on vocals. It was my first serious band. We called ourselves Wadsworth Anthium. We worked hard putting up flyers and advertising locally - we were very serious. And we made money playing gigs and parties. It was truly a great time. By then, we had made enough money playing that we could go into the studio. We recorded three cover songs: "Tin Soldier" by The Small Faces, "Inside Looking Out" by The Animals (we did the Grand Funk Railroad version), and "I'm Tired" by Savoy Brown. That was my very first time in a studio and my very first record. It really was a great experience. We were always playing, and the only downside was not having a car. Hauling a drum kit from Jim's garage to home, and then to a gig, and finally back home, was not easy. Sometimes Jim's mom would pick up my drums and transport them, but a lot of times I would just call a cab and shove them in the back seat and in the trunk.

    We hooked up with another kid in high school, Bill Ward, who set us up with a massive backdrop and a rear screen projector for a major school dance. The backdrop was the typical effect of the time – psychedelic patterns flowing in and out. We had a lighting rig as well. That school dance was my very first "wow" moment, the very first gig that had some professional touches. We played mostly Creedence Clearwater Revival songs for the packed auditorium. It was so much fun, and for us at the time, it seemed like the biggest concert in the world. Anita Diliberto sang for us for a few shows as well. Anita was gorgeous, and she had a fantastic voice. We landed a lot of gigs with her on vocals. She was a huge draw. (Anita eventually went on to sing for the Glenn Miller Orchestra during the '70s and early '80s). I have so many great memories from that period.

The band eventually dissolved, as most high school bands tend to. We all went our separate ways. However, Jim and I remained close friends. We tried to start another band, which we named CaNu – a mishmash of our last names. It is hysterical when I look back on it, but back then we thought it was ingenious. We had cards, stationery, and envelopes printed up - everything to market our latest venture. But we did not need any of it as we had to yet to play a gig. We were young and inexperienced, and back then there was no internet how-to guide. There were not even library books on such subjects. Back then, you learned from personal experience and wisdom passed down from others.

Jim and I lost touch in the following years. But around 2004 or so, David "Rock" Feinstein gave me a message. He said, "Hey, this guy named Jim Nunis called the restaurant [The Hollywood, which is owned by David] looking for you. I took his number down." I called him immediately. We quickly reclaimed the friendship of our youth, talking for a few hours every week. During the years of our distance, Jim had become an accomplished guitar maker. He worked for a large company before launching his own brand in the early 2000s. He had been that way since we were young. Jim was so into guitars that he would sight down the neck to see if there was a twist or bow. He even learned to make his own headstock nuts out of bone. He was into guitars from day one. It was a natural fit for him to be a guitar builder. At this point, he was doing his custom work from his garage, and he was trying to get a facility for production. One night we were talking on the phone, and he mentioned his shoulder was really bothering him. It did not seem like a big deal, and I certainly did not think twice about it. The very next day, he briefly mentioned it to a doctor friend who in turn urged him to see an oncologist. It turned out to be a rare form of cancer. Three months later, Jim was gone. I was absolutely devastated.

Jim was a massive influence in my life. Especially early on. My father was not around, and Jim, being a bit older, had taken on a very important role in my youth. He was very knowledgeable about music and how it fits into a particular lifestyle. He knew a lot regarding the aesthetic of the early rock scene - the clothes, the style. He guided me in that area and really drove me musically. We would jam day after day, inspiring each other to get better and more refined. I learned a lot from Jim, and he had a large impact on my early life. I have so many great stories from those years.

One of my most memorable experiences was the time we took a bus to New York City. I was 15 and Jim 16, and neither of us told our parents. Of course, we did not have any money. But Jim took a handful of valuable silver dollars from his mom's hutch. They were probably worth 20 times their face value - but we really wanted to go to NYC and hang out in The Village. Once we arrived in the city, we ate at the Port Authority. Jim had a rare burger, and it was but a few hours later when Jim came down with violent food poisoning. He ended up doubled over on the sidewalk in excruciating pain; I thought he was going to die (and so did he). I tried everything to get an ambulance for Jim - he clearly needed one - but everyone passed us off as ailing drug addicts. Eventually, we made it to the hospital, and much, much later we had the luxury of staying at the same rat-infested, filthy hotel that The Lovin' Spoonful had stayed in. Which to us was fantastic. Due to the hospital stay, Jim's mom found out where we were and the next day, she picked us up from the city. She was not happy to say the least. But we had a blast. It was well worth it. We always had so much fun, and there are so many great memories from that era. Jim was a great friend and was an amazing human being. Rest in peace, Jim.

During our trip to New York City, Jim and I were able to visit Manny's Music. Manny's Music was an iconic music store located on West 48th Street, in Midtown Manhattan. Manny's was legendary. We had heard stories of the owner, Manny Goldrich, closing the store early so that Jimi Hendrix could shop. All of our guitar heroes shopped at Manny's. We had heard that this was the place to be, and we wanted to see it ourselves. The walls were covered with autographed 8x10 photos – all pictures of famous musicians. It was really exciting to see that. It was like a museum for musicians who love music history. Jim and I spent a lot of time there that day. And as the years progressed, I visited Manny's a number of times. Manny's was very important to me.

Every time I went to New York City, I would call Billy Hilfiger. I grew up with Billy and his brothers, Tommy, Andy and Bobby. Billy had moved to New York City and got a job at Manny's. When The Rods got signed, Billy took our 8x10 and put it on the wall at Manny's. That was huge for me because I would always go there to stare at all the iconic artists plastered on Manny's walls. And here we were, The Rods, with our very own photo on the wall! That was really cool, and Billy was always great. We were good friends and Billy would visit me at my house from time to time. I would visit him in New York every time I went there. I was visiting him one day and Billy told me, in a hushed tone, that this guy was just in – he was from England, and he bought a bunch of these brand new, very, very expensive guitars. We were in awe. Billy said, "I don't think he plays." I asked Billy what he was going to do with the guitars if he couldn't play them. And that was when Billy told me that the guy was opening a restaurant in NYC. He was going to hang them on the wall in the restaurant – which was to be called Hard Rock Cafe. We were all like, "What? He is hanging brand new guitars on the walls as art?" That was unheard of. As starving musicians, the thought of hanging a beautiful Stratocaster on the wall and not playing it was just blasphemous. So anyway, Billy and I stayed in touch throughout the years. Billy was wonderful and I can't say enough good about him. I miss him to this day.

I came into Manny's store one day and Billy said, "Carl, take this number." And he gave me the phone number for Tony Williams, who was a famous jazz drummer. Billy said, "I think he's taking students - call him." I called Tony Williams and sure enough, he was taking students, and I started taking lessons from the legendary Tony Williams! I even got to play Tony's iconic mustard color set! I had been a huge fan of Tony's, so it was a great experience for me. Tony wanted me to play with a traditional grip and he had me playing it with my ring and little finger. It was very tight, holding the sticks that way. That was really hard for me because I've always played matched grip but now, I had to play traditional grip for him. Lesson after lesson, he broke my balls. He was all over me: "Come on... you got to be able to do both!" Well, he was right, and to this day, I still play with a traditional grip occasionally. Especially if the song is a ballad, a slow song, or has a jazzy swing beat. He lived in a high rise, and he kept the window open – with the drums by the window. I asked him, "Don't the tenants complain?" And he said, "No, I own the buildings." I was scraping money to pay for my lessons, so the fact that he owned these huge buildings in Harlem was pretty impressive. I remember Tony was performing a couple of shows at The Bottom Line, and I went to see him both shows.

Both times I was up front, just off to the side so that I could watch him play. He played match grip, the entire show, for both shows. It was incredible, but he was playing match grip after telling me I had to play traditional grip - and really hammering me about it! And so now, at my next lesson, I said, "Tony, I don't get it. You're killing me on this traditional grip thing. And you played two sets, both with match grip." And he started laughing, and then he didn't say anything - he knew he was busted. So after that, for the lessons I went back to match grip, and he didn't say a word. But one of my take aways was that he was a really kind guy. And he was patient, and he wasn't condescending in the slightest. He was miles above my ability. His understanding of music and drumming was so far beyond what I was even capable of understanding, let alone executing. For my final lessons with Tony, they were really not even drum lessons. They were just philosophical discussions about music and approach to music. We talked about how to approach it and the whole vibe of the song and the pulse of the song. Those conversations taught me so much. Now I think of Tony Williams every time I start to work with a band or a song that I'm doing an arrangement on. His words really stuck with me. There is one story I have about Tony Williams that I will leave you with. Remember, I was a fan, so meeting him, I was in awe. He was my hero. My idol. And so, after our lesson, he wanted me to give him a ride downtown. Before we left his place, he lit up a joint. He said, "Hey, do you want some?" Well, I did not, but he's Tony Williams. He's like the coolest jazz guy out there. And so of course I've got to do something. So I took the tiniest hit - I barely inhaled. It was just enough so that I would look cool. I gave the joint back to him - and now I had to give him a ride. Once we got downstairs, the air hit me – and then the weed hit me. I had never been higher in my life. I was so stoned. And there I was, driving Tony Williams, nervous as hell, and driving in heavy Manhattan traffic. What a nightmare. It was awful. I couldn't wait to drop him off. And thank God, I was able to make it home. I don't know what kind of weed that was, but it was some serious, serious ganja.

So back to Billy Hilfiger, because Billy is always connected with hooking me up with Tony Williams. Billy was such a great guitar player. He had a great tone. He always reminded me of Mick Ralphs (of Mott the Hoople and Bad Company). He was a great player and a great guy. Everybody loved Billy. To this day, if you post something about Billy, there are tons and tons of replies and comments. Everyone loved Billy. Before he passed away, Billy wrote to me; I think it was a four-page letter, two pages, both sides. He wrote that he'd been having seizures, and apparently, he was told that he did not have a long time to live. He was told to start reaching out to people. It was heartbreaking to read. At that point in my life, I hadn't really experienced a lot of loss from friends. This was devastating. It was devastating for everybody who knew him. As time went on, he struggled. He told me that Tommy, his brother, had helped get him the best care possible. Tommy had sent him to the best people in the country - his care couldn't have been any better, but sadly he was still in decline. I remember his brother Andy calling me and telling me he had passed. I was actually doing something for the Red Cross, a benefit I was involved in. And I had to excuse myself and I sat down and wept for quite a while. It was tough for me. Thankfully, his brother Andy and I are good friends. I love Andy the way I loved Billy. Andy was gracious, and he really understood the loss that I had. I can never thank Andy enough because after Billy's death, I was kind of lost, because every time I would come to New York, I would have this great sadness. But Andy was always there for me. He never made me feel like I was imposing. And I'm always grateful to him for that.

Not only did I take lessons from Tony Williams, but I also took drum lessons from Carmine Appice. When I was 20 years old, I belonged to the musician's union. The union had a monthly paper. I looked in the back of the paper, which I would always do, and found an ad from Carmine Appice, who was accepting students. So I placed a call, figuring somebody else would answer - but Carmine answered. Carmine had been my hero since I saw him on *Ed Sullivan* in the mid-60s with Vanilla Fudge. He answered the phone, and I was in shock. I was in awe. I was a fanboy, and I arranged to take lessons with him, and it turned out to be the best thing I could have done. He changed the way I played. He was so positive and helped me keep the things that I was doing, which technically might not have been correct, but were cool. And he helped me refine things that were not working. He taught me to play faster and longer without stress. He took me through some books, including his book, *Realistic Rock*. I just can't say enough about how positive he was, and I pass his advice on to young people all the time. He said, "If you're playing because you want to be rich, famous, or get laid, you're playing for the wrong reasons. If you play because you love it, you'll have it your whole life." And certainly so - here I am, having had it my whole life.

# On the Road

After high school, as mentioned, I took a few months to work on my technique. For months, all I did was practice. Once I got to a point at which I felt I was ready, I resumed playing in bands. The years following were spent traveling, touring, and playing in different outfits - paying my dues. My high school friends had dispersed, some going to college, some beginning careers or families... but I hit the road. Early on, I was a bit hesitant about a career choice. I wanted to play the drums and I had not even thought of another option, but few make it in the music world. I had mentioned it to my former English-teacher-turned-good-friend, Henry "Hank" McBride: "I do not know what I want to do. I want to drum but obviously, Mom does not want me to play drums for a living." His response was simple yet profound. "It really doesn't matter what you do... as long as you do it well. That's all that matters." That was it. That statement really resonated with me - it was simple, yet it was very effective and very empowering. That one line created the mindset and raw determination that mapped out my future.

My first effort was to record a seven-minute drum solo. I took it to the Valex Agency. The Valex Agency was a talent agency/recording studio. Terry Singleton, who ran the agency, gave it a listen. Surprisingly, he listened to the entire tape. Afterwards, Terry turned to me and said, "Well, we do not have any bands that need a drummer, but we will keep you in mind." And here is where the charmed life makes an appearance: It was the very next day when I received a call from Terry. "Right after we heard your tape, a band notified us of needing a drummer," he said. So right away, I landed a job with a band called Big Daddy and the Duquenes. The very next week, I was traveling throughout the north east, playing clubs with Big Daddy. It was my very first touring outfit. I was only 19 and I was playing in packed clubs. Back then, a typical draw at a club was 500 or more people. Big Daddy was great fun but the experience did not last more than a year; the singer resumed his career as a chef and the band members went their separate ways. Once again I reached out to Terry Singleton: "Terry, I am out of a gig, do you know any bands that need a drummer?" Terry's response was the same response as the first time: "We don't know anyone who needs a drummer. Everyone hires drummers they know personally." And what do you know - the very next day Terry calls me: "Hey Carl, right after you called me, a band reached out to me looking for a drummer."

That band was Raw Meat. They were signed to RCA for a brief period (as Brian's Idols). They were strictly rock and played covers of bands like Yes, Jethro Tull and Deep Purple. Raw Meat was killing it at the time. They were touring and playing packed clubs and colleges. I quickly signed on. We toured non-stop throughout the East Coast. It was a lot of fun. The guys in the band were fantastic. It was as good a gig as you could get (for a cover band). It was everything a 19-year-old kid could ask for. But after two years, I felt there was something missing. There was nothing wrong with the band, those guys were great, but I was hungry, and I knew there was something bigger out there, so I left Raw Meat. They did not want me to leave - they thought it was foolish to leave. We were making money, we were having fun and we got along well. To them, it did not make sense. It was walking away from a sure thing. I was intent upon finding a band with major label aspirations. There was just one problem - I had no plan. I was going off pure gut feeling.

I did have a small traveling job after Raw Meat. It was for a top 40 band that toured the Midwest. They had the Holiday Inn circuit. Which at that time meant the players were faceless. You were basically a human jukebox. People just needed background music for their attempts at hooking up. It was incredibly boring. But it gave me some money to finance my future trips. I had a pick-up truck by then and kept my money stashed under the truck liner. Not the best place to keep your entire savings.

I spent the next few months traveling. I went to San Francisco, Los Angeles, and New York City. I did not know anyone in any of those cities. Not a single person. I had thought I could find a band and audition and things would just happen. But no such luck. I think if you are just looking, if you do not network, and you do not know anyone in the local scene, it is tough to come across the right opportunity. I really did not know how to network either. I was fresh out of high school - I really did not know better. But I was hungry, and I was persistent; I was not going to give up, so I tried the fourth city on the list: Boston. Right away I found a band in need of a drummer and landed an audition. That band was Jack Stella and the Northern Lights. I felt I did not do well in the audition - I really thought I blew it. A few days later I got a phone call. "Carl, the band loved you! But Jack [the frontman] thought you were too good, and you took too much attention from him. So sorry, it is a no-go." I auditioned for a couple of other bands, and I had no luck whatsoever. I packed my bags and headed home. I tried four massive cities and came up empty. Maybe leaving Raw Meat was a bad idea after all? I returned home defeated, my savings exhausted.

It was two weeks later, and I got a phone call. "Carl, we tried another drummer, and he was terrible. The band really wants you!" So I packed my bags once again and headed back to Boston. I was now the drummer for Jack Stella and the Northern Lights. That was quite an experience. The band had a full horn section. They were fantastic. They were brilliant musicians - most of the members were graduates of Juilliard and the Boston Conservatory at Berklee. They were pros and I learned a tremendous amount from them. However, there was one issue. The singer had one of the largest egos I had ever encountered. When we started a show, we would play our intro and Jack would come out like Tom Jones. He would play these little keyboard solos - more accurately described as horrible noodling. One time, Jack messed up his solo. When we got back to the hotel later that night, Jack began screaming at everyone. The guys were looking at their feet while he was yelling at the lineup. He told us, "You were trying to make me look bad!" (He did not need us to make that happen.) No one spoke out. And that was my first lesson on the road - the boss is always right. This job was quickly beginning to lose its luster.

    Luckily, a band called The Criminals reached out to me. They were looking for a drummer. The Criminals had a house in Needham, Massachusetts. They all lived at the house and rehearsed in the basement. The guys in The Criminals were outstanding - all great guys and we got along tremendously (not what you would expect given the band name). By then, I was more than willing to leave Jack Stella and the Northern Lights.

# The Annual Half-A-Beer

Early on, I made a firm decision to never play drunk or high. I did not want my playing to be hindered in any way. It just was not worth it - I wanted to be at my absolute best. For years, others would poke fun at me; people would say, "Maybe Carl will let loose and have his annual half of a beer tonight!" I was never a teetotaler - I had some experiences early on. But I never felt the need or desire to partake, especially while performing.

My very first time smoking pot was with Jim Nunis. I remember we were in his room listening to Mountain. We were so high that I could not understand any of the vocals. Jim's mother came in and started talking to us and asking us questions, and I could not even reply. I could not utter a single word. I could only sit there and laugh – on the floor, wrapped up in a blanket. I am certain she knew. While it sounds fun, I did not like the feeling of not being in control. After that episode, I figured I should try the second most popular drug of the era: LSD. A friend hooked me up with some acid for my 18th birthday - which was to become my first and absolutely last time doing LSD. It was not a pleasant experience. I figured it would be a great way to celebrate my 18th year. The friend took some as well, and I assume he was the paranoid type when high, because he spent half of the night questioning me. For some reason he thought I was a cop or narc and subsequently he ruined the experience for both of us. He was following me around all night and asking about my intentions. Another time, I was given mescaline. There was one small problem - I did not know what mescaline was and what it did. We were playing a show in a church basement, of all places. I don't recall much, but I do recall attempting a drum solo. I stopped mid-solo to announce, "I broke my drumhead," while the audience just stared at me with hollow eyes. I think everyone was high. It was not a pleasant experience, and it was my last experience of the sort.

Going back to the guy who gave me my first hit of acid… he showed up at the next birthday party and tried to give me heroin. He said, "Hey, I got you a great birthday present! It's heroin! Let's do it!" I told him, "No way. No thanks." He really pushed me to try it. He was very persistent. He kept saying, "It is your birthday present! How can you say no?" Finally, I put my foot down and told him there was no way in hell I was trying that.

In all honesty, I have never been drunk. Sure, I have one or two drinks occasionally. But being drunk has never appealed to me. Being in bands at a young age, I saw a lot of that. I witnessed musicians drink and do drugs and go to jail - and get totally trashed. Some of them turned it into a full-time habit. I am not judging those that do. It was just never for me. A good friend of mine, who shall remain nameless, was really having trouble with alcohol. He approached me and asked for help. I told him, "I can't help you until you are willing to help yourself." We had reached the point of 'tough love.' But you must do something. Because it must end, or they end up hurting others or themselves. After some convincing, I was able to get him to go to Alcoholics Anonymous. He had one condition - that I go with him. He was terrified to go alone. It was such a big step for him. Side note: I had to pretend I had a drinking problem to go. It was the only way that I could accompany him – AA had a strict policy regarding bystanders in attendance. So we would go to these meetings - and they were powerful. Many attendees were powerful people talking about the tragedies and the sorrow in their lives, all brought about from their addictions. This went on for a while, until eventually he was able to say, "Thanks, I think I can take it from here." He is still sober to this very day! For me, it was an eye opener, from the standpoint of being in a room where you must trust people, often strangers, to not discuss anything outside of the room. We heard the craziest, most heartbreaking stories. AA works, folks.

While I was not fond of drugs, I soon discovered that like most male teenagers, I was quite fond of women. My girlfriends were almost always older - I was in high school and I was primarily dating college aged women. This was one of the many benefits of playing in a band, and playing the occasional college party. By then, Mom worked third shift sorting mail at the post office. She would constantly come home in the morning and discover one of my dates still at the house. Surprisingly, she was cool about it. She would make us breakfast and was always respectful to my guests, but eventually she pulled me aside and said, "I know you are not going to stop, so can you at least have them park down the street, so the neighbors do not know what you are up to?" (This was at a time when this sort of thing was often frowned upon, especially in a small community such as ours). This was also around the age when I met Dianne, who was a few years older than me. Spoiler alert: I eventually married Dianne. We will get to that later in the book.

# Kelakos

Right after I joined The Criminals, the band changed their name to Kelakos, which was derived from the name of frontman George Michael Kelakos Haberstroh. The guys in Kelakos were superb. They were easy to get along with and I fell in place quite well. Kelakos was everything I was looking for. They were excellent musicians. And most importantly, they had major label aspirations. From day one, Kelakos wanted to have a record deal. We were all so naive about it. We had absolutely no clue what to do. After playing the Massachusetts bar circuit for some time, we thought, "Well, why don't we move close to New York? That way we can approach the big record companies." George's brother lived in Matawan, NJ. It was an hour of a drive into the city, but the housing options were much more practical. All of us moved into a small house and we would practice each day. All our equipment was set up in the living room. We were practicing a lot and as a result we were getting tighter, but nothing was really happening. We were quickly running out of money. We ended up finding a manager named Louie Zichino. That helped us land some gigs. Things slowly picked up. We were getting some auditions, finally, but nothing that moved us closer to a record deal. We were playing small clubs. This was the mid to late 1970s and disco was king. It was massive in the Jersey area. This was right before *Saturday Night Fever* was released. The rock scene was small and consisted mostly of cover bands doing Ted Nugent and Queen songs. But we still were able to get gigs and get a few bucks to eat.

We used to play in Dubois, Pennsylvania, at a place called The Hitching Post. It was a decent club with a decent stage. We would play there for two weeks at a time. The Hitching Post had their own accommodations, but when we first went there, we were too poor and too stupid to know that we could demand a decent hotel room. Instead, we used the Hitching Post's accommodations – and the rooms were godawful. Behind the venue, there was a rundown motel, but it was basically abandoned. And that was where they stuck us. There was no heat. One time we were playing there in winter, and we finally got the nerve to say, "Look, we can't stay here anymore." There was no door to the bathroom, and the place was freezing. I know they had a maid who came around once in a while, but it was awful. Though it was fun to play The Hitching Post. And one of the most important things that came out of playing The Hitching Post was meeting a man named Andy Weis. Andy would come and watch us play. For some reason he saw something in my drumming. Andy was an N.A.R.D. drummer (National Association of Rudimental Drummers) and he eventually tested me. Because of that, I was able to get my N.A.R.D. certification. I've always been proud of that, because my first teacher told me that I sucked and that I would never be able to get certified. Getting it was a vindication and I am very proud of the accomplishment.

We played the New York City and Northern Jersey area for almost a full year. By then, we were slowly becoming a great band, but there was no interest from the record companies – which is why we had moved there in the first place. I suggested we move to upstate New York because I knew there was potential there. Not so much from record companies, but the upstate club circuit was massive. The music infrastructure there was strong. Upstate had a healthy supply of recording studios, venues, industry people such as managers and promoters and, of course, rock fans who pay to see shows. The Valex Agency (who I had worked with multiple times) was also located in upstate NY and I knew they would help us book shows. While disco was massive in NYC, upstate New York had a solid rock fanbase. I threw it out there, and surprisingly the band agreed. We left right away for Ithaca, which was to be our new home base.

In no time at all we were playing gigs – and a lot of them. Instantly gigs were booked, and we began building a fanbase. We were consistently playing five or six nights a week. As a result, our financial situation improved greatly. We were making a living solely by playing gigs, almost every night. Back then, a good cover band could tour a healthy circuit and make a comfortable living. If you had some worthy originals, you could build a brand. We were beginning to amass a following. In a short period of time, we had enough money saved to record some songs. We recorded two original songs: "There's a Feeling" and "Funky Day". As soon as we got our stack of records back from the pressing plant, we drove to New York City. We spent an entire day walking around Manhattan knocking on the doors of assorted publishers, music executives and talent agents. We tried to get that single in the hands of as many people as we could find. And every single one of them could not have cared less. Those singles most likely ended up in the garbage as soon as we left. It was all, "Thanks but no thanks." They couldn't have cared less that we were doing very well in upstate New York. But it was my first official record. We did not have a record company, but somehow, we managed to get it in the hands of a few jukebox vendors, which to us, made us somewhat legit. We kept playing gigs and we kept saving. Since we had little to no luck with the single, we were determined to go to the next level on our own, which was to write, record and press a full length album. Full length albums had a fallback option. If the record companies were not interested, we could at least sell it at shows, and to local record shops, and give it to local radio stations to play.

When we had enough songs, we booked some studio time with the intention of making an album. While we should have focused on the basics (knocking out some great rock songs), instead we focused on creating something deep and colossal, and as a result, we were about to get in over our heads. We were young, eager, and inexperienced in the studio. None of us had spent much time in a recording studio before. We spent a ton of money and brought as many superfluous instruments as we could find - xylophones, strings and horns. We wanted to take it over the top. We brought in David Kant, who was the keyboard player for Hall & Oates. We had guest musicians. Whatever instrument or addition we could conceive of, we went for it. We were spending crazy money. After more than 350 hours of studio time and exhausted savings, we ended up with a complex and diverse album, which was sonically week. The album just did not sound very good. We were bummed. It sounded nothing like how we initially envisioned, or at least hoped it would. It was a massive disappointment. Looking back, I am glad we did the album because much later it resurfaced. A few years ago, we re-released it. I had all the masters transferred to digital. Linc remixed it and we ended up releasing it - almost 40 years later. It got some great reviews. That was a vindication of sorts. It was something we could hang our hats on. That album became our legacy, decades later. But getting back to the original recording... after that album, the demise of Kelakos began. We were burned out. We had been gigging non-stop and had spent every penny we had (and then some) on a record that we were not happy with. Linc went back to school to pursue his masters, so we got Craig Gruber to help us out. Craig had played with Gary Moore and Rainbow. With Craig on board, we booked a tour throughout New York, Pennsylvania and New Jersey. That tour was highly unsuccessful. We were playing mostly empty rooms. We had an album out that was getting absolutely no airplay. We spent money on radio ads and even those did not help. After that failed tour, we agreed to call it quits. We divided up our stockpile of albums and everyone went their separate ways. Just like that, I was back to doing nothing.

**Linc Bloomfield;** *Kelakos*

*"We had a lot of inspiration from The Beatles, including songwriting and singing, which was fundamental. Anyone who was brought up under The Beatles understood that the appeal of popular music starts with singing. The rest is important, but without the vocals, you are just not at a high level. So that is how it all started. We played on the south shore of Massachusetts for a while. And Carl said, 'We are just not going to go*

*anywhere unless we do something different.'* So, in 1975 we relocated. George and Mark and I moved into to a house in Matawan, New Jersey, which was not far from New York City. It had access to Long Island, New York City, Hudson Valley, and the Jersey Shore. Carl lived in a nearby town with Dianne. And the thing that we did not count on was the explosion of disco in the mid-seventies. If you think disco had a big impact in upstate New York or New England, it was huge in the metro New York area. In New Jersey, all the club music was disco or retro oldies acts. And it was a more organized music market. There were much bigger venues, and we had to work through agents and managers who wanted the acts to be a lot slicker. We played in some of the worst clubs in Asbury Park, and remained in New Jersey for a year. And then Carl persuaded us to move again. He said, *'Back where I come from, there is a great music infrastructure that can help us. There are a lot of gigs and good managers. I know the studio people. Let's give that a try.'* We were ready. So, we relocated again in 1976, this time to Ithaca, New York. Everybody found a room to rent. We made Ithaca our base. That was really the heyday, if you will, where we played hundreds of gigs over the stretch that we were together and wrote original music on our time off. It was like two and a half years, until the fall of 1978. We cut our first record in 1976 – a single: *'There's A Feeling'* and *'Funky Day'* – and then we worked hard to scrape the resources together to get in the studio and do a full album. It was not easy.

"Financially, this was the height of the 1970s recession. We were not paid a lot, and we had to keep trucks moving and the roadies paid, even as vehicles and equipment kept breaking down during a couple of brutal winters. We wanted to invest in higher fidelity equipment and pay for time in the studio. So that takes us up to finally getting into the studio, which was Pyramid Sound in Ithaca. I think any manager would have said, *'Keep it simple. Pick one style that you think is your best sound. And do seven or eight songs that are kind of in that vein, and do not change any of the instruments.'* Well, we did the exact opposite. We thought we were going to do a record on par with the Beatles' White Album. We all were guilty of shooting for the stars, and we were not going to hold back. Carl brought in a violin section from Ithaca College, and I had to write some charts for them on the spot. We brought horns in. I mean, it was unbelievable. We brought in a guest electric keyboardist from Hall and Oates. We played a Hammond B-3 and Leslie speakers, and grand piano parts. Carl had multiple unique-sounding drum kits. Every song was different.

"The production on each tune was different. The instrumentation was different, as was the key, the tempo, the style, and the vocals. Like The Beatles: you cannot name two Beatles tracks that sound like each other. They always made each song special. And that approach was in our DNA.

*We were never going to make two songs the same because then one would be better than the other. Why would you do that? So, we did this album, Gone Are The Days, and we finished with 13 days of intense mixing trying to get it finished and pressed. I went off to graduate school weighing 135 pounds. I mean, it was just completely exhausting. We burned off all our energy, and all of our money. That is when I left the band, and the others continued for a while promoting the album and doing some local TV performances."*

# The Brotherhood Begins

Historically, New York City tends to get the publicity and recognition when East Coast rock music is discussed. But in the mid to late '70s, there was not much of a rock scene in NYC - it was mostly punk and disco. We had a running joke that you could have Jesus introducing The Beatles on a weekday (in NYC) and no one would show up to the club. The real happening rock scene was found throughout Long Island and upstate New York. There were plenty of great venues, clubs and colleges that always hosted bands - and eager crowds that packed the venues. It was a fantastic place for a musician; so looking back, what happened next was not out of the norm.

Brian, the singer from Raw Meat, owned a music store in upstate New York. I was in there perusing and hanging out, just chatting with other local musicians. And in walks Denny, who had worked lights for Kelakos at one time, and he proceeds to tell me in a very formal manner: "Mr. Feinstein [David 'Rock' Feinstein] and Mr. DeMaio [Joey DeMaio] would like to speak with you. They are in the car outside." So out I went.

I had met both in the past - Joey played for a local band called Thunder, and David I knew from the local circuit. David "Rock" Feinstein was the cousin of Ronnie James Dio, and he played guitar in Ronnie's band Elf (previously known as The Elves). David also played in Thunder for a brief period. David was an amazing guitar player. Since we were often working the same circuit, and I would go to see Elf perform frequently, we would occasionally run into each other. So, I climbed into the back seat - David and Joey were sitting in the front - and Joey turned around, looked me in the eyes and said, "Do you want to play with boys? Or do you want to play with men?" I instantly said, "Men."

That very night we rehearsed at my house, David on guitar and vocals, and Joey on bass. We practiced a couple of times more... I really cannot recall for how long, but it was not much. Joey left early on. I believe he ended up getting a job as a bass tech for Black Sabbath and he went out on the road with them. That tour was responsible for the formation of Manowar (which we will talk about later). Once Joey left, David and I decided to keep going. I really liked David. We had similar influences, we shared the same vision and we found we worked great as a team. Both of us had spent many years touring and we both had songwriting and studio experience. Now we needed a bass player. Luckily, David knew a guy from his previous band,

Mickey Rat. That bass player was Steve Starmer. Steve was a great guy and a great bass player. Steve came on board, and we immediately felt the chemistry. We also tried to get a singer. David wanted to focus solely on the guitar, but it never worked out. David started singing, "until we could find a singer," but we found David's voice was, in fact, the perfect fit, and allowed us to create our sound. I do not think The Rods would have had that heaviness if it was not for David's voice. Now keep in mind, this was before 'heavy metal' became a household term. The New Wave of British Heavy Metal had not even hit our shores. There was only 'hard rock' music. There was no immediate decision to start playing 'heavy metal' – it was not until late 1979 that we began to see that gradual shift in music. David's vocal range and guitar tone led favorably to the harder edged rock. It was not a deliberate decision - we did not sit down and say, "We are going to play really heavy and loud!" It was just natural for the three of us. So that is how The Rods were born.

Our first order of business was to find a place to rehearse. Luckily, Al Falso Music, which was a legendary upstate New York music store, had a rough and uninsulated extension built onto the back of it. Al was kind enough to let us use this as our rehearsal room. This room was not heated - and if you have ever been in upstate New York during the lengthy winter, you'll know it can get blistering cold. Which it was. We were separated from the elements by thin sheets of particle board. We had a small kerosene heater that did almost nothing. And of course, during summer, it was like an oven. There were no windows in the space. But hey, it was a place to practice. We would practice every day from 10 to 12. Then we would go to my place and build equipment. I also had a silkscreen, and we would make t-shirts, getting a jump start on merch. After hours working on equipment, we would go back to Cortland and practice from 6 to 9 PM. Al's daughters told me they went to bed each night to the sound of us rehearsing. Al's shop was instrumental to the formation and longevity of The Rods - it is an important part of our history. (Al Falso eventually became known as The Rodfather. The song "Music Man" was written for him). Al was such a character. He really took the time to ensure we were taken care of. He treated us like his sons, and he took on a fatherly role with us. Especially with me; I had lost my father at an early age and it was Al who really became the prominent role model of my early adulthood. Al was a great man and because of him, we had a place to practice, working equipment, and the always important fatherly advice.

With all that rehearsal time under our belts, and with some freshly built equipment and plenty of merch, we decided it was time to play some gigs. We had some issues getting gigs, even though there were plenty of venues, as we had trouble getting an audience. We were unknown. We had no fanbase and we were playing hard rock; at that time, the masses preferred softer rock - bands like The Eagles and Journey. Harder-edge rock really did not hit the masses until late 1979. It was rough at first. Even though we were all somewhat accomplished, and had come from successful local acts, we were starting from scratch. We were right back at the bottom. We knew we had something great. We knew getting the word out was important, and we vowed to take any gig. Any gig that would provide us with a little bit of cash - or enough to eat that day. We were not picky. We just wanted to play. At this time, we were playing mostly covers - you really had to at that level. No club would hire an "originals only" band with no existing fanbase. One early gig was especially memorable. It was at the Arcade in Ithaca. It had been a theatre in the '50s and '60s and they basically pulled out all the chairs and opened it up as a live music venue. The floor was massive. There were around 250 people there before we went on, which would have made for a great night. However, by the end of our first set, almost every person had left. We had peppered our set with a few original songs, and to see everyone leave was a huge blow to our self-esteem. Only the girlfriends and the road crew remained. It was now a big empty venue. And because of our contract, we had to play the rest of the night. Talk about embarrassing.

We played the Arcade again a few months after that. The turnout was not much better; why they hired us again I will never know. But that show was memorable for another reason. After the show, Drew, who was a local guitar tech and who knew me from a brief stint in The Dean Brothers, approached me. Drew, who was quite drunk, said, "Carl, the 1960s are dead man. Why you play that shit is beyond me. You are ruining your name. You will never amount to anything playing that crap." For a moment, I wondered if he was right. Was I making the right decision? Was this the right path? It was hard to argue against it as we were not pulling big crowds. I always thought of Drew as a nice guy – but finally, I realized he was being a drunken idiot. Ultimately, I went with my gut feeling. There was something about The Rods that felt right, even though the early days were rough. If we could make $100 for the three of us (and the road crew) to split, then it was considered a good night. Thank God for the friends, family members and girlfriends who supported us and fed us. We could not have done it without them.

Just when we hit peak frustration, things seemed to take a turn for the better. It was not overnight, but we noticed a small but growing fan base. To start, it was not much, but we began seeing the same faces return (always a good sign) and the crowds intensify in volume and energy. That made us want to work harder. Eventually, we packed the venues - but we had to pay our dues to make that happen.

**Steve Starmer;** *Founding Member of The Rods*

"Well, in Cortland, there were a lot of bands around. Everybody kind of looked up to Ronnie (Ronnie James Dio). Everyone used him as a benchmark on what to do and how to succeed. Back then, I was playing with a band called Mickey Rat [Note: Not the West Coast Mickey Ratt which featured Stephen Pearcy]. Ronnie used to have us open for him. When we played the bigger clubs, he asked us to open and at that point, David was Ronnie's guitar player. We were all in a hotel room after the gig and David came in and said: 'I just quit Elf.' He just quit the band. Then he says, 'Would you guys like a guitar player?' Now I guess the difference was, we were a part-time band. Ronnie had a full-time band. And David had some other things going on in his life. I believe he was building a cabin. So, David joined my band back then. We played for a while, and then we broke up. After Mickey Rat broke up, David went with some other guys out of Auburn. And I think his band was called Thunder or something like that. So, he played with them for a few years. (The same Thunder that Joey DeMaio was a member of). And I played with some other bands for a few years. When David and Carl approached me with The Rods project, it was good timing. We aspired to get signed. It was going to be a full-time thing. I mean, I had a job back then. I left my job to join the band. We struggled, of course, financially. We put in our time rehearsing - and we built our own PA. We would spend half of each day rehearsing our music, and the other half we were building our PA system and equipment. We were serious about this, and we were not young kids at the time either. We thought that this might be our last opportunity.

"In the beginning, we were kind of a cover band. We did a lot of Ted Nugent, UFO-type stuff. It was not metal but hard rock. And basically, we were a cover band. What happened over time is that David wrote some material. He would write the riff and he would come to us with an idea, and we would put it together. We had a few songs to start and then Carl started writing also. Carl was instrumental in hooking us up with the recording studio in Fredonia, which is where we recorded the first album. This was probably a year after we got together. We would go out and play three or four nights a week, and then we go and record for three or four days. It was bizarre. The early shows were okay. As we got going, and as the months progressed, the shows got better and better. We would play clubs, and they would have to rope it off, because there were so many people there, but in other cases, not a lot of people cared. But for the most part, we got more and more people and they were slowly getting interested in the band. That album took six months or so. Because we, we were paying for it ourselves. So, we go out and we play, make money, and then come back and pay for a session or two, then we go out, play some more - to make some more money.

We never made any money for ourselves. Everything we made went into the band and album. We had girlfriends at the time. They helped. And we did not eat much. Eventually we started getting more gigs. We started opening for bigger acts. And that was fun. People started recognizing the band for what the band really was, and that kind of thing."

**David "Rock" Feinstein;** *Founding Member of The Rods*
"I met Carl at a time when I was not actually playing. I had left the band Elf. After leaving, I was not doing anything - well not with music anyhow. Why did I leave? There were a lot of personal reasons - I did not leave the band on bad terms with Ronnie or any of the guys., But I had some personal things that I needed to clear up on my own. And I really did not feel like I was going to be leaving the band forever. I just felt that I needed some time away from the band and the music business. Because that is all I had ever done since I was a young kid. So, I needed to get away from it for a while. I really thought I would come back to the band down the road. Well once Rainbow was formed (Ronnie disbanded Elf to join Rainbow), and that whole thing happened, there was never going to be another Elf again. But I missed playing and I wanted to put a group together, basically just to play bars and then play some small gigs and make a few bucks. I only wanted to survive and play some bars - I never really thought it would turn out the way it did. When I quit Elf, I got away from music completely - I did not even listen to the radio, I even took the radio out of my truck, I did not want to have anything to do with music, I needed to get away from it. But after a while, being a musician is like a drug - it always brings you back. So, I thought, let me just see who's out there, let's see who is available to play. A friend told me about Carl. At that time, he was playing with Kelakos. A few weeks later, Kelakos was playing close to Cortland. So, I went there with a friend - just to check out their drummer. I met Carl that night, it was on a break (or after the show) and we had a discussion. I said, 'I'd like to start a band and, you know, just play around some clubs and stuff like that.' He was interested in doing that. So that is when I first met Carl. From there we planned to get together. It was Carl and me. Of course, we were looking for a bass player. At that time, it seemed like everyone was looking to put a band together, and there was a small pool of musicians that revolved through each other's bands. And when Steve came, it really worked out great. Steve was such a great bass player. I played with him in a band previously.

"The Rods were a cover band at first, and Carl and I each began to write songs. New Wave of British Heavy Metal came about after the band got going - because I do not really recall that term being used when we formed the band. So, it was something that we got categorized under (heavy *metal), all because we were there at the beginning of it. We were not aware of it when we formed the band, we just played in that style of hard rock. We started playing a lot of cover material, and of course, I started writing again - I was an avid songwriter. And suddenly,* I had some original songs and Carl had written songs, and we started playing those songs out live. And then we got someone who wanted to be our manager - and suddenly, we had a manager. And then we had a record deal. We did not form this band thinking we were going to be rock stars, and travel and make records - it just kind of happened naturally. We had planned on bringing a singer into the mix, but there just was not anybody. So, as it turned out, I ended up singing and Steve ended up singing. And we did songs, only cover songs at first, that we felt we could work with our vocal abilities. Eventually, we funneled into one direction - even in the writing of new material, whether Carl wrote, or I did, it was geared towards a three-piece hard rock band with vocal parts that could be handled by the ability to vocalize with what we had. So, that is pretty much it. But from the very beginning, we were all on the same page - so it made it relatively easy for us."

# The Music Man

Before we venture too much further into the history of The Rods, I want to speak a bit more in detail about Al Falso. He was a critical part of the success of The Rods. He was like a second father to me. I loved him so much. There was a point when Al was ill, and he was dying - he was in the hospital, and I was talking with him on the phone. I remember he said, "Carl, I will never play drums again." He was very emotional. It struck me hard, and I was so sad for him. I realized that, one day, that is going to be me. I am no longer going to be able to play drums and it is going to hurt. It was a little window into my future. I loved him and hated to see him lose something that he obviously loved that much. As far as Al goes, there are so many stories in which we had no money, and he took care of us. We would come to the store to rehearse, and he would say, "Hey, will you guys go get me coffee?" He would pull out some cash and he would send us across the street to the donut shop to get coffee - and he would pay for our coffee. But he never made us feel like we were mooching. He was such a great guy. After The Rods got signed, we were to go to England to record.

We were fortunate enough to be going on a British tour with Iron Maiden, as soon as the record was finished. I did not have the money to take drumheads, drumsticks and cymbals - all things I needed. Well, Al loaned the equipment to me, I want to say on credit, and he let me take whatever I needed. I must have taken $1,200 worth of equipment to England. That was a lot of money back then. I do not know how I could have done the tour without it. I simply did not have the money. Al fronted us, and luckily, I was able to pay him back right after we returned. I was so grateful for that.

On our first album, David wrote a song by the name of "The Music Man", which was inspired by Al. For another album, we wanted to record Al playing the harmonica. He played harmonica really well. He played harmonica aside from being a drummer and a singer - he was very talented. So I wanted him to come into the studio... and he comes in the studio and is walking around as nervous as can be. Al's wife, Mary, said that he was up all night, he was so nervous. I told Al: "Go in the booth and practice a little bit before we record." Then, I had the engineer hit the record button while he was warming up. So what you hear at the very end of *Heavier Than Thou* (also called *The Music Man*) is Al warming up - he did not know he was being recorded, and as a result he was loose and played some great stuff.

Al said to me one day, "Carl, you're losing a lot of your finesse." He had a little drum kit downstairs, right below the storage area where The Rods played, and he said, "Sit down there and let me hear you go around the set with doubles." So I played doubles around the set. And it was pitiful. I had not realized how pitiful I had become with my doubles. Al sees me do this pathetic roll and pulls his glasses down over his nose. He stares at me; he doesn't say a word for 20 seconds and then shakes his head. And I could not stop laughing - but I got the point. He was right. I was letting part of my technique go.

In the early 2000s, Al came and performed with The Rods at Beaudry Park. He came up on stage and we played "Route 66", which I really did not know too well. There were a couple of stops I missed, and I was a little embarrassed. Al, on the other hand, played fantastically well, and the crowd really loved him. Al was such a great guy and I miss him to this very day.

Also instrumental in our early success was Arden Schneider. I had met Arden somewhere around the demise of Kelakos, and we had become fast friends. Shortly after we had met, she had started her own booking agency. She became quite successful with it. She named it the Mctara Agency. Since we were just starting out, and heavy rock was not very popular – this was the tail end of the '70s and it was disco, punk and new wave that was happening - we had a very difficult time getting booked. Clubs wanted known acts – and there were many - or top 40 acts. Not new rock acts. But Arden took a chance on us. She backed us fully and got into our corner. No other booking agent was willing to give us a chance, but she did, and as a result, we got gigs. Those gigs turned into more gigs, which led to opening slots, festivals, and theaters. I will be forever grateful to Arden. If it was not for her, who knows how far we would have made it?

**Dianna Falso Petrella;** *Daughter of Al Falso*
*"Carl and I are close. Carl was one of my father's favorites. My dad really talked about Carl a lot. They practiced next door - our house was right next to the shop. They practiced in the shop - there was an addition upstairs, at the back part of the store. I do not think there was heat up there. And there were no windows up there. They would just practice and practice and practice and practice. My father really helped everybody. He came from a poor family and back then if you wanted to play an instrument, it was not easy. Instruments were expensive. My father wanted to make music accessible to everyone. People tell me stories now. They say, 'Because your father gave me credit, I was able to play music.' When you are a poor kid from upstate New York and you get credit, that is a huge deal. They come*

up to me and tell me, 'I am the man I am today because your father nurtured me.' He was not about the money. People would come in and out of the house a lot in those days - there was a sense of family with the customers. My dad went out of his way to make everyone feel like that. But Carl was like a son to him. My father never had a son - it was just my two sisters and myself. And in the house were my mom and grandma. So, he lived with five ladies. Carl had a key to the shop. Can you imagine that? Giving a rock band the key to your shop? But he trusted Carl and Carl really was a responsible guy. He was so proud of them. He loved all his customers. But The Rods were his buddies. He wanted to help them, and he felt very close to them. He loved that they looked up to him. There was a donut shop across the street - my dad was always buying donuts and lunch for them. That was probably the only time they ate. I do not think they had much money at the time. But Dad really got a kick out of seeing them grow in popularity, get a record deal, and start touring. Carl gave me the tour jacket from the Iron Maiden tour. I still have it to this very day."

## Paying Our Dues

When The Rods first started, it was tough to get a crowd. We were playing to nobody – and for no money. It was the end of the disco era for sure, but nothing was happening. It was a short, but strange sort of limbo in which the next big thing had not yet arrived, and people were not sure of where things were going. People would usually leave by the end of the first set, and most of the time the places were empty, so it was a rough go at first.

I remember playing upstairs at a club in Syracuse. We had to carry our equipment up a rickety fire escape. We could barely fit ourselves, let alone our equipment, up the rusty metal stairs. There were rats running around on the ground and alongside the building. While we were carrying our gear up that metal staircase, it was like, "I guess this is what paying your dues is?" Well, we were most definitely paying them. But we hung in there, and thankfully, we gradually started catching fire. Gradually. It started at first in some of the more rural areas - we started getting a following and it was quite remarkable. We were building it up to the point where we were packing the places. But we still were not making much money. In fact, we were flat broke. In one of the more memorable clubs, the owners also owned a bakery and would load us up with day-old baked goods. While the club itself was not remarkable, the shows were fun, and we were able to subsist on bread for days afterward. We were starving, so free baked goods were a massive help. It was the small things like that which got us through. Also, until we got signed, we always shared a hotel room. The girlfriends, the road crew and a few friends of the band all piled into one small, cheap hotel room. It was crazy. Eventually, when we started booking bigger clubs, we were able to get a separate room for the road crew. Slowly, things got better.

**Steve Starmer:**
"People would always try to give us drugs. And we always wanted people to think we were cool - but none of us used drugs. So, we would take the drugs and give them away to other people. We were really serious. So, we really did not take any drugs. But when somebody offered them to us, we did not say, 'No, I do not do this.' We would take them and give them to the roadies. And then everyone is like, 'Man, those guys are so cool! They are giving out drugs!' But honestly, we did not use them because we did not know what the hell they were they were giving us. I remember one time at a show, we were playing 'Sympathy for the Devil'. And what I would do is

*I would come out with a torch on the end of my bass. And with a mouth full of accelerant, I would blow fire. Basically, we put 180-proof alcohol in my mouth, and I would spit it out resulting in a giant fireball. Anyway, it looked like I was breathing fire, right? Well, there is one time I blew the fire, and we also had flash pots - the fire caused the flash pots to ignite prematurely. They blew up. It scared the shit out of everybody. It singed a girl's hair in the front row. Carl was so nervous about getting sued - so we gave her a ton of merchandise. Another time, we were doing a soundcheck and we had a new roadie, and we were trying to teach him what he had to do in order for me to breathe fire. And he had to do it in sequence. Well, I had on this big sweater. And as we were starting the process, this guy did something and I laughed – and spit the liquid all over my sweater. Which resulted in my sweater catching on fire. That gave me a nasty burn on my arm. To this day, the hair on my right arm is gray. And the hair on my left arm is brown. I look back and laugh, but it was scary at the time - and Carl and David were laughing hysterically. I thought Carl was going to pee his pants. We had a lot of good times. No harm, no foul. It was a lot of fun - but do not get me wrong - it was a lot of hard work. It was two and a half years of my life. I absolutely loved it."*

We had plenty of fun on the road. Two of the most amusing memories were of The Golden Calf and Rods Law. When gigging, we had something called the Rods Law. When we would declare "Rods law," we had to abide by it. And one of the rules was: "No sex before a gig." The law actually was "No loads before a gig." Of course, that is crass, but we were young and a bit crazy. We had lots of Rods Laws. Another was: "You can not be with any woman who is closer than 50 miles from your home." That way, they would never show up and bother you when you were at home. There were a bunch of rules that we had, and while created jokingly, they probably saved us some hassles on the road.

The Golden Calf was our band car. And it was not a Cadillac, but it was bigger than the largest Cadillac model of the late '60s/early '70s. It was a big parade float car and it had a ghastly retro-gold paint job, so I named it The Golden Calf. We had a nickname for everything. That heap gave us so many memories, most of which will not appear in this book! But it was a great band car and it lasted forever. One time we were coming back from a gig in Watertown. The car was clearly on its last legs. And I remember the engine light came on – the engine was done. Back then, when the engine light came on, it meant it. That usually meant the end was near. After a quick glance under the hood, it was clear The Golden Calf could not be saved. We wound up driving it from North Syracuse to Cortland with a rapidly fading engine. It was about an hour's drive. The car was overheating, smoking, and making all types of strange noises. We parked it in a garage in Cortland. We got out of the car, and we never looked at that car again. We left it right there. After that, we saved and purchased a Cadillac. A nice one at that.

**Steve Starmer:**
*"At the time, band names like The Cars and The Police were coming out. We considered 'The Hot Rods'- following that style. Now, at that time, I was working as a buyer at Smith Corona Typewriters - I was purchasing different parts and a lot of those parts were these long rods, which would get cut and processed. So, with that in mind, and with hot rods and being a little dirty, I had written down 'The Rods.' Of course, it was a double entendre. I remember we did a radio station interview, and the female DJ asked us 'What does "The Rods" mean?' I leaned into the microphone and zipped my jacket down really slowly. She was stunned, to say the least. Of course, we were laughing hysterically. We had fun with it."*

# Two Inches of Hard Rock & Roll

We had been going at it for almost a year when we decided it was time to record an album. Initially, David's intention was simply to play some shows and have fun, but things quickly turned serious. Perhaps it was the chemistry the three of us had that was responsible for changing David's mind. From the start, I wanted a major label deal. And recording an album was a necessary step to achieve that, being that we were out of the jurisdiction of most major record labels. By then, I had written a few songs and David had written a few. We did not have enough for a full album, but we found our original material came together rather quickly when we started working on the arrangements. There were plenty of studios, but of course, money was in short supply. Gigs were getting better, but it certainly was not enough to finance a studio album. My best buddy, Greg Bubacz, had a brother by the name of Chris Bubacz, who was a student at nearby Fredonia University. He majored in sound/production. Fredonia had a decent studio, from what Greg had told us. We went to Fredonia to meet Chris, who agreed to take us on as his class project. We would have to donate a delay line to the school, which was around $1200-$1400 at the time. That was a lot of money for us. Especially as we did not have it. After borrowing some money from family members, we provided the delay line to the school. So that is how we came to record the first album, which we released as *Rock Hard*.

    We did not record it in one shot - it took months. We had to find time in between gigs and of course wait until Chris was able to book the studio, which he had to share with the other students. That was fine with us as we could not afford to give up two or three weeks of gigs, which were our sole source of income for the three of us. We would play a week or two of shows, then go to Fredonia and record a song. A lot of the time, we were writing at the studio also. We were working it out on the fly. Recording the album was interesting. We would stay at this cheap hotel in Fredonia when we had to record. We had to carry our two-inch tapes around with us - there was no vault at Fredonia. Our entire efforts were on these two-inch reels. There was no backup. We had to go to great lengths to keep the tapes safe as they were extremely fragile. Excessive heat, cold and moisture could easily render the tapes useless. These things were heavy; keep in mind this was before the digital age, and we could not keep everything on a computer. We would determine who had to haul these tapes around by a simple coin toss.

Whoever got the worst of the coin toss was dubbed "The CEO" and had to lug the tapes to and from the hotel room. It was not fun, especially in the seedy hotels we often stayed at, where in order to get to the room we had to travel down multiple hallways and corridors. But we always had fun laughing at the poor sod who had to lug these things around.

Because the recording process was taking so long, we figured it would be best if we released a single first. We wanted something to give to local radio stations, send to record companies, and sell at our gigs, so we released a 45 featuring "Crank It Up" and "You Better Run". Back then, the only way to communicate with radio or record executives was by standard mail or via the phone, which was quite expensive. We would send these out in the mail, and then follow up with a phone call. Calling some of these radio stations was nuts - often you would have to wait on hold for hours to speak with a program director.

We had sent it to a radio station which, I believe, was near Rochester; I cannot recall the name of the station, but their slogan was "Crank It Up." When I finally got one of their DJs on the phone to see if they had received the record, I introduced myself and the DJ said, "Hey man, it sounds great! We have been playing it constantly!" That was huge to us. To finally get airplay was a massive incentive to keep going. Back then, putting out a single or album on your own was not as easy as placing an order at the record pressing plant. First, we had to go through the union. We registered with the American Federation of Music and had to set it up through them using an attorney - it was a very lengthy and expensive process. This was needed if you wanted to be the registered owner of your music. It is not as simple as saying "I wrote this" - you had to follow the process and it was not cheap, nor was it easy. Especially when everything was done through standard mail and via phone. But that is what we did. I had set up an actual organization to ensure that we owned our own product. All so that we could get royalties in the future; if we were lucky enough to have any. I am sure there was a shortcut, but we did it the legal way. The long way. All of that for a simple 45. To accomplish that, we had to borrow even more money from friends and family. I wrote a lot of IOUs at that time. Thank God we got signed, and we were able to pay everyone back.

**Steve Starmer:**
*"I had been in a studio three or four times before that, doing singles and demos, but I had never done a full album before. It was my first time making an album where you had to do your parts over and over and over. You had to do them until they were 'just right.' Most of the material was written in the studio. I remember one session in particular - we were there recording two other songs. Carl says, 'I have an idea for a song, I want to call it*

"Woman". ' I said: 'Well how does it go? ' Carl said, 'I do not know - I only have the drumbeat.' So, all we had was a drum track. David listened to it and came up with a riff and melody. I put a bass line on it. Right then and there we built that song - while recording it. If you listen to the track, it starts in one time and speeds up and ends in another time. It came out great. We did a lot of the album like that. It took us around six months or so. Because we were paying for it ourselves. So, we go out and we play, make some money, and then come back and pay for a session or two. Then we would go out, play some more, and make some more money. We never made any money for ourselves. It all went into recording the album. There were a lot of expenses for that album beyond recording – we had to pay for the photo shoot, the layout, and the initial pressing. With living expenses, travel, etc. it was not cheap. We had two sound engineers - Chris Bubacz and John Petrie. They really knew what they were doing. God, they were just fantastic. It was a lot of fun. We also recorded some parts in Ithaca, and then we went to another place in Rochester for a track or two. It was really scattered - the album was slowly patched together. And it is amazing how cohesive it sounds."

### David "Rock" Feinstein:
"There was never really any friction as far as the sound went. With things like that, we pretty much agreed with everything that was happening. Carl and I produced it. We had the same influences and vision of the end result, which made it easy. Writing was the same way. I had some originals and Carl had some originals, and the three of us would get together and work out the bits and pieces. It was really easygoing."

Once the recording was finished, we rushed to get it printed. It was not cheap to press a run of 1,000 albums. Thank God for the friends and family members who helped us out. We were in debt for $32,000 when it was all said and done. We were really depending on this album. At that point, we really needed a major label contract. Management put us on a per diem of $5.00 a day - for all three of us. We were happy with the end result of the recording. For the pressing of the album, we decided to use a company in Texas, which did a great job pressing our single. Our contact at the pressing plant was a stern, by-the-book lady by the name of Vera. Vera was German and she was tough, with a thick accent. We really enjoyed working with her. For the cover design, we sent Vera a poster that had our picture and logo on it. Underneath, it said, "12 inches of hard rock and roll." Of course, it was a double entendre, but we thought it was clever. We sent her the poster in the mail. Weeks later we got a proof in the mail. It had the same image and the same font, but "12 inches of hard rock and roll," was now "2 inches of hard rock and roll." Of course, she did it on purpose - she was fucking with us. That gave us a laugh.

We ended up pressing one thousand LPs. The very day they arrived, we split them into thirds. They did not last long. Most of them went to radio stations and record companies, but it is amazing how quickly 1,000 albums can disappear.

# Bad Advice

Doug Thaler (a founding member of the band Elf, who later went on to work with Motley Crue), was helping us out during our first couple of years. Doug would help us book shows and would give us the occasional much-needed guidance. He had been part of Elf and had firsthand experience in what it takes for a successful local band to join the big leagues. Due to our rising popularity, Doug recommended we take on a manager. He told us, "There are two avenues you can go. You can go with Cedric Kushner, who is a great promoter, but you will most likely receive less attention than his bigger acts. Or you can take on a guy like Peter Morticelli who is not as well-known but will give you plenty of hands-on support." Ultimately, we decided to go with Peter because he was a local guy. Peter put us on a $5.00 a day per diem. That five bucks had to feed the three of us, pay for our gas, and anything else we wanted. Steve was a smoker so that left us with $4.00 and some change. We were always hungry, to say the least.

Doug still connected us to Cedric Kushner, who, with Doug's urging, was willing to add us as support act attached to some bigger bands that were scheduled to play in the area. Cedric agreed to add us as support for Judas Priest for one of their shows in upstate New York. This was huge. Priest had just released *British Steel* and they were pulling in some massive audiences. This new thing called "heavy metal" was starting to take off in a big way. We were finally going to play in a stadium. But there was one major issue - we had never played in a venue of that size. We had no clue about monitors. As a result, we had one of the most terrible shows of our lives. We could not hear each other during the performance. All I could hear was a massive roar. It sounded like a jet engine. I could not hear David and I came in with the drums based on a guess. It was atrocious. It was embarrassing. Imagine three different instruments starting the same song at three different times. The worst was yet to come. Cedric Kushner was quite powerful at the time. His name carried a lot of weight. After the show, Cedric approached David and said, "You need to fire your bass player." Right then and there the pressure was on us. We had just released an album and we thought listening to Cedric would help us get to the next step. Unfortunately, we took Cedric's advice and fired Steve. Now, Steve really did not have a downside. He did not have any addictions or an ego. We got along well with him. He was a great player. It still bothers me to this day that we let Steve go. Steve was from a well-known family in Cortland.

Everyone loved and respected the Starmer family; so when we let Steve go, we were hated immediately by a large percentage of the locals. To this very day, there are still people pissed at us for getting rid of Steve. It was something I have always regretted. Looking back, it was probably the best thing for Steve - he was able to focus on his family and have a career that was more stable than the music industry. But I really liked Steve. When you are young you tend to take the advice of any manager who has a big name and a bit of experience. You really do think they know best.

**David "Rock" Feinstein:**
*"It was definitely a management type of thing - a pure management decision. You know, Steve, he is a great guy. We love Steve. I know Steve's whole family - they live here in Cortland. Carl and I hated it when we had to let Steve go. First of all, he was a great bass player. Second, he is a great guy. He is really funny. There was really no reason that I can remember why Steve would ever have to leave the band. I think it was a power play with the management. I am sure they still do it. These record companies like to put these boy bands together - they put these individuals together that do not even know each other, all because they match physically. They look the part. And I really think it was something like that. Carl and I were basically forced, which made us feel really bad and put us in a really bad position. With Stephen, everybody that knew him loved him. He did not do anything wrong - that is for sure. I still regret it to this very day."*

**Steve Starmer:**
*"Well, I think it was the managers at the time. I do not know, maybe I did not come across the way they wanted. I really do not know. But it was not a happy ending. I mean, what the hell? But yeah, I am not sure. I am really not sure where the responsibility lies for me leaving. I do not know if it is because I had too much baggage. I had a daughter at the time, and I was supporting her and that was playing on my mind constantly and that kind of thing. And at the time, my family was splitting up. And that is what made it difficult. I had some responsibilities that I had to take care of. That was more important. And it came out in my music. I think one of the reasons that I lost. Looking back, I am grateful for it. We had a terrible manager - I thought that from the very beginning. I did not trust him from the start. He and I did not hit it off. And I cannot recall if Carl and Dave agreed with me or disagreed with me, but it was at the point where he really did not like me. I did not like him. I did not trust him. And I was pretty good at summing a person up. I could tell a good character in a person when I met them, and he just did not strike me as a guy that was honest. So, we opened for Judas Priest. And we had a horrible, horrible night. I mean, it was terrible. We*

*could not hear anything. I know that the potential manager was there. But after that, I was pretty much gone. I was bummed. I put my bass guitar in my case. And I got a couple of calls. One wanted me to come to Louisiana. They had heard my music and they wanted me to play for them and they sent me an airplane ticket. There were a couple of other things that I was asked to do. But my heart was not in it anymore. I put my guitar down for about 10 years. I did not touch it for 10 years!"*

# Manowar

While the Rods were making a name for themselves, I was playing in another band. That band was Manowar. This was in 1980 or so, right when we began recording *Rock Hard*. We were a small community of musicians so it was common for things to get a bit incestuous. Manowar began when Joey DeMaio (bass) met Ross the Boss (guitar). They found a local guy to sing: Eric Adams. Eric was such a great singer. A real powerhouse. Joey asked me to join them on drums. Which I did. At that point, I was committed to The Rods, and I worked well with David, but I was curious to see where Manowar was going. Heavy metal was a new thing at the time and Joey really wanted to take this new style of music to the next level. I spent a few days rehearsing with Manowar, and it was a lot of fun. I had been with the band during the writing process and while they were fleshing it out during their genesis. I also flew to New York with them to meet with EMI. There was one main problem: Manowar was Joey's band. If I stayed in Manowar, I would have been relegated solely to a drummer. A supporting player. But with The Rods, I was an equal. I wrote songs, produced, and contributed equally. For me, that was important. At one point, we were in Rochester recording a piece for The Rods' first album and Manowar happened to be in the same studio, a few yards down the hall. I worked on the two Rods tracks and the next day went and did the Manowar demo. Right after recording the demo, I decided to leave Manowar. It was a tough decision. It was not a popular decision, and I think Joey is still upset with me.

**Ross The Boss**; *Ex-Manowar, Ex-Dictators, Ex-Shakin Street, Ex-Manitobas Wild Kingdom, Ross the Boss band:*
*"I got a demo budget from my friend at EMI, Bob Curry. We (Joey DeMaio and I) decided to make a demo. Joey says, 'I know this guy Carl Canedy who plays the drums. He is unbelievable... he is great!' So, we scheduled it (rehearsal). I know we practiced a couple of times. And then we went into the studio. That is how I met Carl. He did that original demo. I wanted him to be in the band. He was just impressive - a really impressive drummer. And he played beautifully on the demo, and obviously, that is the demo that got us signed to EMI. He passed on Manowar because of The Rods, which I respect of course. I respect his decision. And you know, we remain friends to this day. Can you imagine Carl in Manowar? Man, that would have been awesome. He was amazing."*

Remember how I said things could get incestuous? Let me backtrack, as this happened prior to the Manowar demo. After Steve's departure, we needed a bass player. Right away our friend Craig Gruber agreed to help us. Craig had played with Rainbow and was well-known on the scene. We knew he would not stick around long. He was getting a lot of offers at the time. Craig was an amazing bass player and said he would play some gigs with us until he got a call. We also brought Eric Adams in for vocal duties. That would be the same Eric Adams who would go on to sing for Manowar. David had always wanted to bring a vocalist in so that he could focus on guitar. We really could not find an appropriate singer until Eric came along. Eric was awesome. He had a great voice and was very charismatic. Well, our manager suggested we get rid of Eric. "He is not a good fit for The Rods," he told us. And we listened. It never went beyond that practice session. But everything worked out in the end. David's vocals were a great fit for The Rods. Months after joining, Craig got a call from Black Sabbath. This was when Geezer left Sabbath. We knew the day would come when Craig would have to leave us, so we had been thinking about another solution for a few months. We knew this guy who lived in the area by the name of Gary Bordonaro. He had the look, and he had the chops. A friend had told us that Gary's band was going through some difficulties, and they were on the verge of breaking up. So we reached out to Gary and invited him to join. Gary was the perfect fit. He was easygoing and he was a serious player. He had some great stage moves. It was a no-brainer.

**Chris Bubacz;** *AKA Dr. Metal, Recording Engineer*
*"I was a senior in college, and we had to provide what they call 'the senior project'- which is our final work before we graduated. I wanted to do a full album from start to finish. So, my brother Greg introduced me to The Rods. Now, most students recorded other students, so they did not really incur a lot of costs, but the fact that these guys were a professional band, and we were going to be recording them was really cool. The school felt a donation would be appropriate and the suggested donation was a Lexicon delay line. It was an inexpensive way to record a whole album. I got a good grade. Yeah. I got a good grade, and everybody was happy with the recording other than me. I think that I really did not have any professional experience up to that point. They were a great band, and I was in the right place at the right time, so to speak. And I was happy to hear that they got signed - for sure. The Rods helped me to land Metallica, which really started everything. There was a classmate of mine that was offered a job in Rochester. He worked with me on Rock Hard - John Petri was his name. He was offered a job as a chief engineer in Rochester and did not*

*want it - so he suggested that I investigate it, which I did. And I got the job and then I moved to Rochester. Jonny Z, who was the president of Megaforce records, was looking to record an album upstate for a new band by the name of Metallica. There was another band called Manowar - they were like the nemesis of The Rods. They had kind of a feud going back and forth. And they had recorded at the studio that I was working at in Rochester, but they would not work with me because I had worked with The Rods. So, they (Manowar) would not work with me - they wanted to work with another engineer. Jonny Z was looking for a place to do Metallica and he talked to the guys in Manowar, and they said, 'It is a great studio but do not deal with an engineer named Chris Bubacz.' Not that they would know - they never worked with me. They hated that I was close to The Rods. So, when Jonny Z calls to book the studio, the only name he can remember is 'Chris Bubacz.' So of course he asked for me because he did not know any other names. And that started my career with Megaforce - they (Manowar) really did me a favor in the end. If you want to look at it that way."*

# Getting Higher

Our manager, Peter, was using an attorney in NYC by the name of Jonathan Blank. Johnathan had a lot of major label connections and knew a lot of people in the industry. Through Johnathan, Peter was given a contact at Ariola records. Ariola was a subsidiary of Bertelsmann, which was a large German media conglomerate. Peter gave them a copy of *Rock Hard,* and shortly after, they offered to sign us. Warren Schatz, who was the A&R for Ariola, pushed to sign us. We were finally there!

Or were we? The ink was not even dry on the documents when we got the word that Ariola had just been purchased by Arista Records. Typically, when a record company purchases another, the new and underperforming bands are quickly shelved. They tend to keep the anchor acts (bigger acts that consistently provide income and airplay). Traditionally, the A&R reps are often dismissed as well. But the charmed life makes an appearance - and this is where we got lucky: Mike Bone was an A&R rep for Arista. He took one listen to *Rock Hard* and fought to keep us on the roster. Mike loved us. Who knows what would have happened if Mike had not backed us. Keep in mind, this was in 1980, and at that time, record companies were still cautious when it came to new hard rock acts. This was before the "sign every band with long hair" trend that occurred later in the decade. Mike was in our corner and thanks to him we were able to keep our contract. We were really worried for some time.

While it was great to have a major label backing us, we were on the same label as Air Supply and Aretha Franklin. I remember Pete coming back from a meeting saying that we did not get the tour support we were asking for because Aretha Franklin "needed record store promotion," and Air Supply needed these massive glowing rocks for their stage set. So we got the shaft on tour support for glowing rocks. Thanks, Air Supply.

As for being signed, that was an amazing feeling. It was a total validation of everything we had been working for. With our advance, we were able to pay our bills and pay back family members we borrowed from. It was also interesting to see the dynamic: suddenly the girlfriends were freaking out, because now we were going to be gone for a lot longer and a lot further away. Few relationships survive the world tour. I was so focused on getting a deal, it never occurred to me that this was not going to be a win for everybody. There was another side as well - the side of jealousy and anger. One guy said to me, "You guys got signed? Wow, if you can get signed then anyone can get signed!" Suddenly, some people started treating us differently. As for us, nothing changed. We did not make any money. We were still playing clubs, and we were still struggling. And I did not notice it at first, but old friends would suddenly call, and they would start kissing your ass. Friends who had made no effort to converse with you for years. It was disappointing in a way to see how human nature works and how we were perceived and how it changed. It changed the dynamic. Al Falso was the one person who was unfazed and unchanged by it. He was the man. He was in our corner. He was not looking at us like we were big rock stars. Al was like, "You're the same bums you always were." But he was really happy for us.

### David "Rock" Feinstein:

"Well, we went through another bass player before Gary, and he was from Cortland - Craig Gruber. We shared some history. He played with Gary Moore. He was in Rainbow for a while. He had some credentials, and he was a good bass player. And he was a local guy. And at the time, he was not doing anything else. He played with us for a while – for a few live dates. Craig was a great guy. And he was a great bass player. But it did not have that magic, you know what I mean? In a trio, you really need to have that magic. Chemistry is important. Otherwise, with a trio, it sounds too thin. It was another month before we found Gary. He was another local guy that was playing in a band. We met Gary and he looked really good. He was younger than Carl and me. He was such a great bass player. He had a great look. He was a really good singer. We had a rehearsal with him, and it was the kind of magic we were looking for. We felt it right away. We were like, 'This is it man. We are complete now!' He was definitely the right guy."

### Warren Schatz; *Record Company Executive*

"I was running the Ariola division. Peter Morticelli called me up, told me about The Rods and sent me a package. I listened to them and signed them right away. I had not dealt with Peter in the past, but I knew he was booking acts in Rochester. He had this little production company or label and he was recording some of these bands. When I was at RCA, I signed bands like Triumph, which was also a trio - a heavy, hard rock trio. And then at Ariola, I also signed a band called Krokus. I thought that The Rods fit into that kind of world. With those kinds of bands, I was not concerned about whether they had a hit single or radio friendly single - bands like Rush and Triumph were not particularly known for their individual songs as opposed to their high energy stage performance. So, I thought that The Rods were easily in the same class as all those other really good rock bands. I really did not know that much about the whole heavy metal scene. But *when I played the record, our promotion guy went nuts. He went nuts over The Rods. So that was a sign to me that at least I was not crazy. I thought the record was really well done. And I knew that Peter really believed in them, and he knew what he could do with them up there. Also Peter did not beat me over the head with a big advance. Normally, we did not really look at unsolicited stuff. It either came through people I have known in the business or through lawyers. Now, my thought is that if someone was spending the money on a lawyer, then they definitely believe in themselves - and we would always give them a listen. They obviously believed in what they had because New York lawyers, even back then, were charging a minimum of $5,000 just to walk down the street and take your tape. Ariola was one of the largest companies in the world. People were not bugging us with garbage music. Peter had a plan to tour them, and he did not beat me over the head with a big advance. It was a very, very reasonable deal financially. So, they made it easier for me to just move things forward. Kudos to Peter. Otherwise, it would have been very difficult. For me it was all an upside. An easy sign. Just before the record came out, we closed Ariola and I left - and my whole staff left, and there were a lot of records that never got put out."*

# Arista

When I was around nine years old, I watched a movie called *Circus of Horrors*, which frightened me. I thought it was terrifying, but I loved it. There was a song in the movie called "Wish for a Star". I bought the 45 and I played it to death. I was just getting into music. And as I've mentioned numerous times, I was sad and lonely at that age. I remember walking around the backyard feeling lonely and singing "Wish for a Star". I was hoping that something was going to make things right, something or someone was going to take away the loneliness, the sadness, and that somehow all of the things that happened to me would somehow be taken care of. Years later, when I took up drumming, I thought that if I could just get signed, that if I could get a major label deal, that it would make all of the emptiness go away. Flash forward to when The Rods were finally getting signed, and we had to do a showcase for Clive Davis. Clive founded and oversaw Arista Records, so it was a big, big deal. The showcase was at the legendary CBGB's. After the gig, I walked to the corner to a pay phone, and I called my mother. I told her that we had been signed to a major label! Getting signed had been a big goal of mine, so I was thrilled. She was like, "Oh, well, that's nice." She had no clue. But I was thrilled. And then I started crying, because up to that point, I thought all of the sadness in my life would be taken away by achieving this goal. I thought that once I got a major label deal, that would make me happy and take away the sadness and the emptiness that I felt. And... that didn't happen. It was a bittersweet moment. I realized that nothing in my life had changed. Nothing took away the sadness, the emptiness, that empty feeling inside, the hollow feeling, whatever you want to call it.

Now that we had a record contract, the next step was to release an album. Arista was happy enough with *Rock Hard* that they wanted to release it - almost as is. That says a lot; that an independent album, recorded with no outside production, that utilized first-time student engineers, and was recorded over many months at a small upstate college, was good enough to be re-released with the Arista name on it. For the Arista version, they remastered the album and had us go into the studio to record two additional songs: "Nothing Going on in the City" and "Ace in the Hole". We quickly recorded those two songs at Music America Studios in Rochester, NY. They removed the following songs: "In Your Panties", "Sit Down Honey" and "Getting Higher". They also removed *Rock Hard* as a title, and it was launched as a self-titled LP. Arista quickly repackaged the album and out it went. We were now officially major label recording artists!

Right away, it became clear that Arista was not going to give us much support. We hired AEI as our booking agency. They managed to get us some shows, in addition to the gigs Peter booked for us. We were still playing clubs. Outside of upstate New York, we were back to square one - trying to build a fanbase. We did not get new equipment, a stage set or a tour bus. Honestly, not much changed. Arista released "Power Lover" as a single, with "Nothing Going on in the City" as a B-side. Our friend Victoria phoned to tell us we had a review in *Sounds* magazine. *Sounds*, a British publication, was much more in tune with the newly developing rock scene than American publications were. American magazines (such as *Cream* and *Circus*) were focused on the mainstream rock acts and did a poor job of trends abroad such as the New Wave of British Heavy Metal. Outside of Black Sabbath and AC/DC, heavy metal had yet to hit the newsstands in America. England, thanks to birthing the New Wave of British Heavy Metal, was at the forefront in terms of heavy metal. Victoria called us to tell us that *Sounds* had given our album five stars. Five stars in *Sounds* was quite an accomplishment. In the review, they called us the "American Motorhead" - we had no idea who Motorhead was, so we went to the record store and picked up the album *Ace of Spades*, which Motorhead had just released. We were blown away by the look and attitude on the album cover. The guys in Motorhead looked legitimately badass. *Sounds* gave us a huge compliment.

We spent the rest of the year touring. We played some dates with Foghat, which went very well. We did some shows with Benny Mardones and Point Blank. It was a strange time in which the booking agency was adding us as support for any rock band with shows booked in the northeast – but during 1980, there were not a lot of major label American rock acts touring. Of course, that was to change once the 1980s got underway. We played central to western New York State as part of our routine. One gig was in Canandaigua, NY. It was the first time we played there. In the crowd, there was a very nice-looking girl who Gary spent the night with. She was very attractive, and she seemed really nice. She was not your typical groupie. She had a girl-next-door vibe. Gary really liked her. But Gary came back a day or so later, and he said, "I think I have crabs. I am not sure where I got them from." And Gary definitely had crabs. He was freaking out and he had to buy the shampoo that gets rid of them - or whatever you buy for that kind of thing. David and I were messing with him. We said, "Gary, you know you got it from that girl in Canandaigua, right?" He replied, "No way. She is so sweet. She is so innocent." We could not convince him that she was the source, and most likely, she was sleeping with a lot of guys. But he swore up and down. "No, no, no, no, it could never be her. She is an angel. She is so sweet." David and I would laugh and laugh about it. We continued to bust his balls, saying that she was not as innocent as he thought. Gary was not convinced. We ended up playing there a few months later and once again, Gary hooked up with this girl. Well, he came back a day later to find he had crabs once again! We were dying laughing. Poor Gary had to admit that yes, it was more than likely her. That sweet little angel had crabs and passed them generously on to Gary - twice. As broken-hearted as Gary was, David and I were merciless. We did not let him live it down and Gary was a good sport.

Meanwhile, we were starting to write and record demos for the second album. Back then, you were expected to record an album every year - and tour to support it. The record companies really put the pressure on in that respect, to keep that momentum (and the sales) going strong. We were still broke, and consequently I was living in this rundown shack in Cortland. My friend Greg was rooming with me. We called it "the Nest" - but it should have been called "the Dump". It was a mess. Every day we would wake up to slugs, snails and mice roaming the floors. Many songs were written there, though. I was constantly writing and recording songs on my TEAC 4-track recorder. David was doing the same, so when it came time to record the next album, we had plenty of material.

**Greg Bubacz;** *Longtime Friend*

*"We were living in a shack. I had a full-time job, and Carl was with The Rods. The neighbors had three dogs that were constantly barking - every time we left the Nest, the dogs would go absolutely crazy. They were tied up – thank God. But that is where the idea for the three headed dog on the Wild Dogs album cover came from. Our place was so bad. One day I was with a female friend and her young daughter, and we were on the way to see Carl, and the young girl goes, 'Mommy, are we going to go visit the man in the broken house?' It was on stilts - it did not even have a foundation. We were both very busy, so we were rarely there. What a dump."*

# Wild Dogs

As the first tour came to a close, Arista called us in to discuss the second album. We really liked working with Chris Bubacz and John Petri, and we recommended to Arista that we use the same team (with David and me producing) for the second album. They shut down that idea right away. Arista was insistent upon a well-known studio – and a well-known producer to boot. One of the first names recommended by Arista was Chris Tsangarides. We had not known of Chris at the time. We had only heard that he produced Tygers of Pang Tang. We, being young and inexperienced, passed on Chris because "We do not want to sound like the Tygers of Pang Tang." We passed on Chris - which is insane as Chris went on to produce hit albums for Thin Lizzy, Anvil, and Judas Priest. It is a huge regret to this day that we passed on him. Of course, that reasoning has come back to haunt me many times over. Years later, when I started producing, new bands would pass on me because "We do not want to sound like Anthrax" or "We do not want to sound like The Rods." Of course, the reality is that if you have your own identity, a producer and/or engineer cannot make you sound like something you are not. Looking back, Chris would have been the perfect producer for *Wild Dogs*. I would have loved for Chris to produce a Rods album, but it never came to fruition, and sadly Chris passed away in 2018. Mark Dodson was also recommended. He had worked as an engineer on Joan Jett's first album. Of course, we passed on him because "We do not want to sound like Joan Jett." And once again we missed out on what potentially could have been a great producer. So, after we passed on two great producers, a producer by the name of Martin Pearson was recommended. Martin produced Krokus's *Metal Rendez-vous*. He only produced one Krokus album, and was not asked to do the follow up, and we later realized why. He was a nice guy, but he was not an effective engineer, in my opinion.

Having secured a producer, Arista booked us at Parkgate Studio in Sussex, England. Parkgate was located far out in the English countryside. We were stoked to be recording there. Around this time, I started to have these fierce premonitions. It felt like a panic attack – but it was not a panic or anxiety attack. It was a sudden and overwhelming feeling of doom. It was quite strange how they came on rather suddenly. I knew that something bad was around the corner. I could feel it. I had this enormous feeling that I was going to die before the album was finished. Death felt very, very near.

I was not sure why I was getting these intense premonitions all of a sudden. They kept getting increasingly worse and only a couple of weeks before we were to leave for England, I received a call from my cousin Ann. Ann was a nurse at St. Joe's hospital in Elmira. She told me that my mother had come to the hospital earlier in the week. It was not good news. Mom had a very serious form of cancer, and unfortunately that cancer was spreading rapidly. I was able to speak with Mom's doctor. He told me that Mom did not have much longer to live. The cancer was terminal. We were only days away from going to Sussex to record. It was scheduled to take two weeks, paired with an Iron Maiden tour that would last for an additional 30 days. That was not something that could have been postponed - both the studio and the tour were booked. We were contractually obligated to do both. Further, Mom's doctor and Mom assured me there was plenty of time. Both urged me to finish the recording and the tour and come home to spend the remaining months with Mom. Dianne and Greg moved in with Mom to take care of her while I was in England.

Parkgate Studios was beautiful. The studio was in a large barn. It was in the country - very secluded, quiet and peaceful. Kind of an odd setting for a hard rock album. The lord of the manor was there to have dinner with us the first night. I remember him asking his wife, "What's for puddin' love?" It took me a second to realize he was asking her what was for dessert - I thought that was the strangest thing. It really was a new experience for us. But I loved everything about England. The people were fantastic. The countryside was beautiful. I felt I could be content living there. The next day we began working on *Wild Dogs*. Martin Pearson came in and he started telling us where the drums would fall in terms of frequency. Martin wanted the drums really loose, so loose that my drumheads were barely on. This really bothered me. Martin did not even take a few minutes to observe how I play and analyze the tuning based on that. He wanted me to just slam the drums rather than use my standard style of playing. In order to get the sound that he was looking for, I ended up breaking a bass drum beater. In all the years I have played, no one has ever asked me to play louder. I was only told the opposite. It was definitely a new approach for me, and I hated every second of it. It was like clubbing the drums.

After destroying my drum technique, Martin moved on to the guitars. He made David's guitar sound razor thin. It made for a terrible guitar sound. For the bass, Gary's sound was traditionally mid-range. But Martin pushed for an opposing range. How Martin liked his bass sound was the opposite of what we preferred. But that was his choice and that was what we went with. Live, the band had a strong bass sound, and that was what we wanted to convey. This was not starting off well. For a band who had been producing their own material, it was especially difficult. Well, we were young, and cocky as well - I do not think that helped either. The record company was also pushing some cover songs on us, songs owned by their publishing company. We really did not like the songs they were pushing. I cannot recall what they were; they could have been good, but we really had our minds made up about the songs on the album. I think they were trying to give us some radio-friendly material. There was a lot of pressure on doing two of these songs, and we fought back. Peter ended up getting involved and there was a big pissing match. Peter was pissed at us, and rightfully so. Mike Bone was our A&R guy and was adamant we record these songs. He had not steered us wrong on the first album and we should have given him the benefit of the doubt. We should have recorded our songs and the two songs he requested. But it was black and white for us. No one showed us that there are gray areas. So we did not do the two songs. It was a lot of pressure up to that point from Mike Bone. We refused, and we thought we had won, but looking back, this most definitely hurt us. Eventually we finished the album, having pissed off the record company in the process.

Having finished the recording of *Wild Dogs*, we headed off to do our first set of gigs in England. By now, Arista had released an EP in the UK, which was basically six songs from the first album (our first album did not have distribution in the UK). We were also getting some press in the magazines, so the response at the gigs was fantastic. I have some great memories from that time - going through Stratford and past Shakespeare's house, seeing all the historical sites - things you hear about in America, but few ever have the opportunity to see them. We got to tour the Marshall factory with Jim Marshall. It was amazing to see how they were made. They were handmade at that time (in 1982). We've all grown up with Marshalls - they were the amplifier of the day, and to see them being made by hand was really cool. Peter was with us, taking pictures of us with Jim and of the Marshall production line. After leaving the facility, we were in the van and Peter said, "Oh *shit*!" He had just discovered he had not loaded any film in the camera. He had taken all those pictures with nothing to show for it. So we turned around and went back - just to get pictures of the factory.

We had a fantastic road crew. They were dedicated and they were loyal. Jeff Tarbell was my drum tech. He did a great job. In fact, after the *Wild Dogs* tour, we came back to America, and Jeff was offered a gig with Bon Jovi. And after he had been out with Bon Jovi for a while, I asked him how it was, working for Tico. And he said, "Carl, after working for you, it is a breeze!" He was being funny but there is some truth to that. I was anal about my drum equipment. All of my drumheads were numbered. Each drum had a specific drumhead that was used on that drum. I sorted my sticks, by left hand, right hand, and by weight. I would have sticks on the left and sticks on the right. And while I was playing, if I stuck my left hand down, Jeff would put a stick in it. If I held my hand out in the shape of a U, he would put a drink in it. We had a system. There was a science behind it. And we had it down. Being organized allowed me to play very comfortably and with total freedom. So I can imagine that when he went with Tico Torres (Bon Jovi's drummer), he probably did not have to have that intense work the entire show the way he did with me. Jeff was truly fantastic. And he was beloved by everybody. I do not think I ever saw him get angry, no matter what was thrown at him. When we got back to the States, and our equipment had been brought back, Jeff opened the cases, and everything was in pieces. Apparently, customs went through everything looking for drugs. I mean everything was taken apart. Everything. And they did not put anything back together. Jeff said, "Well that sucks, let's get it back together, shall we?" It did not even phase him. He had a great attitude.

As the gigs continued, the band got tighter, and the fans were responding unbelievably well. The Iron Maiden tour was fantastic. After the first show, it was clear that this was going to be a great tour. We got along really well with the guys in Maiden. Unfortunately, two nights into the Maiden tour, I got a call from Dianne. Mom was getting worse. Her health was rapidly declining, and the outlook was not good. We really had not expected that this soon. We knew her time was limited, but this was only weeks after her diagnosis. I booked a flight back home with Peter. While at Heathrow Airport, I called Dianne to let her know we were on the way and relay our ETA. She told me "No need to hurry," which was her way of letting me know that Mom had passed. I had lost my father at an early age, and now I had lost my mother. It hurt even more that I was not there for her final days. Nor was she there to hear about our newfound success. Thank God for Dianne and Greg, who had been taking care of her. We would have to miss a few dates on the Iron Maiden tour. The guys were more than understanding. I flew home to take care of Mom's affairs. It was a long, heartbreaking flight. Once again, I found myself on a plane to find a dead parent. I was back home only for a few days - I had to come right back. There was no time to grieve, to mourn, or to drown my sorrows. It did not even seem real. It felt like a dream. I had not even begun to process my emotions.

When I was around 15, I began to worry about my mother dying. My fear was that if my mother died, I would be alone in the world. And that used to terrify me. My entire life to that point had been my mother and me. So I began asking Mom to stop smoking. This was the era when people were becoming aware that smoking caused cancer. I would constantly ask Mom to quit smoking. I would say to her, "Mom, if you quit smoking, you might live an extra day, and that extra day might be very important." I would beg her to stop. I had asked her a number of times. In the end, it was lung cancer that got her. And when I was flying home, I realized that I did not get that extra day.

Speaking of important days, one of my big regrets is that Mom never got to see me play an arena show. Playing your first arena show is a huge milestone. For our first arena show, The Rods were booked to play in Binghamton, opening for a Blue Oyster Cult. It was our first big show, and it was kind of our hometown area, so we were really excited. I really wanted Mom to be there. The plan was, as my mother did not drive, that Dianne would pick her up and bring her to the arena. Mom had never obtained a license, so she was at the mercy of other people. Diane was driving from Ithaca with a friend, and unbeknownst to me, Dianne had changed the plan and decided not to pick up my mother. When Dianne arrived at the arena, I was shocked because Mom was not there. Sadly, my mother never got to see me play again, and she never got to see me play an arena show. That is a big regret. It was no fault of Dianne's, but nonetheless, it was painful and remains painful to me.

Once back in the UK, we rejoined the tour, and the response was increasingly enthusiastic. The fans were absolutely rabid. Maiden hired one of our roadies, Warren, to dress up as Eddie each night. This was the early days of Eddie - at that time, he was essentially a guy in a cheap costume. It was nothing like the massive Eddie of the late 1980s. For the second to last show, we played the Hammersmith Odeon. At the Hammersmith, we were in the dressing room getting ready to go on. Joe Elliot from Def Leppard came through. He was not particularly nice. He was kind of arrogant – he stood there, said nothing, and then left. He would not even talk to us. Aside from that, I think we had a really good show. The last show was going to be at The Marquee. We were excited to move on to the next task (the mixing of the album) but we were sad to see the Maiden tour end. We had so much fun, and we really enjoyed the UK. Personally, I had held it together for all those weeks on the tour. I suppressed my hurt. After we finished our set at the Hammersmith Odeon, the band and the road crew were celebrating in the dressing room. But not me. My mother's passing had finally hit me... I found the bathroom backstage and broke down in tears. I had kept it together the entire tour, but at that moment, completely alone in that crappy bathroom, I was finally able to let my emotions out. Here I had just finished playing at a legendary venue and was soon to play another - both The Marquee and Hammersmith Odeon were arenas of legend - and I should have been ecstatic, but the loss of my mother weighed so heavily on me, I locked myself in the bathroom and had a much-needed cry. Everyone was celebrating and I was in the bathroom crying. The pressure of pretending to be ok finally hit me. My mother was such an important part of my life, and now she was gone.

At The Marquee, we intended to record some of the show. Once at the venue, I ran through some notes with some of the sound guys. The Marquee was cool - they had a recording setup attached to the stage. The Marquee is the stuff of legends. The dressing room was plastered with graffiti, writing and doodling from the many previous bands. We were in awe as we found signatures and scribbling from some of our favorite bands. It was very surreal. Oh, and we were headlining this show. Iron Maiden had finished their dates and we were on our own for this one. It was a monumental moment. I remember going on stage and seeing a massive crowd - the energy was intense. The Marquee lights were set low, and of course, I had a large drum riser... well, those lights were so hot and so close to my set that I touched the rim of the drum to adjust it and burnt the shit out of my hand. I had not even started playing and I had burnt my hand - but there was no stopping. We went right into it and the crowd went crazy. After a few songs, David began his guitar solo, so I snuck backstage to get a break from the sauna created by the lights. I was covered in sweat. I had to get a towel. I moved the lock on the dressing room door and ended up slicing my hand on a piece of loose metal. My hand was now bleeding. And then I heard David's solo in high gear. I ran into the dressing room and reached for a towel when something caught my eye. Standing in the corner, staring at a scantily clad outfit on a hanger, was a very naked woman. It turned out that Peter had hired her to dance on the stage. I definitely was not expecting that. She smiled and said hi. I ran back on stage and got behind my kit. One burnt hand and one hand bleeding - that was rock and roll. A few minutes later, we started playing "Violation" and the stripper came out on stage. No one expected it. David started rubbing his guitar on her ass. The place went crazy. What a great way to end the show and wrap up the England experience! It was such a mix of emotions. It was such a great time for The Rods, yet it was colliding with one of the worst events of my life.

**Ann;** *Cousin*
*"Another family member told me America (Carl's mom) was at the hospital and was really sick. I was working a shift, so I went to see her. They had diagnosed her with pneumonia at first. After some more testing, they discovered it was cancer and it was terminal. It came about quickly. Really quick. I recall when she had gotten so bad that she was admitted full-time to the hospital. It was really tough. We are Italian - we were a very close family. Carl had been through a lot as a child. And he was still considered young when he lost his mother."*

Next we had to mix the album. To do so, we had to rent some outboard gear, compressors, and delay lines from Pink Floyd. Pink Floyd had so much equipment that they would rent it out when they were not on the road. When we started the mixing process, England had the worst snowstorm in decades. Now, we were upstate New York boys - we were used to snow. Heavy snowfall was part of our climate. Heavy snowfall for us was 3-4 feet. For England, it was a mere few inches. England was not equipped to handle so much snow. The town we stayed in did not even have a snowplow. No salt trucks. No snow removal plan - nothing. The town shut down completely. Nothing was open. And we could not go anywhere. All because of a few inches of snow. Some of the locals were hired to provide the food and cook for us over the coming week. On our first night there, we arrived to find a large feast waiting for us. This was some feast, and we were more than willing to demolish it. Which we did. And then we finally put two and two together and realized that they had made all of our food at once. This was the sole food for the coming week. They had prepared it and left it out and we consumed it thinking it a gracious welcome meal. So, with everything shut down, we had no more food for the coming week with no way to purchase or prepare food. I remember being very hungry that week.

We finished mixing the album. Looking back, I was not happy with the result. Overall, the drums were overpowering, the guitars were thin, and the bass was weak. I am partly to blame. We all had our hands in it. But at the end of the day, Martin was not the right guy to produce that album. Our second album should have been over the top. Arista pumped a ton of money into it - at least compared to what we spent on the first album. *Wild Dogs* should have been harder and heavier. It had a thinner sound in comparison to what other bands of the genre and era were doing. It was wimpy. Writing-wise, I felt we had some great material. Much of this album we still perform live. Some great, great songs are on that album, but unfortunately, the production did not convey that. To this day, *Wild Dogs* is our most well-known album. Is it our best? I do not think so, mainly because of the production, but the material is strong. *Wild Dogs* was the album that solidified our brand. It also taught us a lesson – that David and I needed to produce our albums. No one understood our sound, and the end result we were seeking, better than us. To date, this was the only Rods album not produced by David and me.

**Peggy;** *Cousin*
*"I remember Carl came to visit my mother in the hospital. This was the early 80s. I was there with my kids, who were very young at the time. Carl walks in with his heavy metal outfit on. He had on leather and chains, and it was all black - we had never seen anything like that. My mom thought it was the strangest thing she had ever seen. Here was Carl, dressed in chains and leather. My kids still talk about that to this very day."*

A review on Amazon for *Wild Dogs*: *"Hard rock at its best without the spandex and women's makeup"*

**Mike Bone;** *Former VP of A&R and Promotion for Arista Records*
"When I joined Arista, they were a pop-leaning label. They had Barry Manilow, Air Supply, and Whitney Houston - that was sort of their stock in trade, they were not really a rock label. I mean, they had The Outlaws and a couple of other bands. I do not remember all the artists on the roster, but I was a rock guy, I had worked at Mercury in Chicago and worked with Rush and Thin Lizzy. I wanted to have more bands of this type. And so that's how we came to sign The Rods. As for Krokus, we had the option of picking them up for North America. And so that was just a contractual thing - we had the option to pass on them or pick them up and we decided to pick them up. But The Rods was more of an A&R thing, where we actually went out and saw them live. I forget who the A&R person was at the time, but they made the decision to sign them - which I was supportive of. I had a relationship with their manager Peter as well. I do not remember fighting with the guys about recording the two cover songs - that was 40 years ago.
But it sounds right. I was a promotion person. It was my job to get records on radio stations. So I was always looking for material that I could get on some radio station somewhere. I may have sent them some songs that I felt like that, if they covered these that I might, it might make it easier to get them success on the radio. As a promotion person and the time and rock radio being what it was, you had to do things like that. Airplay was important. If you were not on the radio, then most likely you were not making any money. I was always looking to put records on radio stations.
So anyway, that was my job. I remember commissioning someone to do the album artwork for Wild Dogs. Which, in hindsight, was pretty cool. But at the time, I went to the art department, and the guy who ran it - I cannot remember his name, but he really knew his stuff. I said, "Look, this is what I'm looking for. We are looking for a three-headed animal, aggressive and mean." So he came up with the cover that you see today. Look, to me, it looks like the dog is backing up. He is kind of backed into a corner and snarling. I was looking for something like the dog is on the hunt or on the attack. Aggressive and lunging forward. I remember he and I had a long discussion about that. He was like: 'You know, we have spent more money on this fucking album cover. I cannot go back to the artist and make the dog go forward instead of backing up'. So it was never fixed. I felt like that would have been a better album cover. I think the fact that here we are 42 years later still talking about this is indicative of the fact that something was going on with the band. So anyway, they were, they were good people.

*And I wish that I had been able to give them a larger platform. As far as their demise with Arista, and I do not know this to be a fact, I left and went to another label. Once I left, there was nobody in their corner. There were no hard rock/heavy metal fans in upper management. Everyone else thought heavy metal really does not fit with Barry Manilow or Air Supply."*

**Les Edwards;** *Artist of the Wild Dogs album cover*
"Most of my work, at the time and for most of my career, has been in publishing and painting book jackets - with only the occasional diversion into movie posters or album covers. In fact, I've only done a few album covers: a job for the rock group Legs Diamond and some artwork for The Prodigy. One of my paintings was used by Metallica but was originally done as a book cover. I do not remember much about the job (Wild Dogs) but it would have come through my agent at the time, much like all of my other work. I do not recall having any contact with the band and I do not know why I was chosen for the job, except that I was pretty much the go-to guy in the UK for that sort of imagery. As a rock fan, I was aware of The Rods. My original sketch for the cover was just a single dog's head but someone decided that a full body was necessary. I do remember that they insisted on the dog holding its paw out toward the viewer. I was uncomfortable with that as I did not think it looked natural and I've never felt it looked quite right. I think my original idea would have had more impact but I'm sure the band or their management had reasons for their decisions. The client is always right. I occasionally get asked about the cover. It always amazes me when someone wants to know about the work that I did such a long time ago. One of the surprises of advancing years I suppose."

# Elf and Ronnie James Dio

I was only 18 when I met Ronnie James Dio for the first time. At that point, he fronted an extremely popular local band called Ronnie Dio and The Prophets, and he later went on to form The Elves with his cousin, David "Rock" Feinstein. The Elves later shortened their name to Elf, and Elf became massive locally - and as a result, they got a deal with Epic. They toured heavily throughout the northeast. (The same circuit The Rods later played.) In the early '70s, I would see them perform as much as possible. As a live act, they were absolutely amazing. Always. They had such charisma. But they were not demonstrative on stage. Nobody was going crazy or running frantically around the stage. They did not need to, as they played hard, and loud, and they were really good. They were just so much fun to watch. They were also the coolest-looking guys. They inspired all of us upstate guys and every musician in the area looked up to them. I cannot emphasize enough how great they sounded.

At the time, The Elves consisted of Gary Driscoll on drums, Doug Thaler on guitar, Mickey Lee on keyboards, David "Rock" Feinstein on guitar, and Ronnie on bass and vocals. They played very, very loud. Gary was a phenomenal drummer - he was bombastic and unpredictable, but it worked. Sometimes he would lose the beat and he would turn the beat upside down. But it would always come after a brilliant fill that nobody else could play. But then he would come out of it. Now they are called linear rudiments, but back then, none of us had heard of linear rudiments. Gary would play a linear rudiment and then instead of coming out on the one he would come out on a two and then he would roll his cymbals. He would just stop playing and crash his symbols until he could hear when to come back in. As a drummer, it was funny because he was so brilliant, yet losing the beat is such a simple thing. But what a phenomenal drummer he was. In fact, I put a Gary tribute in a few songs... it is a little foot thing that is similar to Bonham triplets. You can hear it in many of my recordings. I always add a little piece in there just as a tribute to Gary.

I was 19 when I moved in with Dave Porter. Dave and I played together in Raw Meat, and we practiced each day in a furnished garage attached to our house. Doug Thaler lived nearby (with our bass player Joe Leo) and that was where Elf rehearsed. They rehearsed in this really small house. It was cramped and crowded. Gary only had a three-piece kit. He had a bass drum facing the wall, one tom tom, a snare drum, a hi-hat, and one cymbal.

That was it. And I thought that was the strangest thing. It was the polar opposite of my massive kit. Later in life, when I matured a little bit and understood things, I realized that it was actually very smart of him to keep it simple. I also remember they had this long gravel driveway, and David had a truck at the time. Doug had a Firebird, and Rock would always hit the gas and kick gravel toward Doug's car. Doug would come out screaming at David. It was always hilarious.

When the first Elf album came out, we all rushed to buy it. We thought it was absolutely spectacular. They really were special and unique for that era, as evidenced by the fact that everywhere they played, they drew massive crowds. When we heard their first album, we recognized right away that they had something else that was special – they were great songwriters. In the club circuit, they were mostly doing covers, so we were all blown away by the album. Later, when The Rods were formed, I would always hear stories from David about Ronnie. David would tell me how Ronnie was a one-take guy. One take - that was it. David said it took him one take to record the vocals, every single time. He never did more than one take. He was always flawless and spot-on. It was no surprise to me that Ronnie was fantastic; but one take only? I was starting to think this was a case of skewed memory. I had never heard of anyone nailing 100% of their songs in one take. Statistically, it seemed impossible. In September of 2007, David and I went to see Heaven and Hell (Black Sabbath with Dio) perform in Binghamton, NY. We were backstage with Ronnie and the Sabbath crew.

This was before the show, and Ronnie was talking to everyone - he was very mellow. Very relaxed. He was extremely intelligent and was a great conversationist. And suddenly, they got the call to go out on stage, and Ronnie stood up, and casually walked out on stage. No warmup, no vocal exercises, nothing. Never had I witnessed that. Well, I have seen some singers who did not warm up, but you could always tell because their vocals were mostly terrible. But not Ronnie's. We watched the show from the audience, and his voice was perfect. As the show progressed, he got better and better. He was singing his balls off - it was so powerful. We were by the monitors, and it was mind-blowing.

Not long after, we were getting ready to release a new Rods album (and David was intending to release a solo album), and Ronnie agreed to sing on two songs - "Metal Will Never Die" and "The Code". I wrote "The Code", so having Ronnie sing on a song that I had written was a true highlight. I had sung the song previously in demo form. Ronnie came into the studio and listened to the demo version. He went through it verbally with us. And then - he did it in one take. One take! He was able to knock both songs out in one take! David was not bullshitting me all of those years. For me, Ronnie James Dio is the best metal singer of all time. His tone, his lyrics, his performance, and his vocal range and ability, all add up to him being the absolute greatest. Hands down. His work with Elf, Rainbow, Black Sabbath, and with his band Dio, left a body of work that is unparalleled in heavy metal. I can never thank David enough. Because that was a huge act of kindness on his part. He could have just had Ronnie sing two of his songs - he had plenty of great songs. Ronnie loved David. And even though they were cousins, he loved David like a brother, and would have been happy to sing any two of David's songs. But instead, David thought that "The Code" was the right song for Ronnie's voice. I will always be indebted to David for that. That was a career highlight.

Once we completed the recording, Ronnie and I talked a little bit. He was telling me about some of his travel experiences. It was a conversation that I will never forget. It was just a short time later when the world lost Ronnie. It was very sad. The songs he recorded with us were the last two songs he ever recorded.

# Wild Dogs Tour

After the somewhat unpleasant experience of mixing *Wild Dogs*, we returned to America. Back home, we patiently waited for the album to be printed and distributed Stateside, which happened relatively quickly. The obvious tactic was for us to get out on the road and perform. Back then, you sold albums by touring. The more you toured, the more albums and the more merchandise you sold. Which meant you could pay for the album you just recorded. But Arista was holding off a bit so that we could open up for Judas Priest, who were set to release and tour for the album *Screaming for Vengeance*. Priest was working on a massive stage production. It was to be enormous. The stage was so large that a single crew could not put it up and tear it down in a single day. Because it needed a full day to set up, and it needed an additional day to tear down, they had two full stage sets that required two separate crews. They had a build crew and a take-down crew - not to mention sound and lighting guys who traveled with each team. The first crew had to travel one city ahead of the band. A secondary crew was to follow behind by a day and take down the stage. With such a heavy production, the Priest tour kept getting delayed. Which meant that our album was out in the stores, and we were stuck waiting.

We did get to do a show with Iron Maiden at the Palladium, which was very cool. We were able to open for Rainbow in DC and Myrtle Beach as well. But it was the Judas Priest tour that we were waiting for. During this time, our manager told us that AC/DC had offered us the opening slot for their England tour. By then, British rock magazines such as *Kerrang* and *Sounds* were giving us fantastic reviews from our recently concluded Maiden support dates. We had developed quite a solid fan base in England, and after reading the positive press, AC/DC wanted us as the support act on the *For Those About to Rock* tour. But to return to England, the buy-in would have cost us around $40,000. That was a lot of money back then. We did not have it and Arista was not willing to put it up. Peter did not fight it. There were other outlets - we could have borrowed the money. The first England tour with Maiden went extremely well and opening for the biggest rock band of the time would have been massive for us. The return on investment was a sure thing. But Peter was firm and told AC/DC no. We simply did not have the money. I felt we should have cut ties with him that very night. I feel bad for Gary and David, because I kept them up all night venting about Peter. I felt Peter should have realized the opportunity that was being offered to us - and it was certainly better than the nothing (waiting) we were doing at the time. I made it very clear that, in my opinion, we needed a new manager. But The Rods were a true democracy. We were a team, and getting Gary and David on board was difficult. Their concern was that we did not have anyone to replace him. Not only that, but Peter had helped us land a major label deal. I gave David and Gary a hard time because they were afraid to make a move. I understood that. But we should have made a move. To quote Gary, "They held out the brass ring and we said no." Looking back, Peter was only being realistic – it was a lot to repay, and it came with no guarantee.

Eventually, we wound up doing the tour with Judas Priest. We received a great response from the die-hard Priest fans. I had a large drum riser, and due to Priest's expansive stage set, often I could not fit my riser fully on stage. There were times when the road crew had to hang my riser partially off-stage. The road crew would often have to hold it in place while I played. It was a little bit frightening as there is typically a lot of movement and vibration, but our road team was absolutely incredible. It would not have taken much for my riser to slide off the stage. But what a great tour that was. Every night I would sit in the audience, slightly off to the side. I would watch the entire Judas Priest set. Night after night. They were flawless. I became friends with their drummer at the time, Dave Holland. We corresponded via snail mail for years. He was a really good guy. And I know he had some issues later in life, which was surprising to hear. He was always nice to me. The most interesting thing on that tour was that the road crew would rope off an area, and then select the most attractive girls and put them in the roped-off area - all of them on display. Kinda like a new car lot. Post-show, once guitarists Glen Tipton and KK Downing finished showering, they would come by and take their pick of the litter. Every night, Glenn and KK would leave with four of the most beautiful women that particular town had to offer. One on each arm. That was two very attractive women for each guy – every single night. We were a little bit envious of that. It was also the first time I got to witness a video shoot in action. We were off to the side watching the director doing edits live - it was intense. He was saying things like, "Go to camera three, now go to camera one and stay on this." It was fascinating to watch. Keep in mind this was the very early 1980s and the music video was in its infancy. Large-scale video shoots were an extremely rare expenditure and reserved only for the biggest bands. The Priest tour showed us a side to the music business we had only read about in magazines up until that point. It was a blast living it.

With every series of highs, some lows are certain to follow. This is the rule of life, and while some have more highs than lows, we were not so fortunate. We were just beginning to develop an international following.

Heavy metal was relatively new and was beginning to take the world by storm. We were starting to get airplay and plenty of great press. We were all excellent musicians, and we could write great songs. But right after the Priest tour, Arista informed us that they would not be renewing our deal.

I placed the blame on our manager, Peter. And I wanted to fire him. Gary and David were hesitant. After all, he was the one that got us the Arista deal to begin with. At the time, we were planning and writing our next album. Peter knew I was pissed and tried to do some damage control. He said he was flying in Ashley Howe from Atlantic Records. The thought was that Ashley could produce our next album and get us signed with Atlantic. Ashley had produced Hawkwind, Uriah Heep, and a multitude of great bands. Ashley was all about screening songs. And so that is what he wanted us to do. He listened to our material. We performed three new songs for Ashley: "Love Is Pain", "Cold Sweat and Blood", and "Stay on Top".

Looking back, it was a poor choice of songs. None of the three songs were very heavy. He thought "Stay on Top" was a hit, and he eventually gave it to Uriah Heep to record. Ashley was also big on click tracks, which was a big wake-up call for me. So we were in the studio with Ashley Howe, and he wanted to do a click track. I had never done a click track in my life. I had no clue how they worked. Ashley gave me no guidance either. That was actually good for me later on as a producer, because I've been able to pass that insight on - but I did not see it that way at the time. When we did the Thrasher album, I had a song called "Black Lace and Leather" in which I wanted to have two drummers. I wanted Gary Driscoll (from Rainbow and ELF) to be the guy because Gary had always been kind to me, and he was a kick-ass drummer. Gary said to me, "Working with you as a producer, it is the best experience I've had in the studio"- all because I gave him some proper input and guided him on the click track. But Ashley Howe did not give me any input. Nothing but "Start playing."

Ashley put a click track on. I was upstairs of the control room, with a camera pointed directly at my face so that they could watch me from downstairs. I could only communicate with them by yelling because I did not have a talkback mic. I could hear them in my headphones because they did have a talkback mic. He started the song: *click, click, click, click*, and I started playing to the click track. As mentioned, up until that point, I had never played on a click track. I was trying to match every eighth note to the quarter note. And it was impossible to play it at first, solely because there was no feel. So, I was playing along to the click track, and I got through maybe a minute, and I heard this loud noise - which was the sound of the tape slowing down. Ashley said, in his thick British accent, "Right. Let's do that again." I started the song again. And again, I was trying: *tap tap, tap, tap, tap, tap*. I had to match every click on the metronome. It's nearly impossible to figure it out on your own unless you are experienced with click tracks. I had no clue how to work with it. Overall, my feel was garbage. We did this several times. I heard nothing from Ashley. I could only see the camera. I knew they could see me, and I knew that I was playing horribly, and I knew that they were now talking about how horribly I was playing. After what seemed like three minutes, in his thick accent, he said, "Right. We will drop in." A 'drop in' is what we also call a 'punch-in', which is marking the tape and picking it up from that location, so that you do not need to start at the beginning every time. I do not know how many times he had to punch in, but it must have been quite a bit. It took me forever to make it through "Cold Sweat and Blood", which was a simple four on the floor - the most basic beat. Two and four on the snare drum and 1,2,3,4 on the bass drum. It does not get any simpler. I had to be punched in constantly just to get through that song. By far, that was the most humiliating experience that I have ever had recording. Remember, I had just come off a tour with Iron Maiden, Judas Priest and Rainbow, playing to thousands nightly. Killing it with my drum solo nightly. And here I was, having a hard time with the most basic exercise. It was humiliating. I went from a big stadium rock drummer to the crappiest drummer of all time. And that is the tape that went to Atlantic.

Atlantic did not want the band. Aside from my drumming, the production was way off. Ashley did not grasp the band, and ultimately, he was the wrong guy. He was looking for hits. He wanted an FM radio hit. FM radio was very limited at the time. Just as Iron Maiden had never really had a radio hit, The Rods were never going to have a radio hit. We did not play pop music and we were not that type of band. Though as a result of that experience, I bought a drum machine. I started practicing to the click. And I have never looked back. And I have been able to help other drummers use the click by explaining to them how I use it. I learned to play ahead of the beat, behind the beat and on the beat to the click track. Nowadays, I will not record without it. Everything I have recorded since then has been to a click track, with the exception of *In the Raw*. The first time was like being stabbed with an ice pick every second - but I conquered it and now it is a friend. It is a very beneficial tool, and I will not record without it.

# In the Raw

After the disastrous Atlantic Records demo, we decided to go back to Chris Bubacz, who had engineered the very first album. Chris was a great friend and we felt he had done a great job with *Rock Hard*. By then, Chris was far from being a student - he was working at Music America and had a few more albums under his belt. There was one issue, however - we had no record company backing us and therefore we had no money. Chris was kind enough and cut us a deal with Music America. If we agreed to record on 2-inch tape, and if we would work quickly (when the studio was not booked), then he would get us on tape. This album was going to be on a shoestring budget. Which did not bother us a bit. Some of our best work was done with very little financing. I learned early in the Kelakos days that a large amount invested into recording does not always equate to excellent product. Especially with a band such as The Rods - we played raw, unadulterated, stripped-down rock and roll, and a simple recording process was all that was needed. We could have shopped for another major label, but we figured it would be easier to do what we did with the first album – record it, produce it, mix it and take our chances. So we went to Rochester, NY.

I did not bring my drums with me. Chris said he had existing studio drums (familiar studio drums would be more efficient to mic). Once there, I looked around the studio... there were no drums. Only pieces of a set. I dug through every closet and storage area, which ultimately left me with a double bass kit with five toms. It was a real Frankenstein kit, and it was actually pretty cool to play it. Gary and David were in the same room as me. The bass was fed directly into the console. David was in a booth with an amplifier. This was basically the way we recorded the first album. There was no click track. We simply counted off the songs and played them live. In my opinion, that is the reason the fans love this album. It truly lives up to its title: *In the Raw*. It solidified what The Rods do best - play hard rock live.

We did the entire album in two days. That was all the time we were able to get from Chris. We went directly into mixing. We'd only had three or four hours of sleep by then as we had really cranked it out. Chris had very little time to mix it. We were regulated to a very fast, down-and-dirty mix. It was essentially a demo. However, when I say demo, it was made by the three of us working to give our very best performance. We also tried to get the best sound initially possible, as we would not have time to clean it up post recording. Chris put his heart into it and gave us his absolute best. Perhaps it might have benefited from a little more time, but maybe excess time would have watered down its ferocity. Ultimately, it was a fun process, even though we were exhausted by the end of it. We also had that camaraderie - and you can hear it in the songs. We really knocked those songs out. We did minimal overdubs. David, Gary and I added some harmonies. There were no session players and no outside backup vocals. David added some solos. It was truly very raw. We did not overthink it. To this day, I still love that album. It has some really great songs. I really enjoyed the process. When you are a band, it is always the best vibe when you are performing that way in the studio. Because the studio can be an extremely sterile environment. It is very clinical - every little noise, every little movement is under the microscope (technically the microphone). We went in and we played live. We were conscious of playing the songs with the right vibe and getting them down on tape fast. So that required a self-conscious performance. We knew we would not have the ability to do multiple takes. There is no doubt that a major record label never would have let us record in this manner. They would have sent us to some far away studio, paid big money for a well-known producer, and then sent it off to be mixed at another location. The entire process would have taken months and cost a ton of money - and then they would have billed the band for the entire process. And if we had recorded it that way, I do not think it would have sounded as good as it does. The songs on that album work perfectly with a stripped-down recording style.

On another note, our manager was unable to get us another major label deal. Mike Varney, of Shrapnel Records, agreed to press and distribute the album. Shrapnel was a very small (and somewhat young) record label. They wanted to get the album out quickly as we were fresh off the Priest tour, and they did not want to lose that momentum. Peter came in during the recording sessions and snapped a quick photo of us. We had been up for two days straight by this point. We looked terrible. Peter turned that photo in to Shrapnel. If you look closely, you can see the bags under our eyes. We looked so rough that Shrapnel put a red filter over the picture. For such a solid album, the cover is a real dud. Instead of giving us the opportunity for a proper band photo, Peter gave them something so bad that Shrapnel had to put a filter over it. The color was atrocious. It was not creative. That photo was not fit for the back of an album, let alone the front of an album. So that was the cover - and I think that it really hurt us. Keep in mind that during this era, it was common for many people to purchase an album (from a band they had never heard) based solely on how the cover looked. Cool covers sold albums. We were proud of *In the Raw*, but the cover was a huge disappointment. We weren't pretty boys.

Mike Varney of Shrapnel Records was cool. Mike did a great job of promoting the album. We were not paid a ton of money, but we were paid. And I think we had some royalties for a while as well. I was always suspicious as Mike Varney and Peter (our manager) later started Magna Carta Records together. Our manager was basically in bed with the record company. I have always wondered what would have happened if we had used *In the Raw* as a demo and shopped it around. Would we have gotten another major deal? Would we have picked up a label in Europe? It would have been a great deal for any record company, and the album could have been remixed and released properly (like *Rock Hard*). That would have been a very low dollar advance, a great bargain for any record company.

The time was right - heavy metal was quickly gaining notoriety. Why Peter did not push to shop this around is beyond me. Perhaps he, like us, was burnt out after the loss of the Arista deal. David was fed up with the music business before we even formed The Rods. We also knew that having a big record contract did not translate to a big payday. The other downside with a major record company is that there is a large focus on 'radio hits,' which was something we really did not concern ourselves with. We just wanted to make great rock music. But, in the end, we made a great album, something that still holds up and is a fan favorite. *In The Raw* is an album we are proud of. It has some great songs, and it sounds good considering the amount of time we put into it.

If you've made it this far, you have most certainly noticed that I was upset with Peter Morticelli. What I have written was simply my take at the time. That was also a long time ago. Do not get me wrong, I do not think Peter is a bad guy. Quite the opposite in fact. It was simply a difference of opinion. And I am sure we each have our own take on the events.

At the end of the day, Peter did a lot for us. To show you what a good guy Peter is, we reached out to him for commentary. Peter went above and beyond and answered all of our questions and even provided his take on The Rods. Thanks Peter!

**Interview with Peter Morticelli;** *Early Manager of The Rods, Pelican Marketing & Management Inc., Magna Carta Records*

**Question:** How did you first discover The Rods?
**Answer:** *I knew a friend of the band's, Doug Thaler, who lived in New York and was a booking agent for a big agency in New York. Doug knew that I managed another band for whom I had secured a major label record deal and he thought that I could do a good job for The Rods, who were hoping to get signed.*

**Question:** Did you sense potential right away or were they a bit unpolished?
**Answer:** *I sensed potential when I first saw them but, honestly, they were a bit too polished when I first saw them. They were wearing satin outfits; not even close to being hard-edged in terms of their image. That was one of the first things that I addressed with them during our initial discussions. They were doing a lot of cover songs at the time because they were trying to balance being a working club band with being a hard-edged recording band. When I first met the band, they were part way through recording a self-produced album and I ended up helping them finance the completion of this production.*

*I had seen Dave Feinstein in Ronnie Dio and The Prophets, The Electric Elves, The Elves and Elf. We had never met prior to The Rods but you could say that I followed him throughout much of his musical career.*

**Question:** What events/decisions led to Steve's departure?
**Answer:** *I wish I could help with the question regarding Steve Starmer leaving the band. He was not around for very long once I began talking to the band. But to the best of my recollection, I had the impression that he seemed to be unwilling to make the necessary commitment that it would take to pursue a recording and touring career. I think he may have been a little fearful of the unknown. I could be way wrong about that but that is what I can recollect. I just cannot remember much about him other than the fact that he seemed like a very nice guy.*

*His replacement, Craig Gruber, had been a member of Black Sabbath for a while and really did not seem as if he had the desire that would allow him to struggle from the ground up with The Rods in their building process. I felt that he was a disruptive force within the band. I let Carl and Rock know that I would not be able to work with them if Craig was going to be part of The Rods. In the end, I think they knew that the chemistry was not right among the three of them and they were lucky enough to find Gary Bordonaro locally, who was young, talented, and good-looking.*

**Question:** How did the Arista contract come about? What led to its demise?
**Answer:** *I was good friends with Mike Bone, who oversaw A&R radio promotion at Arista. I had met Mike four or five years earlier when he worked for Mercury Records, and I managed another band on that label. We had always gotten along well, and I knew that he liked heavier rock. Arista did not have much in the way of rock on their roster. But I went to him to give him the backstory of The Rods. He knew that Arista would not sign a band like The Rods but, after a time, he directed me to a label called Ariola America that was a German-owned label that was related to Arista*

*in terms of ownership. They were even located in the same building. Ariola was a bit more eclectic from a musical perspective than Arista. They had an executive there by the name of Warren Schatz who was a good record man. He was intrigued by the fact that The Rods had recorded an album on their own. That was an attractive aspect for a label in signing a new band. They were not really taking a gamble on the development of a young artist. They were acquiring a finished product which they were able to judge for themselves. Unbeknownst to many people, Ariola America was having problems internally - and financially. I had just completed the deal for The Rods, and I went to New York to meet with the label and collect our advance check. I was looking forward to that because by then I had made a considerable investment in the band, and I wanted to be made whole.*

*After I picked up the check, I stopped off to see Bone to let him know about my meeting with Warren Schatz and their plans for The Rods' release. When I got to Mike's office, I received a bizarre call from Warren advising me to deposit the check in the bank as soon as possible. Apparently, an abrupt decision had been made to close the label with no notice to the employees or artists signed to the label. Naturally, my concern was what would happen to The Rods and the deal we had just signed. I was told to wait for a couple of days until the dust had settled. But Mike told me that even though it was probably unlikely, he would do whatever he could to try to acquire The Rods for Arista. Finally, the word came down that Bone was able to make it happen. They allowed him to promote the band on Arista with the understanding that the label would not do much in the way of financial support. But Mike knew me and my ability to get things done against difficult odds. So he told me that it was going to take a lot of extra work and that he would need me to be even more dedicated to figuring out ways to squeeze resources from whatever targets possible. Additionally, he told me that my years as a booking agent would be put on display because he wanted The Rods to play as many dates as possible, whether they were high profile tour dates or simply regional club shows. Over the next couple of years, he and I did stuff that helped the band complete tours that cannot be discussed publicly. It is doubtful there would ever be another record executive who would be willing to put himself on the line like that for a band.*

*The Rods always had a desire to do things on their own terms, which on the surface seems like an admirable stance for a young artist. However, this does not always play well with record companies (and their staff members) who question a new artist's ability to make judgements that affect the future success of both the band and the record company. Especially when they have never been involved in the business before. That bothered a lot of people at the label. Mike Bone protected them from the backlash. But there* were times when they did not want to follow Bone's direction either. I was always caught in the middle, trying to defend the band's position but knowing that the label understood the realities of their business far more than The Rods. I often had to try to make the band understand why the label wanted to do the things that they wanted to do. It was true that the label did not have a real affection for the band. We had some allies there that wanted to see the band succeed for Mike Bone's sake, but there was also a contingent that wanted to get rid of the band more for aesthetic reasons than for anything else. They just did not feel The Rods had the "class" or correct "image" to be part of the Arista family. Most of them simply did not care for what the band was doing and did not feel it was "special" enough to warrant investment and attention.

Mike Bone, and a couple of others at the label, did what they could do to muster some support for the band. Mike and I concocted several "schemes" that enabled The Rods to get some of the Arista departments to do some things they would normally do for acts that were more of a priority. I was able to generate a good deal of press for the band based on their image and reputation. Granted, much of this was "hype" but, at the time, it was all we had going for us. There was a significant amount of airplay on "Power Lover" off the first album, but we could not get it to grow once it got added to stations' playlists and, as a result, did not stay on playlists very long. There was never a strong effort by the label to get records in the stores in markets where airplay did occur.

There was a lot of push and pull between the label and band when it came to recording the second album. The location, producer, material and artwork all became topics of stressful discussions. A very brilliant solution to the location was worked out that allowed us to take advantage of a tour opportunity that looked as if it could be an opening to break a career wide open. Iron Maiden was just about to become a legitimate headliner with the The Number of The Beast album, which featured the radio hit "Run to the Hills". They were interested in The Rods as their opening act on their tour because of the massive amount of press we had received in England. It was all built around the wild image that the band was purported to have. A lot of this was built around some backstage photos that showed The Rods with some young ladies with exhibitionist tendencies and the band's obvious enthusiasm for these girls. When it became apparent that we were not going to get much support from Arista, Mike Bone and I determined that these types of photos were going to be the basis of our promotional campaign. So that became one of the reasons why The Rods got so much attention in the English music press and why Iron Maiden took notice of them. I was asked to put together a bare-bones budget that would allow the band to go to England, record an album, go on tour for a month, mix the album and *return home. It was a tight budget that allowed for nothing to go wrong during all that activity. Obviously, rock 'n' roll does not work that way.*

*The big rub throughout The Rods' relationship with Arista was the strength of the songs. Arista felt that The Rods' material was not consistently strong. Dave wrote the best, most Rods-like material. But Dave had been through so much in his career that he was no longer interested in participating in the inner-band power struggles. When material from other band members was introduced, it basically diluted the stronger material and reduced the impact of Dave's songs. This was not something we ever talked about or discussed as a band/manager conversation in those terms. It would have been too difficult and too personal. I knew that each band member wanted to write and contribute but the fact was that many of the songs were mediocre at best. And the individuals always 'felt strongly' about their own songs. The right thing to do would have been to have a forthright conversation and be brutally honest with them. But I really did not think that they would have accepted my appraisal and it may have created enough dissension within the band that it could have broken them up. They probably would have fired me on the spot. I was not afraid of that because that is usually what happens when a manager tells a band something they do not want to hear, but I just wanted to see if we could get the project back on track somehow. I always try to see things through to whatever end there is. So, I just tried to encourage them and stay positive.*

*But the main reason why the band never broke through to a wider audience is because they never came up with that one song that defined them - the song that got on the radio and stayed there for a sufficient amount of time to garner public awareness. There were several occasions when outside material was suggested to the band. There were two outside songs on the first Arista album and one of them got airplay. I do not recollect what outside material was suggested for the second album other than when we were in England, I was directed to an English producer that had some pop hits who proposed doing a Motown song. There was a lot of pushback (as usual) about the suggestions but The Rods ended up doing "You Keep Me Hangin' On" with the arrangement Vanilla Fudge had recorded in 1967. The thinking was that it had been so long since they had their hit, it could be brought back by The Rods and have it seem recognizable, yet fresh. Unfortunately, the label was not interested in promoting the song to the radio. But beyond that, I do not remember the other songs that were proposed by the label. Whatever they may have been, obviously the band did not do them.*

*The final nail in the Arista coffin was probably the funniest thing that I have ever witnessed in all my years in the business. In an effort to demonstrate the appeal of The Rods to Arista once and for all, a showcase* was arranged in New York City so that we could finally convince the powers that be at Arista (mainly Clive Davis) that this band would be a worthwhile investment for the label to continue with in the future. It was a hot and sweaty summer night in New York and the band was prepared and ready to put forth their best performance. Rock had recently acquired one of the very first wireless setups for his guitar and that allowed him unlimited movement on the stage and throughout the club itself without being tethered to his amplifier by a cable. Unfortunately, Mr. Davis was very late to arrive at the club and the band's performance kept being pushed back and back. Mr. Davis finally showed up with his assistant and his publicist, resplendent in a finely tailored white suit. The club (The Great Gildersleeve's in New York's Bowery just down the block from CBGB's) had long, banquet-style tables laid out vertically in relation to the stage. Finally, the show began, and The Rods began their typically high-energy performance. At one point, Rock leaped off the stage and jumped onto one of the long tables. These tables were filled by Arista employees and their guests. It just so happened that the table that Rock had jumped on was the table where Mr. Davis and his party were seated. At a certain point, Rock reached the area where Clive was sitting. Suddenly, Rock accidentally kicked a beer glass which landed directly on Mr. Davis and soaked his beautiful white outfit. Without much thought, Rock pushed himself and his guitar against the boss's assistant.

You could say he was humping her. I could not really determine whether she was horrified, excited or amused. It might have been a combination of all those things. But within a matter of seconds, the fate of The Rods at Arista Records was sealed. It is doubtful whether Rock had done those things with any forethought. It looked like a very spontaneous, theatrical, rock 'n' roll moment. Certainly, he did not kick beer onto Davis on purpose. It just happened in the moment. I found it incredibly hilarious, but I knew in that very moment that it was over for The Rods at that label. And so it was. There would be no third album on Arista, no recognition of the band as a valued artist on that label, no investment of company resources in the future of The Rods.

**Question:** Their lyrics are all about partying and rocking but they are all pretty tame in real life. Any truth to that or did they have some wild moments?

**Answer:** *The members of The Rods were so low-key behavior-wise, so uninvolved with alcohol and drugs, that it made working with them on that level one of the easiest bands that I have ever been involved with. That is not to say that they were the easiest to work with on a personal basis. The reputation of The Rods as a hard-partying, womanizing group of reprobates was the farthest thing from the truth. But it did not take long for* the realization that the band was not what their press coverage said they were. In that instance, it probably did not help the band. I think the fans were disappointed when all the stories about The Rods proved to be little more than stories. But what hurt the band more than anything was that they did not impress as a live act any more than an above-average hard rock band. Each member was talented at his instrument. I would even say that Dave Feinstein is underrated as a guitarist. He certainly is not a member of the classically influenced virtuoso school of guitarists. But he plays in a blues-based style as if he is walking a high wire without a net, blindfolded.

He has an extremely rhythmic style and within the three-piece Rods set up he combined beautifully with Carl's muscular playing and Garry's steady, solid bass lines. It was and still is a very impressive lineup. But it was not one that captivated audiences or stretched boundaries. The band played numerous live shows in front of big audiences. They always played well but there was never anything that stood out to make audiences feel as if they had seen something memorable. Obviously, these are all just my opinions, but I had seen at least a hundred Rods' shows and felt that I could read an audience's reaction accurately. I just hoped that there might come a time when the band came up with better material and their entire presentation would be raised to a higher plateau. Sometimes it could take three or even four albums before bands would find the spark that takes them to a place where they could feel confident that their efforts were embraced positively by larger audiences.

The Rods always put on a high-energy stage show. They never phoned it in. Like many bands, they had a difficult time trying to make an impression on audiences as an opening act in theaters and arenas. Their most effective shows were as headliners in large clubs. When audiences were face-to-face with the band, they were always able to connect more successfully. In my opinion, this would change over time, but the band did not get this opportunity. I just wanted to sustain their career until I could land them another major label contract and give them a chance to achieve the potential that I thought they possessed. I had very good luck obtaining multiple major label deals for another band (three, in fact). I had relationships with a number of major labels, and I was really surprised when I got no interest from these labels. It was always the same story. No one heard material that they felt was strong enough to warrant signing them, despite their previous record deal and touring history. I had a number of labels come to see them perform. But there was seemingly no interest from major labels for the band. This was very disappointing to both me and, of course, the band. It came to mind that we needed to continue to keep the band in front of the fans. So, I suggested that the band release an album on an independent label in order to establish their continued presence in the marketplace. We did this with some mixed results. The album was not a breakthrough for the band in terms of material, but it was not inferior either. I continued my efforts to get the band connected to major labels, but it became all too apparent that there was no interest at the time in signing The Rods. I honestly do not remember how or when the band and I stopped working together.

In retrospect, there was a short window in time when it appeared that there was an opportunity for the band to break through to a larger audience. One thing to keep in mind is that The Rods were the first of the so-called New Wave of American metal bands to be signed to a major label. So, the release of their first album put them at a competitive advantage. We had made solid inroads on the radio and the press and it looked as if we were strategically positioned to move forward. With the upcoming tour of England with Iron Maiden and the release of their second album, there was an opportunity for The Rods to carve out a segment of the growing metal fan base for themselves. But when the tour did not create the kind of excitement for the band that we had hoped for and the album did not generate the airplay or sales that the label was hoping to experience, things took a quick downturn. When the label showcase did not go in The Rods' favor and Arista decided not to continue with them, it was a a very low point. At the same time, there were many other bands that were being put in front of audiences with significantly better results. Musically, things were changing as well. Younger groups with newer, exciting styles and images were emerging. Metallica, Motley Crue and Slayer were suddenly in the marketplace and were creating excitement among fans and doing solid business in record sales and live appearances.

**Question:** AC/DC asked for The Rods during a tour of England, but the boys were waiting for the Judas Priest tour. Do you think that would have made a difference for them?

**Answer:** *To the best of my recollection, the AC/DC tour was a non-starter. I believe the tour was going to be in Europe and there was no possibility of support from Arista. Additionally, even though they were unwilling to support the band financially on tour, they wanted us back in the US to promote the second album. We had that opportunity by being added to the Judas Priest Screaming for Vengeance tour. I wish I could tell you the stories about how that tour was financed but some people would lose their jobs and others would go to jail. Now that I think about it, some of that actually happened.*

**Question:** You went back to Elmira with Carl when his mom passed. What memories of that do you have?

**Answer:** *I have many, many memories of that particular event. This would take a long time to describe the whole adventure. But here is a stream-of-consciousness version: We got the news of Carl's mom being close to the end after an Iron Maiden show in England. Manchester, England's airport closed at 10 P.M. I could not make airline reservations until the following morning. There was a baggage handlers' strike in England during that trip.*

*So, in addition to handling my own bags and Carl's massive suitcases from several airport doors to the airplane, I had to steer Carl himself, who was grieving and had taken some medication to calm his emotions. I had no idea what was happening most of the time because Carl was unable to communicate any details with the exception of when he spotted Cozy Powell at the airport in London. I did not know exactly where we were headed, how we were getting there, and what was supposed to happen once we got there. I did know that we were in the middle of a big tour, and I had to make sure that the other two Rods and the crew were still in England and had to be taken care of until we returned (if we returned). Arriving at JFK and seeing a guy holding a sign with our names on them, I thought we might be driven to Elmira. But as we followed this guy through the bowels of JFK, we ended up getting on board a twin prop, four-seater airplane. I did not have much time to consider what was happening because the past 24 hours had been so crazy and exhausting. I fell asleep immediately upon takeoff, only to wake up 45 minutes later. When I looked out the window of this small plane, I was shocked to still see the lights from JFK. It had taken us that long to gain the proper altitude and move away from the airport a few miles. The only thing that was more discouraging than that was looking at the pilot and co-pilot in the seats in front and finding out that they were using a road map from the AAA to navigate our trip to Elmira. All in all, that was a trip I will never forget.*

**Question:** What are your overall thoughts and your impression all these years after?
**Answer:** *I think that we all did everything we could to try to make the most happen for the band that we could. Each of us did our utmost individually and as a unit. I will never think that they gave anything less than 100%. But there is part of me that feels as if they made some poor decisions regarding the direction of their career. They tended to overthink some issues and feel that they could not trust anyone else. Yet, they would take input from people outside their organization and let it influence their actions. And, from my perspective, this is what hurt their ability to succeed as much as any deficits they may have had artistically. The leadership of the band was somewhat fluid. So, as a result, there was never a consistent direction within the band.*

*I think Dave let it happen this way simply because he did not want the aggravation of being the leader of the band. But I think he regrets approaching it that way. Sometimes Dave led the way, sometimes it was Carl. It was never Gary, probably because he was younger and the "new guy". I imagine this was not always pleasant for him, but I only seem to remember him getting frustrated about that a couple of times (that he actually verbalized it).*

*I did not follow the band after we stopped working together. I was so wrapped up in the things I was working on that I did not keep up with what they were doing. But I must respect the fact that they are still making music together 40 years after they started the band. I have kept in touch with Rock over the years and have a good relationship with him. On the rare occasion that I saw Gary, we also got on well and I kept track of him through Rock. I did not have the same connection with Carl. When I spoke to Rock we really did not talk about The Rods. It was not an uncomfortable topic, we just had more current things to talk about.*

*We laughed a lot during the time that I worked with The Rods. They were bright and had some cutting observations about many of the people they came into contact with. There were a lot of memorable experiences that I recall. I certainly wish that we had more tangible rewards from our efforts but that is the risk taken in any business that relies upon the creative output of individuals that is then presented to the public for judgment. The fact that the band is still presenting themselves to fans that have stuck with them throughout the years is a testament to the fact that they found something that continues to resonate with a segment of people. We all did what we thought was the best for The Rods during those years. It is certain that we all made some mistakes. But that is bound to happen. To try to point fingers at this stage of the game is senseless. Trying to rewrite history is equally pointless and somewhat pathetic. One thing that people do not realize is that the record business (like almost any other business) needs a good dose of luck in addition to all the positive strengths that you can bring to it in order to succeed. Unfortunately, for all those who were involved, luck was not something we experienced very often. We were always struggling from the bottom up. We needed to make something out of nothing. But, as I had previously stated, we were basically trying to do all of this without much (if any) belief and support of the record company. At that point in time, the record label and, by extension, its ability to generate radio airplay were the key components of any band's success. Without that, it was practically impossible for any band to make any kind of progress.*

*One thing that should not be forgotten: The Rods were important to the emergence of the metal scene and the many bands that followed them. They created a template for the look, image and attitude for the American metal bands that followed. But when the onslaught of bands occurred and began to morph into bands that experienced great success, The Rods became a lesser footnote in the large portrait of those times. And time has not been kind to their legacy. But, as I have said previously, the fact that the band still performs for appreciative fans gives validity to the entire existence of The Rods. To me, that is success.*

# Metallica & Jonny Z

This chapter is about the many moments which I like to classify as 'Forrest Gump Moments.' In the movie *Forrest Gump*, the main character, Forrest, relays to others his life story, in which he was an accidental participant or onlooker to some vastly important and enormously historical events. That movie really resonated with me, as during the 1980s, I found myself an onlooker or contender in some principal moments in heavy metal history. I witnessed, firsthand, thrash metal evolve from a minuscule underground movement into a mainstream global force. I was fortunate enough to witness and participate in the evolution of Anthrax, Exciter, Overkill, and a host of other critical thrash metal bands. I watched as Scott Ian of Anthrax playfully wrote 'NOT' on his guitar (after using the word multiple times in the studio), to it becoming the band's official slogan, and finally it being stamped on their merchandise and applied to their mascot, Not Man.

I witnessed Manowar become a global powerhouse only a few years after I had taken part in their genesis. I watched Jonny and Marsha Zazula launch Megaforce out of their house and grow it into the most important thrash metal record company in history. That was incredible to witness. Going to school with Tommy Hilfiger and watching him become a frontrunner in the fashion industry. However, observing a band of dirt-poor West Coast kids become the most popular heavy metal band in the world is one of my most interesting Forrest Gump moments. This then-unknown band named Metallica (no one had known of them outside of California except for a few lucky tape traders) came to record in upstate New York.

I had heard about them when Chris Bubacz called and said, "I have this band here - there's something about them. They have huge potential!" A couple of days later I went to Music America Studios and met them. They were very young, only a couple of years out of high school. But they sounded great, and true to Chris's word, they had potential. They had some great songs. They were passionate. They were dedicated and worked hard. Their music was unlike anything I had ever heard. They also partied hard. I know that Chris was having a tough time dealing with their equipment. He said that their equipment was in the worst shape he had ever seen. It took him days to repair and upgrade their equipment to recordable standards. They opened for us a number of times during their time in upstate. While they were definitely talented, I was surprised to see them at an entirely new level many years later. I ran into them in France at the

Breaking Sound Festival. It was clear they were on another level and growing. Every media outlet wanted to interview them. The most beautiful girls were begging to go backstage with them. Metallica shirts were everywhere in the crowd. I have never seen a band grow so quickly as they did. I was happy for them. They were great guys – especially Lars, who always was appreciative.

It was at Music America that I met Jonny Zazula. Jonny had got a mortgage loan and borrowed money from his father in-law (not to mention draining their savings) in order to record and release the debut Metallica album, *Kill Em All*. He believed in them that much. He knew what they were capable of. It was a huge gamble and it paid off down the road, but few would have been that committed. I immediately liked him. He was such a lovable guy. [*Editor's note: Jonny was writing a foreword to this book, but sadly passed before he could complete it.*] We struck up a conversation, exchanged numbers and became fast friends. Jonny had mentioned that Metallica needed a place to stay while they recorded the album and practiced for the tour. Due to their hardcore partying, they were continuously getting kicked out of hotels. I immediately thought of my friend Victoria.

## The Rock & Roll Hotel

Victoria Calandra was a good friend of The Rods. We had known her since the early days when Steve was still in the band. We considered her the band Mom. She really took care of us. When you are a struggling unsigned rock band with no full-time jobs, you are often dependent upon the goodwill of fans, family, and close friends of the band. Victoria was essential for The Rods. She came to our shows. She made us clothes. She cooked these big meals for us. She even provided us with room and board from time to time. She was even in our first, and only, video, which was for the song "Hurricane".

We filmed the video for "Hurricane" on our own dime. This was early 1983 and MTV was in its infancy. I am pretty sure MTV had not even made it to upstate New York by that point. At the start of the decade, videos were slowly becoming more commonplace, but mostly for pop and soft rock acts. Headbangers Ball was not yet a thing and would not be until late in the decade. There was no metal played on MTV aside from the occasional Judas Priest or Maiden video, so MTV was not a possible outlet. In fact, I do not think we even had an outlet in mind when deciding to make a video. One of our sound guys had some experience with editing and camera work, and we just thought it would be a good idea to make one.

We rented a muscle car and set up our equipment in an auto repair warehouse. We filmed the entire thing in a day. For the non-action segments, we all got in the car. Gary and David sat in the front seat lip-syncing. I sat in the back seat with Victoria having a faux make-out session. We were not really making out. The entire time we were whispering, "What do we do now?" It was a blast. Ultimately, the video was never played anywhere. I am sure it is on YouTube now. It is amateurish, but keep in mind it was 1983 and we had little to no money. Videos then were reserved for major label bands. But it was cool having a video - and of course Victoria looks great in it. We could not even afford to pay her. She was more than happy to help us, even if that required her to have a pseudo make-out session with me. That is the kind of friend Victoria was. She supported us and helped us from day one. And she was more than happy to do so. She had all the traits a young and struggling band needed - warmth and positivity - and she was incredibly supportive. She was a phenomenal cook and fed us extremely well. She did it all for the love of rock and roll. So, when Jonny Z needed a place to house his rowdy yet determined band, I instantly thought of Victoria. She had a large house. She could provide meals. And it would be nice to see her get some money for her efforts.

So I approached Victoria with the idea of housing this band who she had never heard of or met. This could backfire, I thought: they could destroy her house with excessive partying. But the kids seemed respectable and were quite determined in their goals. Victoria immediately agreed. That band was Metallica... and they went to stay with her while they recorded their first album and rehearsed for the tour that was to follow. I believe they wrote the majority of *Ride the Lightning* there as well. She would provide their meals and provide room and board, and she would receive some money in return. This was the start of The Rock & Roll Hotel, which was to house so many great and early bands for the remainder of the decade. The Rock & Roll Hotel fostered so many great memories of the early thrash scene. Chances are, if a band was signed by Megaforce Records and recorded in upstate New York during the 1980s, that band stayed at The Rock & Roll Hotel during the making of their album. Raven, Overkill, Anthrax, Exciter and a bunch of others – they all stayed at there. If any place truly deserves a documentary, it is The Rock & Roll Hotel. Sadly, the house is now a frat house for SUNY Cortland. It should have been designated a historical landmark. Victoria and I are still close friends, and she still resides in the area.

**Victoria Calandra**; *Owner of The Rock & Roll Hotel:*
*"Metallica could not stay in any hotels in New York anymore, because they got in so much trouble. So, they were at my house for six months. Thanks to Carl! It was his idea. How did I know Carl? I grew up in the early '70s. I was in high school when I met David Feinstein. He was in Elf with Ronnie Dio at that time. And then they formed The Rods and I eventually met Carl. He became a really good friend. So that is where it all started from. They are amazing musicians - even back then when they were starting out. So, I was always close with them.*

*"So the Rock & Roll Hotel got its start from Carl. Carl asked me if I could house a band and keep an eye on them. I had never heard of them but since Carl was asking, I knew it would be cool. I owned this house in Cortland - and it was only me. It had a few empty rooms. I also enjoyed cooking and can sew, do hair, etc. So I agreed to it. They were really young. And they were kind of well-behaved at my house. I had given them rules. And they rehearsed in my basement. The walls were padded with blankets, and they left behind tapes of them rehearsing. They actually wrote the album Ride the Lightning in my basement. It was when Kurt first joined the band and they had sent Dave Mustaine packing back to California. As for their future success, everybody pretty much knew it. Jonny Z wanted to keep*

*them desperately on his label, but they got signed pretty quickly to a major label. But yeah, everybody knew that they were going to be great. Shortly after, Anthrax came to stay. Then Exciter, Overkill - there were so many bands that stayed throughout the '80s. It was such a great time. They were all starting out – all promising new bands. So, it was exciting to witness the early stages and see them grow. I was an amazing cook, if I do say so myself. I would cook these huge dinners for them. I made it like an actual home, and it was so much better than a hotel. Every weekend we would go to this bowling alley and have an absolute blast. Can you imagine bowling with a young Metallica? It was wild. Raven stayed with me also. It was when they came to the area to record Stay Hard. They were such great guys. The only band that got excessively crazy was Overkill - they partied the hardest. But it was always fun for me and created so many great memories.*

*It lasted from 1983 through maybe 1989. The house is now being rented by college students. Unfortunately, they tore it all apart. It should be a historical landmark. Every once in a while, I will get a call from Lars, the drummer in Metallica. It was such a magical time. I was so happy to be a part of it. When the '90s came, it was a little depressing to me. I could not stand any of that grungy music. It was a real adjustment - being in this huge scene and all of a sudden it is gone. It was kind of a letdown."*

If you drive through Cortland today, it is hard to imagine it was an essential location for the early thrash scene. There is not much there. But back then, we had Pyramid Studios in Ithaca (which recorded so many great early thrash albums) and Music America in Rochester. We had Al Falso Music and a few other necessary music stores. And that area also had some rock and metal history - Ronnie James Dio was responsible for that. So Cortland was actually a great vicinity at the time. The most appealing part for a struggling record company was that upstate New York was economical. You could record and house a band far cheaper than you could in NYC or NJ. After Metallica's stay, Jonny Z began to book all the Megaforce bands there. If they were a band that recorded at Pyramid or Music America, then they stayed at The Rock & Roll Hotel.

**John Gallagher;** *Raven*

*"In the early to mid-80s, we were essentially living in the States. Not officially - but we would only go back home (England) on holidays and such. We spent a lot of that time in upstate when we were recording Stay Hard. We were staying at The Rock & Roll Hotel in Cortland. We had heard of The Rods prior to coming to the States - they had a huge fan base in Newcastle from their tour with Maiden. So we were really excited to meet them. They were such great guys - and especially Carl. One of the nicest*

*guys out there. We had such a great time there and Carl made us feel welcome. David had just bought the Hollywood (restaurant) and we would go there a lot. Such a great group of guys and some really amazing times."*

# Live

After we released *In the Raw*, we considered the idea that perhaps the time had come and gone for The Rods. Perhaps we'd had our shot, and we just were not meant to be major-label players. Most other bands, at that point, would have said "screw it" and gone on to do something else. Doug Thaler even gave me a bit of advice. By then he was managing some very popular bands, so his advice carried some weight. He told me, "Carl, why don't you leave The Rods, move to California, and then join a rising band?" But I just could not do it. Like David, The Rods were my baby. I could not abandon The Rods. Besides, I knew very well that the grass was not greener on the other side. Nor was success guaranteed. I liked what David and I had. I loved what we had built. I liked how we worked together. So David, Gary and I decided to keep things going. Plus, some of the other bands that came out around the same time as we did - Raven, Anvil and Riot - were still putting out records despite record label changes. The demand was certainly there. After we released *In the Raw*, we did not tour to support it. We played some random dates throughout the States, but nothing consistent and nothing that would qualify as a tour. It was a strange time. Do we take a break? Do we release another album? It was clear that we needed to make some changes and the first change I lobbied for was to terminate our relationship with Peter.

While Gary and David were reluctant to let him go, I did not back down. And eventually I convinced them. There were a few red flags. In 1982, Peter pulled me aside and said, "Hey, don't tell the other guys, but I was able to get you an audition with Rainbow. They are looking for a drummer." The following year, when we were doing a show with Vandenberg and Metallica, he approached me with another audition, though this time it was for AC/DC. They were looking for a drummer after Phil Rudd left (or was fired) from the band. While I was flattered to be considered for an audition, ultimately, I do not think I would've gotten either position. Plus, I was not willing to turn my back on The Rods. But Peter approaching me with this got me thinking - if he was encouraging me to join a bigger project, how much faith did he really have in the The Rods? To push a founding and integral member (not to mention one of the songwriters) to leave the band - did he really care about The Rods? The last straw was rushing the cover for *In the Raw*. Peter took a subpar photo, something that would not even be appropriate for a trade magazine, and had Shrapnel Records run it for a cover. We had time (and the resources) to come up with a better cover. In the '80s, the cover was a major contributor to a band's success. This was in the days of record stores and a good cover could sell an album, regardless of radio airplay. So that was the cherry on top. We really did not feel he was in our corner anymore. I am sure he had his frustrations with us as well.

It was a difficult time for The Rods. We really did not know where we were going next. Can we do another five or six years on the club circuit? Should we start knocking on record company doors again? Or should we just put out music and see where it takes us? In 1983, we let Peter go. With no one waiting to take his place, I became the acting manager until we could fill his slot. By then, we had met enough people in the business, and we had our longtime friend Doug Thaler to go to for advice. Looking back, I do not think I did the band justice. Taking on a managerial role was a mistake. I now realize Peter was doing his best to keep us together.

The first order of business was to secure a new record deal. While some bands struggled to write new material, it was not so for The Rods. David and I were always writing. Even during times when we were touring or working on an album, we were still writing material for future albums, so we had a ton of new material. We had some really great songs. We were able to get a two-album deal with Combat/Music for Nations. It was a pretty good deal. With that, we began to plan the next album. So… this next one is my fault - and looking back, perhaps it was not the best decision. But I will take all the blame. I had a thought: what if we record a live album of all new songs? Most live albums are the hits played live. Why not play some new songs live? And release it as a new album? Since The Rods were known as a great live band, why not get that on record - but with new material? And of course, the recording cost would be minimal. So that is what we decided to do.

As I mentioned earlier, we were not touring on the previous album, so we had to secure some dates, which we did. Most of them were throughout upstate New York, and we were able to rent a mobile recording unit. We played a show with Motorhead and Virgin Steele that went very well. Overall, we put on some great shows, and we were able to get it all on tape. The result of that is the album *Live*. What you hear on *Live* is how we sounded in the early 1980s in concert. However, I really wish we had done it as a proper studio album. It had some great songs, and we should have put in time for a proper release. But I am consistently told by fans that *Live* is their favorite live album of all time. It got great reviews and the fans responded well. But I think it would have benefited from the studio treatment. When Jonny Z heard the album, he told me, "Carl, you played a low card!"

**Metal Forces; Issue 3:** *Review by Philip DiBenedetto 1984*
*"The Rods are my kind of band. True rockin' rollers in every sense of the word. Unlike today's 17-year-old poser boy bands, whose biggest worry is to pick out a new pair of leg warmers to match their spandex, The Rods grind out their brand of metal with 'Cold Sweat and Blood'. Although the band seems to be in a rut of late (no major record deal since the old Arista days), they still seem to get records out and keep getting better. This brings us to the new LP Live, which is a no-frills package where you know just what to expect and get it. No ballads, no epics, no nonsense... just pure rock 'n' roll delivered with the exhilarating power so exemplary of The Rods. Out of the nine cuts on the LP, all but 'Hurricane' is new. The new songs come out of the In the Raw mold and performed live proves that The Rods are one of the tightest outfits out there today."*

**Walter O'Brien;** *Combat Records, Concrete Management*
*"Passport Records was distributed by Arista Records. Around the same time that I was working with Passport, The Rods albums on Arista had come out. So, I became familiar with them through working with Arista. I hadn't met them or anything, because up to that point, I really was not very involved in the heavy metal side of things. It was more prog rock and progressive. Meeting Carl and working with those guys was great and a lot of fun. We (Combat) also had a band called Helstar, which Carl produced, and I went to Texas with Carl under the auspices of being an executive producer. Basically, I was there to hang out with Carl and the band. Of course, because of the nature of the music business, I could very easily claim executive producer credits, which I did - because that's what an executive producer does. But Carl did all the technical work of course. We had a great time. And they (Helstar) were teenagers living in a rough neighborhood south of Dallas. It was wild. My favorite story about that session dealt with their drummer. On one of the songs, they wanted to start with a windchime intro. They wanted the windchimes to make a brief whooshing sound. The song was to start slow and then get really heavy. The drummer just could not get it right. He was a good drummer, but he just could not figure out the wind chimes. I told Carl, 'I think maybe if I show him, because I know what you mean.' The drummer never had to deal with windchimes, so he was struggling. But I knew what Carl wanted, so I went over to the windchimes to show him. I went up to it and I faked what a harp player does - with the crescendos and stuff. Carl said, 'Wait a minute, we got to put that on tape.' So, I am credited on the record for 'windchimes'.*

*It was a pretty good record, and I think we made some money from it. I think we definitely sold some. But again, we never broke big on anything.*

"My favorite Carl story deals with Joey DeMaio. I was scheduled to meet Carl at the Mayflower Hotel, which is right off Central Park's southwest corner. We were going to meet the Kerrang writer Malcolm Dome. We arrived a little early. We saw that Malcolm Dome was there already – he was at the bar with Joey DeMaio of Manowar. Now Joey was always friendly to me, but he was not going to talk to Carl. I asked, or maybe it was Carl, but one of us asked, 'Do we really need to go in now? Maybe we should wait for Joey to leave.' And we finally decided to go in anyway. Right away, Joey starts getting into it with Carl. Right at the Mayflower Bar. Joey is getting in his face and saying, 'Let's finish this right now, right here.' Carl said, 'I do not want to fight with you, Joey. We're in a nice bar.' Joey was not backing down. Joey said, 'Let's take it outside.' It was all of the best bully cliches you've ever heard in your life. So, they walk outside and Carl's actually following Joey outside, but clearly, Carl doesn't want to do this. Once outside, Joey starts hopping around. There's a stone wall from Central Park West to where Central Park starts. So, Joey hops over this stone wall. He launches himself over it. Joey assumed it was only about a 3-foot drop, because on our side it was only three feet. But the other side had a drop that was 25 or 30 feet. So, we run over to see if he was ok and there lies Joey - on the ground, 30 ft below. He was shaking his head – just like in the cartoons. You know with the canaries flying around someone's head tweeting? So, Joey, though stunned, looks up at us and begins shaking his fist. He yells, 'This isn't over, Carl Canedy!' It was hilarious."

# Anthrax: Fistful of Metal

Right before The Rods *Live* hit the market, David purchased a restaurant in Cortland, NY, called The Hollywood. He still owns and runs it to this very day. That is quite a feat - the restaurant industry is tough and to keep an establishment operational for nearly 40 years is a difficult task. David always had alternate professional interests, which is incredibly smart as in the music industry only a rare few make serious money. I figured it was time for me to expand my options as well. Being in The Rods was great, but it did not seem like a solid long-term prospect for paying the bills. Since music was my sole interest at the time, I figured production work would be the best option. David and I produced all but one of The Rods' albums, and I felt confident in my abilities.

I reached out to Jonny Zazula, who I knew had intentions of expanding his new label, Megaforce Records. I told Jonny that I was available should he need a producer. I lived close to both Music America and Pyramid Studios, both of which were only a five-hour drive from Old Bridge, NJ, which was the Megaforce Records home base. We also had The Rock & Roll Hotel as an option for lodging. For a new, and financially limited, record company, it made perfect sense. It was a short time later when Jonny contacted me and told me he had a new band he wanted me to work with. The name of that band was Anthrax, and like Metallica, they were young, passionate and dedicated. He said they showed potential, and they had worked really hard to get some quality songs together. Their demo was produced by Ross the Boss and it impressed Jonny enough that he agreed to put up the money for their first album.

So Anthrax came to upstate NY. They were very polite, but they were young New Yorkers - they were brash, they were pumped up, and they had tough attitudes. I liked them from the start. They were very receptive to my ideas, but they were also ushering in the new guard. They had their own vision. Their own concept. This was the early 1980s and there was a new type of metal on the horizon. The Rods were dinosaurs compared to what they were doing. Along with Metallica, Anthrax had a fresh and emerging sound. They really helped to expand my musical knowledge as well. They listened to everything and played it in the studio - that was where I first heard rap music. This was long before rap was on the radio and on MTV.

The original intention was to record at Music America. However, the day we were to start pre-production, we learned that Music America was going through renovations. We moved on to Pyramid Sound, which was the perfect facility for them. We had Chris Bubacz on board to engineer, and a gentleman by the name of Alex Perialas was to be the assistant engineer. Alex's father owned Pyramid Studios. Alex worked with me on the majority of the albums following *Fistful of Metal*, and then went on to become a top producer and engineer. Alex, at that time, was somewhat new - he was essentially a student, but he was a good engineer from the start. He was easygoing and had a great vibe. We were all somewhat new - myself new to production outside of The Rods; Alex, who was early in his engineering career; and Anthrax who were new to recording, with the exception of the *Soldiers of Metal* demo. My goal for them, from day one, was getting them to play tightly as a unit. To play a bit more cohesively. They were a great band, and they had a lot of energy live, but there was a little bit of push and pull that we needed to dial in. My goal was to capture that live power and eliminate any lack of cohesion.

They were all great players and were very aggressive, and they learned very quickly. But they were not used to being under the microscope. Scott Ian was a monster rhythm player. We ended up doubling Scott's guitars, because he was so tight. Dan Spitz had these blazing solos and we really tried to highlight them. Keep in mind that this album, which was to become *Fistful of Metal*, was a completely new style of music. Except for Metallica's *Kill Em All*, there was nothing like it at the time. A lot of people in the industry could not grasp it. They could not understand this new style of music. In fact, I made a bet with a friend of mine. I played him the demos and told him, "These guys are going to be huge." He said, "They sound like insect music" and told me how much they sucked. I bet him that they would, at minimum, be a gold act, if not a platinum act. He called me crazy; and much later, I was happy to prove him wrong. It was the changing of the guard. That change can be very threatening to older musicians who had been doing what they had considered cool for years, only to find out that they had been replaced. It often happens very quickly. I get it - it is not a fun place to be. But I understood, as by this time, The Rods were waning in popularity and a new type of metal was arriving to take over.

The guys in Anthrax were all really great, but there was some developing friction. It was very clear from the outset that vocalist Neil Turbin was not in the inner circle. You could tell that Neil was the outsider in the group. The other guys were tight. And Neil was a little bit on the outside. Other than that, it was a pleasant experience. They were a great group of guys and there were not any issues on my end. We were only together for a brief period - I recall it was only a couple of weeks. We did not have long to record and mix. There was a time crunch. We had an incredibly low budget. They needed to press this quickly. Jonny had taken out some loans and he needed to pay them back – and the only way to do that was to sell records. Ultimately, I thought it was a fantastic album, but I was a bit disappointed in the mix. I think we all were. We just did not have the time and we did not have the budget. Neil did his vocals last, and due to time constraints, he had the least amount of time. He really came through and knocked it out. If we'd had a bigger budget, and some more time, I think it would have been stellar - but I still get a lot of people asking about those sessions. For many metal fans, it is such an iconic album.

**Neil Turbin**; *Ex-Anthrax, Deathriders:*
*"Jonny Z signed us and then told us we would be going upstate. I ended up staying longer than the other guys. I was there for a whole month. We stayed at the Rock and Roll Hotel with Victoria Calandra. Carl lived nearby. I even went to David Feinstein's house - it was a log cabin that he had built himself. There was no electricity, only a wood burning stove. I felt like I was at Lincoln's cabin. It was amazing to have that experience. Ronnie James Dio was from there (Cortland)! So, I would stay at the Rock and Roll Hotel, and I would be shuttled about by Carl. Carl would come and pick me up and we would go to the studio every day. Even if I was not doing my parts I was there to observe, so in a sense I really was in the thick of it.*

*"I was really observing the whole production from start to finish. I was there when they were putting the tape into the machine and starting to record drum tracks. I think what kind of happened is we were supposed to go to Music America studios, where Metallica did Kill 'Em All. We loved the sound of that album and we really wanted to use that studio. We slept on the floor for three nights in the basement of the building, waiting for the studio to be free. The day we were to start, as we were walking down the stairs, the equipment was being brought up the stairs. They were ripping out the studio and they were remodeling it. But we got screwed because that would have been great if we could have recorded it there.*

*"So, at that point, we were there for three nights, and we realized, you know, this shit is not going anywhere. Then we went to Pyramid Studios. That's where we met Carl. The guy who ran Music America was going to engineer our album (Chris Bubacz). I do not know about the production, but I knew Ross was not going to do it because he was committed to Manowar. He was either busy or Jonny was not able to afford him. Johnny did not have the money. He needed to put out the album quickly. I mean he was scraping the bottom of the barrel because he had financed Metallica. He was a person. Megaforce really was not a full-fledged label at that point. He was trying to borrow and take out loans to finance this album. I think Carl came into the picture because at that point, it was panic mode. We*

were there for three nights. Upstate is pretty far from New York City, which is where we lived. Going home was not an option.

"We visited a studio in Elmira, which would have been inexpensive, but the sound would not have been good. It was right behind Elmira Prison. It did not have the right vibe and recording next to a prison was creepy. Then Carl told us about Pyramid. It was great. We loved the equipment. Ted Nugent and The Amboy Dukes recorded there. There was a bunch of reel-to-reel tapes they had in storage - we had a good time digging through them. Pyramid seemed like a better environment. But we were in upstate New York, and it was very cold - and not comfortable. I do not think we even brought sleeping bags. It was rough. Carl was great though. He was always positive. He was a very upbeat kind of guy, and he was very knowledgeable. He was really cool. He would always be chewing gum - he had a great energy. There were other people that were part of it, Chris Bubacz, and Alex Perialis, who were running the studio.

"So, these influences were there. Carl's a drum guy, so he wanted lots of drums, big drums. And I think that was part of the approach. And we definitely wanted an arena sound. He wanted big, loud guitars - crunchy and powerful guitars to cut through. I think we did not spend enough time mixing. I think the budget was a big part of that, but also the way they managed the time. I was up there for 30 days. Carl was basically trying to rescue a situation. Because initially it was a disaster. Jonny Z was not able to come up, because he was running the store (Rock & Roll Heaven). Carl was stepping in and kind of brokered the deal for us. That is kind of how that went down. It ended up being a turning point for Carl. We all learned from the experience. We had other issues as each of us were fighting for more of a prominent sound. Since I recorded last, and with the time crunch, this left me in the back. And unfortunately, Carl could only manage that to a point, because it is not his band, right? I mean, it still came out okay. But for me, I know that it could have been so much better had we had more time. Carl came from The Rods, who were a tight outfit and were able to knock out their albums really quick. They were really dialed in. We definitely were not. We did not have the road time or the cohesion. Dan and Charlie were pretty much new. Rehearsals were very impersonal.

"The cover was another issue. Originally, they had wanted this airbrushed cover of a spaceman thing or some shit. It looked like they had it done at a flea market. It looked like something you would see on an old rapper's car. It was embarrassing. Then I had this crazy idea, about a fist going through someone's head. There was a lot of pushback on that. I am actually surprised it ended up being the cover. It just was not executed the way I would have done it. But it is an iconic cover. People either love it or hate it. The other disappointment was the pink logo. Why the fuck would we have a pink logo? And there was no band picture on the back either. And I will tell you this next story because it is a bit funny, but also because it is history. There was this time when we were in the studio, and I gave Dan Lilker money to go buy Devil Dogs (which were these cool chocolate bones, filled with cream) and for a Yoo-hoo. And at the time, Devil Dogs would have been a dollar for a box of 12. And chocolate milk, you would get a bottle for about 50 cents or something like that. So, the total should have been $2 and change - so I should have had some bills back.

"We did not have much money so every bit was needed. So, Dan comes back from the store, and he says: 'Here's your change, and here's your stuff.' And he gives me some dimes and a few pennies – it was maybe 25 cents. So, at that point, I did not have very much money. And he was taking my money, basically saying that it was $5 for all that stuff. So, I take out some Devil Dogs and smash them right into his face. Just like a pie was getting smashed in his face - and he was wiping the Devil Dogs out of his eyes. He was really pissed after that. Dan Spitz was practically rolling on the floor. Even Scott was laughing. So, it was just always this tension, and always this environment.

"Ultimately, I began to get excluded from a lot of things. There were meetings and they started to leave me out. Carl was unbeknownst to any of this. This was peripheral to him. He did not know the extent of this. But I can tell you this, after he worked with Anthrax on the following albums, and he worked with other renowned bands, Anthrax did not even give him recognition. So it is really a shame that where they came from and who they are, they did not give him any recognition. I hold Carl in the highest esteem, because without Carl and Jonny Z, none of this would have happened. I think part of the first album, there were some hiccups. There were some bumps and bruises along the way, but all in all, the album did what it was supposed to do. Everyone looks at their first album after a few decades and wishes some aspects were different. It was the 1980s and we had very little budget. The album artwork - was that perfect? Was the music perfect? Was the songwriting perfect? Was the production perfect? Was the engineering perfect? None of it was perfect. And none of it was close to perfect, but it was a great effort on all parts. Not only is it one of the first real thresholds, it has also became a template for early thrash. It was one of the albums that helped shape thrash metal."

**Danny Lilker;** *Ex-Anthrax, Nuclear Assault, S.O.D., Brutal Truth*
"We were a New York band, but still we were aware of the international metal scene. We knew that there were some other metal bands from New York State and then even over the lake - like Anvil and Exciter and such. We had a sense that what we were doing at the time was going to be

something special. It was a very exciting time back then for metal because it was evolving. It was getting more intense. And the more you reached out, the more you realized that this was going on all over the world. This is obviously way before the internet. You have to do the work and write to people, go to the post office or whatever. But anyway, there was a certain electricity in the air and there were no blueprints for what we were doing. Sure, we had our influences, but we were shaping it in our own way, too.

"There was a feeling in the air that something was going on that was going to be memorable, I guess, for lack of a better word, going with the flow in one way, because you kind of had to. It was definitely exciting. It was a great feeling. I am definitely proud of that, that I was on some records back then that are considered classic thrash records. So, when we were going to do the first Anthrax album, which we did at Pyramid Sound in Ithaca, it was decided that Carl was going to produce it. Now remember, this is the first record any of us ever did. And we were all just like in our late teens and shit like that. Back then we needed more of a producer because we were very green. We never recorded professionally. Here it is, 40 years later. Now I do not need a producer. I tell somebody I know what I am doing, but not fucking way back then. So that is the crazy thing. Now that it is 2023, that record was done in October 1983.

"So, it is fair to say that the record was done 40 years ago, or at least it was written 40 years ago. So that is fucking crazy. Anyway, Carl did the record. When it came up that he was going to produce the record, we were like, 'That guy seems pretty cool.' Thrash was so new then that it would have been hard to find somebody, an experienced thrash producer. It is easy to do that now. We were doing something that might have been hard for some people. To most people it was the fastest thing they had ever heard. You have to really be on your toes otherwise it might sound jumbly. I've done a lot of fucking records. I've produced a lot of my own shit. And everything must be in its own space. When you're playing fast enough, everything has to be in its own little space in a EQ capacity or shit will get lost. I do not think that record (Fistful of Metal) sounds bad at all. So, I think Carl did a fucking bang-up job. Especially considering that it was so new that no one was sure how to handle it. There was not any kind of template or blueprint for it. You just have to take a deep breath and go, alright, let's do it.

"Well, he (Carl) definitely played a role in changing the way I play bass. I was a nervous kid; I was only 18 or 19 years old. Carl said 'Danny, I want you to try and play with a pick.' Back then, I was all about Iron Maiden. So, I wanted to be Steve Harris and play with my fingers like Steve did. But Carl said, 'Why don't you try to play with a pick?' And that was not the hardest thing in the world for me because when Anthrax had first started, I actually played guitar in the band. That was when we were essentially a Judas Priest cover band. I had never used one on bass. So that came in handy because shortly after that, I discovered that using a pick was the way to go - because you are almost playing like a guitar anyway. You are playing with a lot of speed and distortion. And that's how I've always played since then. So, Carl definitely had a big hand in shaping that. He did not say, 'Use the pick so you can eventually play really fast and loud and noisy.' He said it because that is what he thought would work. But he definitely turned me in that direction and that helped a lot.

"When it was time to go for it, when I was getting into Discharge and Hell Hammer, and writing shit for Nuclear Assault, I was just going heavier and faster and that pick really helped. But obviously I have some bittersweet memories of the time, because as most people know, I was thrown out of the band three months later. I was thrown out of the band three days before the record came out. There really was not a good reason except that Neil hated me. They decided to keep him because he was the frontman. But anyway, so on Fistful of Metal, it was decided that we were going to do a cover of 'I'm 18' by Alice Cooper, which is four fucking chords. It was not really that big of a chore. But when we were recording that song, Carl kept changing the bass line. Now, he was not doing it to fuck with me or confuse me. He was doing his job because he was there to produce the band and make us sound as good as possible. He was kind of experimenting with that. I'd be doing the bass with a certain riff and then he'd stop and go, 'You know what, Danny? When you do that last riff with those four notes, play the third note a little bit later than you did just now.' Then a little bit later it is, 'Wait. On this part I want you to try and play the second note a little earlier.' So, what happened was that while we were doing the song, he would keep stopping and doing little critiques and tweaking it. It took a lot longer to record than normal because he was kind of tweaking it while we were doing it.

"Not to mention, if there were ten different changes suggested in the last five minutes, I, being a nervous kid, would start getting confused about which ones were for what. And even though he would say, 'Do this like that', I'd fuck up and still do something wrong. I had all this shit spinning around in my head that he wanted me to do at the last minute and was kind of experimenting. Now, this is not on Carl, but I will show you what this leads up to. So, after I was thrown out of Anthrax, I saw an interview where they justified firing me by saying 'Did you hear the "I'm 18" track? It took Danny 30 times to record the bass track on that.' They neglected to tell the whole story, which is 15 or 20 of them were Carl changing it up. It is just funny afterwards because I read that and I'm like, really? So, you are going to make it sound like I could not play that? Now Carl's going to read this, *and he is going to fucking shake his head and laugh* [Note: Carl, in fact, did shake his head and laugh when he read this].

"A year later, Scott called me up and invited me to play in SOD. It was more like an insult to injury thing at the time because I had been thrown out of the band. I had written most of the first record and here they are saying that it took me too long to do an easy fucking rock song. Carl was just trying to do the best job he could and just decided that it might sound better if that note was played a beat later. That was completely cool, but it is a funny twist."

## Let Them Eat Metal

We owed Combat Records a second album. In those days, it was typical for most bands to release an album every year. The record companies typically pushed for this. In the 1980s, it was extremely rare for a band to go more than two years between albums, unlike nowadays, when musical acts release albums at their own leisure, with very little pressure from the record companies. Of course, album sales were one of the primary income streams (musically) at the time. In the '80s, you toured to escalate album sales and merchandise, whereas in the current era, you sell albums to increase your attendance at shows and sell more merchandise. Another album was not an issue for us. Between David and me, we had plenty of songs written - enough to complete an album and then some.

For a few months, I had been toying with an idea for a song, something called "Let Them Eat Metal". I thought it was a great title, but I was struggling to lay out a song behind it. So I told David about it and he said, "Let me see what I can do." It was but a few days later when he came back with a perfectly laid out track - which we decided to name the album after. We went through some other songs and arranged what we thought would be a good album, and then went to work on the recording process. With the last two albums being recorded rather quickly, one a live album and the other being put together in only three days, we decided that we wanted to take our time and use a more traditional approach for this album. That approach is to play the parts over and over until they were near perfect. We were given a budget of $10,000. Which was not a lot of money - even back then. This also came at a tough time. My producing career was just getting off to a start; I had a plethora of projects booked with Megaforce, and things on that end were just starting to take off.

Once again, we booked time at Music America with Chris Bubacz. I was scheduled to lay down the drum tracks first. This was a memorable session for me, but for all the wrong reasons. It was an extremely cold winter in upstate New York. It was far colder than usual. Since Chris lived close to the studio, I stayed with him. Chris had meager amenities and I was crashing on the couch. It was a long, cold, and uncomfortable winter. The drum sessions seemed to take forever. They were painfully long. Maybe I was overthinking it. But it was a struggle getting the drum parts down. It did not help that we had not played any shows in quite some time. Chris and I spent weeks in the studio. Just us, with no production input. Looking back, this was one of my least favorite albums to record. The entire experience felt lonely and desolate, and the process really dragged on. I had never spent this much time in the studio doing drums.

With the drum tracks laid out, Gary came in and laid down his bass parts. David followed and did the guitars and vocals. Gary and David's sessions went rather quickly - at least much quicker than mine. We spent a week mixing it and we were soon ready to go with what would become *Let Them Eat Metal*. The cover art alone was to become the most well-known feature of the album. When we were discussing the cover art, I told Gary and David about this idea I had been sitting on for a few months. "What about a woman in lingerie eating a silver vibrator coming out of a banana peel?" I asked. Surprisingly, they went for it. Most of our early album covers were groups shots (outside of the animated *Wild Dogs*), so I figured this was a long shot. But they agreed. Our first task was to find a model who was willing to work for little to no money.

The girl on the cover was Sherry Cosmo, who David had known for some time. Oddly enough, Sherry really was not a big fan of the band. She was, however, part of the local rock scene. She had dated a lot of famous rockers like Alex Van Halen and David Coverdale. We talked about our idea for the cover and asked her if she knew where we could get a silver dildo as a prop. To our surprise (well, maybe not) she said, "I have a gold one." Perfect. The day of the photo shoot, Sherry arrived at the studio already dressed in her skimpy lingerie. The photo shoot was done at a small studio in Cortland that had done PR shots for The Rods on a few occasions. The photographer had an assistant, an elderly gentleman, who must have hit the floor when Sherry walked in. I am sure he came close to having a heart attack that day – her panties came with a prefabricated hole in the crotch, and she was consistently squatting and bending over. Sherry was not shy. Surprisingly, Combat had no issues with it. They loved it. In fact, it was shown on *The Phil Donahue Show* when they did a special on the PMRC and controversial heavy metal albums. Looking back, it is quite misogynistic, but many fans consider it an iconic cover.

As for the album itself, we were happy with it, but it received mixed reviews. At that point, in 1984, we were the old guard, and we were somewhat passé at that time - hair metal and thrash metal were starting to hit. But changing our sound was never a thought. We knew that we had a certain aura and style, and we were good at that. To try and get a more modern sound (by 1984 standards) would have been detrimental. We never wanted to alter or water down who we were. It was a solid Rods album. Quite a few of the tracks are still staples of our live set.

I actually wrote a song about Sherry (on *Let Them Eat Metal*) called "She Is Such A Bitch". I had written the music first and then desperately tried to find lyrics that would match. That is not always the best way to put a song together. When I first met Sherry, we did not like each other at all. She demanded her name be on the guest list for one of our shows. I thought that was rather arrogant of her, so I took her name off the list. When she arrived, she was not pleased. She was with this big guy, Ox, who was one of Ritchie Blackmore's bodyguards (known for smuggling Blackmore out of Germany inside a road case). The threat going around that night was that Ox was going to kill us for not having Sherry's name on the list. She was rude and obnoxious. Maybe it came from being a big deal in a small town? She was pretty, well known and very high maintenance. But we eventually became very good friends, and I am thankful for that.

**David "Rock" Feinstein:**
*"The cover was featured on Phil Donahue as one of the more offensive records of that year with the subtitle 'Has it gone too far?' It was funny to watch because, after Donahue held it up and made his point, he dropped it on the floor where it stayed throughout the show in full view. Every time they panned around the room, there it was.*

*"Ironically, if you listen to Let Them Eat Metal, it is a pristine metal record. It is very clean. We had come a long way in our production and our playing. Carl was getting more and more into producing and he really wanted to do a record that could compete with the others that were out there. Technically, it is very good. I remember thinking to myself, 'This band will never break up, we'll be together forever.' Yet, even then we were three separate people going in different directions. There are things in life, things you do not have any power over. Carl was always interested in the production end of things and by doing that he got to work with other bands and gained a great deal of experience. Without product and without a record deal, you are not working. You can do, and we did, regional shows. But unless you have a hot spot where the people are into what you are doing, you are not going to be there. Looking back, what makes me appreciate The Rods was that we could really deliver and write good songs together. Let Them Eat Metal proved it and I will always be happy we had that."*

# Exciter: Violence & Force

Sometime during the madness of *Let Them Eat Metal*, I signed on to produce the second album from a Canadian band by the name of Exciter. Jonny Z reached out to me and told me about them. Exciter had received rave reviews from their debut album entitled *Heavy Metal Maniac*, which was one of the early precursors of thrash. I was interested in Exciter from the start - they were a three piece like The Rods, but even more interestingly, their drummer was also the lead vocalist. This was no easy task, especially given how fast they played and the intensity of their vocals. Their first album, *Heavy Metal Maniac*, was really great. Their music had a really intense energy. It was raw, fierce and heavy. The lead singer, Dan Beehler, had a voice that was absolutely balls to the wall. Upon meeting them, I found they were three of the greatest guys in the industry. They were super sweet guys. Not what you would expect from the tough-as-nails persona their music conveys. They were not big partiers, but they had such a great sense of humor, and this came in handy during the monotony of recording. This album was an absolute blast to record. We were always laughing. They knew what they wanted, and they were not allowing any partying to get in the way of their recording time. It was a lot of work but a lot of fun.

We did pre-production in the studio. Chris Bubacz and Alex Perialis were engineering. Dan had a fierce heavy-hitting drum sound. We really tried to emphasize it on this album. Al Johnson, the bassist, was a phenomenal player and came with a great sound. The only real work came in getting the rhythms dialed in. The guitarist, John Ricci, was solid at lead takes, but for most recordings, the guitars are traditionally doubled. We really had to push to get the rhythms tight. In the studio, you need everything to be precise down to the microsecond. That was the only area where we really had a difficult time. So that was one of the things I regret on this album. I really wish I had pushed for a more aggressive sound with the guitars.

For one of the standout tracks, "Pounding Metal", we wanted the sound of metal being pounded to accompany it – something similar to a hammer on an anvil. Anvil had done something similar for the title track to their second album, *Metal on Metal*, and it lent some ferocity to the track. Alex went to a body shop that was next door and found a large hood, from what must have been a massive car. It had been ready for the junkyard. He dragged this big hood in the studio. We then took these massive tractor chains and smashed them over the hood – it made an interesting sound to say the least. And those are the sounds you will hear on the album.

Overall, it was truly a pleasant experience. The guys in Exciter are world class, some of the greatest guys out there, and they were fantastic musicians. This was a fun record, and I was happy to be part of it. There are some standout tracks like "War is Hell", "Violence and Force", "Pounding Metal" and "Delivering to the Master", but I feel that it was an album that successfully made a musical statement as a whole. I do not think Exciter got anywhere close to the recognition they deserved. They were pioneers. I wish I had been able to do a bit more for them sonically. But, damn, what a great band. These guys have never been anything but a fucking tank at high speed. And today, they are successfully touring the world to sold out crowds!

**Dan Beehler:** *Exciter*

*"Our first album (Heavy Metal Maniac) was recorded with a 12 channel H&H board - it was essentially a demo tape. We did it in a basement. Jonny Z heard the album and signed us. When we wrote Heavy Metal Maniac, we kept writing and essentially what you hear on Violence and Force is a continuation of Heavy Metal Maniac. We had the songs ready to go. Jonny Z gave us the option on the producer, of the guy who did the Metallica album or Carl. We were familiar with The Rods - they played them at a radio station in Ottawa, so we chose Carl. We were really excited to have Carl produce this album. We stayed in Cortland - in Carl's town.*

*"The recording process was great. Carl is one of the most easygoing people that I have ever met. I was 21 or 22 and in awe of the guy. I had his albums and really looked up to him - I was so excited to meet him for the first time. He gave me so much great advice on drumming and recording - but the best part, in the studio we were always laughing. There were some disputes here and there - mostly over the guitars and whatnot. But overall, the album was very successful. We did a lot of laughing. Carl has got a million one-liners. It was a very family type atmosphere.*

*"Fast forward to 1985 - John Ricci left the band and I was getting threatened by the record company (another label at this point) – they were putting the pressure on us to get another album out. So, we got a new guitarist named Brian McPhee. I called Carl up and asked him if we could use his rehearsal space at Falso Music. He set it all up for us. We stayed at The Rock & Roll Hotel once again. In one week, we wrote the entire thing (Unveiling the Wicked) - start to finish. By Friday, we had all of the songs laid out. I think of that every time I sign a copy of Unveiling the Wicked, I think of that time in Cortland. With the help of Carl and Al Falso, we wrote*

*one of the best Exciter albums. There was a real brotherhood at the time and if it was not for Carl, that album never would've happened. Carl even let me use his old drum set. Cortland was really magical at that time - it was such a great time musically and inspired so much creativity. Recording Violence and Force and writing Unveiling the Wicked was truly magic. It was electrifying. Back then, you could call Carl and he would do anything for you. He would always be there. I still feel that way. I still look up to him. He is a good brother and a good guy.*

*"The scene really brewed out of that area. There was so much happening at that time - it was all starting to come together. It was starting to develop. It was electrifying shit. This musical scene was starting to boom. I could tell you stories for hours - there were so many good memories of the area. If you look at the origins and everything that came out of the area, Carl has his name on most of it. The Rods and Carl really led that scene. They helped to orchestrate it. The Rock & Roll Hotel was the place to be. Great bands were always stopping by. Manowar used to come hang out. I remember walking through downtown Cortland with my Walkman. A lot of ideas for Unveiling the Wicked came that way. Just incredible memories. It is pretty incredible."*

# Helstar: Burning Star

I was good friends with Walter O'Brien, who worked for Combat Records during the 1980s. Walter asked me if I would accompany him to Houston. There was a new band they had signed by the name of Helstar. Helstar had a massive following in Texas. They were leading the early scene there, but they had only released a demo, which never made its way to the East Coast. I was not familiar with them, but a trip to Houston sounded good. Walter had not requested that I produce them, only assist him and offer a few pointers to the young up-and-coming band. Basically, I was to be a liaison between the label and the band. However, I ended up producing the album, which I think was his intention all along. I do not believe I was paid much - or anything at all for that matter. But it was well worth it. I have such great memories of those few days. There was no drama. It was a painless session. Which is quite abnormal for a band who had not been in the studio much, and who were barely out of high school.

We did pre-production in a little shed, which was tough because it was incredibly hot. But they were easy to work with. They knocked the album out very quickly; I believe the entire process of pre-production, production and mixing took only a few days. They were so talented, which made it easy. I am happy I got to be part of it. Especially since it was the debut album that would launch their career. I still talk to vocalist James Rivera and guitarist Larry Barragan frequently, both of whom have dubbed me "Dad." They are still out there kicking ass and I am proud of them.

**James Rivera:** *Helstar*
*"We had no idea that Carl was going to produce our record (or even be there). We thought it was only going to be Walter. So imagine our surprise when we walked into the studio. We had a serious management problem, so we were never told much. So we were really happy to see Carl. We really bonded with him. We nicknamed him Dad, and to this very day he calls us Son. We were very young at the time, and Carl was a few years older - plus he had a ton of experience. He was easygoing. He was patient. He taught us a lot. So he was a father type figure to us. That is why we ended up calling him Dad. There were no issues with the recording. Much of that was because we were extremely well rehearsed. It was a pleasant experience and seemed to go smoothly. Our only issues were with our manager at the time, who really hindered us. We blew a lot of opportunities on what could*

have been a strong start, thanks to him. Carl later had to advise us on managerial issues. I think The Rods might have gone through the same thing, so he really understood and gave us some good advice. Now, the funniest event of the era is Carl convinced me to change my name for the album. If you look on the back of the LP, you will not see 'James Rivera'. But you will see 'Bill Lionel' listed. This was around the time when Mr. Bill was a hit on Saturday Night Live. So instead of saying 'Hey man' to each other (we thought 'man' was a bit hippyish), we said 'Hey Bill' to each other, mostly when addressing each other or trying to get one another's attention. That was our thing. So, Carl hears us saying 'Hey Bill' frequently and he asks us about it. At the end of production, when we were discussing credits and thank-you's for the back/liner notes, Carl commented that my name was not metal enough. He said, 'You need a heavy metal name' and given the Bill thing that was still fresh in his mind, he jokingly said I should incorporate that. So that is where Bill Lionel came from. I went back to 'James Rivera' for the second album, but we had to list it as 'James Rivera; Lead Vocals aka Bill Lionel', so that way people did not think Helstar had gotten a new singer. After you release your first album, you are proud of it - you want to show it off and tell people you were part of it. Of course, when I told people, and showed them the album, well no one believed me because my name was not on the album."

**Larry Barragan:** *Helstar*
"Helstar has been around for 40 years now. In 1983 we recorded this demo that got us signed to Combat Records. Can you imagine? We were all teenagers when we got signed. So going into a real studio and actually working with a real producer was kind of eye opening. We were definitely not used to it - I think I was like, 19. The youngest member was Tom Rogers. And at that time, I think he had just turned 17. So, yeah, I mean, we were so green. And the funny thing was, we all go into the studio, and the executive producer was Walter O'Brien, and then Carl walks in. And I remember going, 'I think that's a drummer from The Rods.' I had just seen them a few months prior, opening for Judas Priest. I was like, 'Oh, my God, it is him, it is really him!' So, there was a little bit of me being starstruck. My first album was also going to be produced by Carl - who had just done the Anthrax album. Once we started working, everything just kind of flowed. And not that there were not any little arguments - because I definitely wanted the guitars to sound a little bit different than what they actually ended up sounding like. But he was the producer. So he won that argument. And we just hit it off as friends. We kept in touch over the years, and he is very much like a father figure. So that's why James and I call him Dad. He has always been a counselor, someone that I can go to and ask, 'What do

*you think I should do?'* We hold his advice in very high esteem. We got caught up in a management situation with Helstar. It was right after that album, in '85 or '86. I called Carl up immediately and said, *'Man, you know, this is what I'm thinking about doing'* and he helped me in what was a very dark period. I do not know if he suggested new management to James at some point. Because a few months later James came to me and said, *'Yeah, you are right, I think we need to make a move. And if these guys do not want to, then maybe you and I should just go ahead and continue with Helstar. And they can go do whatever they are going to do.'* And that is actually what happened. Carl's been there every step of the way. And even now, I talk to him occasionally. Still, after 40 years. You would think, *'Well, he produced one album and that is it.'* But friendship lies a bit deeper than that.

"And another thing, as far as rock and metal, he is one of the greatest drummers ever. I do not say that lightly. There are a lot of badass drummers out there, but Carl is one of the greats. I always would joke with him and tell him *'Carl, would you ever work with another band? I think you are that good.'* Now back then you stayed with whatever band you were in. Back then you did not play in multiple bands or anything like that. It was unheard of really. Now, it is what everybody does. But back then, Carl was like *'The Rods are my band.'* The Rods were badass. They were very tight, very professional. Anytime they played in Texas, we would go see them. We did not do the backstage thing - we were in the crowd. Where the excitement was. We were fans first and foremost. I remember another time we were visiting upstate New York, and Carl took us to The Rock & Roll Hotel. Raven was there. Carl showed us around and we had a great time. He always made time for us. Sadly, Carl will never get that recognition that he really deserves. But he is the man. He is the fucking greatest drummer."

## Jack Starr: Out of the Darkness

Passport Records reached out to me about producing a solo album for guitar virtuoso Jack Starr. I had known about Jack through Shrapnel Records: he had appeared on their sampler *U.S. Metal Volume 2* with his prior band Virgin Steele. Jack completed two albums with Virgin Steele before leaving to begin his solo career (and later a project called Burning Starr). I was eager to participate as Jack would be joined by former Riot vocalist Rhett Forrester. Not to mention the fact that he needed a drummer, and I was more than happy to assist. Gary Driscoll (of Elf and Rainbow) had some free time and agreed to help out on the drums as well. Jack also needed a bass player, and I recommended Gary Bordonaro for the role. Gary was always very efficient in the studio; he got the parts down fast and was easy to work with. He was a fantastic session player.

I booked time with Music America and with engineer Chris Bubacz. I picked up Jack, Rhett and Paul Kane from the airport. Paul signed on to do some rhythm guitars for the album. I immediately took a liking to Jack. He could not have been nicer. Rhett and Paul were great as well. This is a very short chapter for good reason - everyone was so easy to work with. The entire process went smoothly and with no memorable issues. What is typically a difficult part during production, the guitar solos, came off without an issue. Jack is a solo machine. Paul was a superb rhythm player as well. The entire process was a piece of cake. Jack was able to nail the solos in one or two takes. It was unbelievable. Typically, I would have to do multiple takes and cut and paste the best parts. Not so with Jack, who quickly nailed the solos. I had a great time with the guys – the entire project was pleasant and smooth. However, there was soon to be tension with Rhett and Jack; but at that point there were no hints of the drama that was soon to come with Rhett.

**Jack Starr:** *Jack Starr, Burning Starr, Ex-Virgin Steele*
*"I had left Virgin Steele and I had gotten a record deal with Passport Records. At the time, they were a big independent record label in America. I needed a great drummer. Now, I was a fan of The Rods... I had heard their albums, and I was thinking, 'Would not it be great to get a drummer like Carl?' I was not even thinking of Carl himself, I was hoping I could just get somebody like him. In other words, somebody that had his skill set, somebody that could play that hard, that heavy, and maintain an iron sight.*

*I guess I was a little courageous one day, and I said, 'I'm going to try to get a hold of him.' Because maybe he would be kind enough to play on my album. I also remembered that he recently began producing albums for some up-and-coming bands. Now, I did not know him at all, and I was worried he might be full of himself or a bit conceited. So, I called him, and after a minute of chatting with him, I realized he was really down to earth. Just an all-around great guy. We started talking about music and our favorite bands, and we really hit it off. I told him I just got a record deal, and I have a good budget, and then asked him if he would produce the album. I loved his production work with The Rods. And he had a really good handle on what was going on in this up-and-coming scene. The metal scene coming out of America was very similar to the New Wave of British Heavy Metal. Only it was the new wave of American heavy metal which evolved into thrash. He said to me, 'I've been working out of some very good studios here in Rochester.' He told me about Pyramid Studios, where he had just recorded Anthrax's first album. And of course, Music America, where Metallica had recorded their album. Which were two albums that were really gaining momentum. So I was intrigued. I said, 'Well, what is this Music American studio? What is that like?' Carl says, 'Well, let me give you the rundown, Jack. It is an old, abandoned, well not really abandoned, but it kind of looks like it could be from the early 1900s. It has a huge ballroom where I have set up my drums, and they sound pretty amazing.' So right away, I am thinking, Okay, this guy wants the big drum sound. And that was all I needed to hear because I was a fan of Led Zeppelin. Right? And I was reading about how John Bonham and Jimmy Page went to this old, huge farmhouse in England, and it was called Headley Grange. It was this huge place that had wooden floors and had this natural reverb. That really inspired me, and I chose Music America.*

"We also talked about inviting different musicians, and Carl recommended a couple of musicians who are all top shelf. He recommended his bass player from The Rods, Gary, who is amazing. He also recommended Gary Driscoll, who played with Richie Blackmore. Carl said 'I do not want to be the only drummer; I do not mind sharing the limelight.' That guy (Gary Driscoll) had just played coliseums all over the world. Carl said 'He lives in the area. I am going to send him some of your stuff and we'll see if he'll agree to do it.' Like four or five days later, Carl called to tell me that Gary's on board. So, when I get up to the studio, I told Gary (Driscoll) how much I appreciated him helping us out. He really did not have to – he was a massive name at the time. Gary looked at me and he said, 'Jack, if I did not think you were good, I would not be doing this for any amount of money.'

"With Carl, the thing that I really admired about him was his incredible love of hard rock and heavy metal. He was not somebody who was just doing it because it was in style. He was somebody that was doing it before it was in style. And even after it was in style. Look, we are in the year 2022. Heavy metal is not as big as it was in the '80s. Unfortunately, it just is not. It is not even as big as it was in the '90s. But do you think that would have an impact on Carl? No, he is still doing it. And he is doing it because he loves it. And that is the kind of person that Carl is. One thing that I have always remembered, and it is kind of funny, but Carl is very fastidious, very methodical, very well organized. By that I mean that when he walked into a studio, he walked in carrying a briefcase, carrying notes, carrying track listing papers, knowing exactly what he wanted to accomplish that day. It was not some kind of haphazard 'Well, let's jam and we will see what comes out' arrangement. No, that is not how he operated. The other funny thing that I noticed is that Carl always had a toothbrush and toothpaste in his briefcase. I thought that was really interesting. Here is a guy that knows he is going to be in there for like, eight, nine hours, maybe even ten hours. And he is ready. He brought toothpaste, and a toothbrush. I picked up that habit from Carl. Later on in my life, when I would go into studios, I'd walk in there with a briefcase, and I had figured out what I needed to accomplish that day. When you are confronted with someone who has good habits, and who is serious, you are going to learn. And that is how I learned how to handle the recording process. By taking it seriously and doing so in a very organized manner.

"Anyways, when we got into the studio, we started recording Out of The Darkness, there was a plan. It was organized and laid out. We were going to do these rhythm tracks a certain way. We did not need to have an entire band in the studio with us. We did not need to have a track blaring in the control room. You need to get in there with headphones on and we needed to visually communicate with each other. We had to lay down a wall of sound. And that is what Carl and Gary did. And then Gary Driscoll came in and I got to watch him get set up and organized. They were all seasoned and there was no nonsense. It was like having a master class in recording... and not just in recording, but a master class in heavy metal.

"Here is another little story. There was a song on the album that was an instrumental. I said to Carl, 'Just to switch things up, what if we got another bass player to play on the instrumental track?' Carl said, 'Well, I know this young guy named Ned Meloni, who is really great, and he plays in a popular local band called Icewater Mansion - but he is only like, 17 or 18 years old.' So, I told him that I do not have a problem with it. If Carl recommends him, he obviously must be good. I said, 'Okay, that's what I want.' I want people that are intuitive. Not just people that are reading off a sheet of music, but people that are intuitive, and play organically. So anyway, he brought in this young guy, and this guy had hair down to his waist - he almost looked like a girl. Probably better looking than most girls that I had known. After I heard him play, I told Carl, 'You are batting 100. Brother, this kid is great.' And that was really the foundation of my 40-year association with Ned Meloni. Ned played on many of the Burning Starr albums. It was a call from Carl bringing him into the studio that day. Another thing that inspired me from those sessions - I was recording some guitar tracks, and Carl looked at me, and said 'Jack, do you need all that distortion? Do you really need all that delay to play?' I said, 'Well, I do not know, that's how I usually do it.' And he says, 'Jack, you are a better player than that. You do not need all those crutches. But if you do, I am going to do something for you. I am going to let you hear all that in your headphones. But we are not going to print it.' I did not know what he meant. What does 'not going to print it' mean? Well, what he meant was, that stuff will be coming into my headphones, but we are not going to record it. Back then you have to remember everything was done on two-inch Ampex tape. It was not done digitally, but what we are going to print on the tape is the actual clean sound. And if we want to, we could augment it with different sounds. He made me believe in myself, he made me believe that I did not need all those crutches, as some guitar players have to have, tons of distortion and delay. They cannot do any solos unless there's a wah-wah pedal. And he just looked at me, he goes, 'You do not need all of that stuff.' I listened to him, and we were able to pull a great performance out of every single person that played on that album, myself included. If you look on the back of the album, you can see Carl's drum set in the Music America ballroom. It was a great time and a great era. Carl was at the epicenter of the movement. The experience was really great - I have so many great memories of that time."

**Monte Connor:** *Former Senior VP of A&R for Roadrunner Records, Current President of Nuclear Blast America*

"Obviously, I was a Rods fan from the beginning. I had followed the band throughout their early career - with all the records, whether it was on Arista, Shrapnel or Combat. In fact, I actually met Carl in the old days. In the early '80s, the band did an in-store appearance at Zig Zag Records. Then they were going to play at L'Amour that evening. They were having a drawing at the record store where you put your name into a box. If your name was drawn, you would win one of David 'Rock' Feinstein's guitars. So, I actually won his guitar! And they presented it to me at L'Amour that night. The guitar was totally beat up. It was the kind of thing that Rock would have used to smash onstage, because the guitar looked like it was ready to be tossed in the dumpster. It was not like some new guitar; it was basically a piece of crap. But I was absolutely thrilled to have anything that Rock had touched. And I certainly was not a musician. So, whether it was like a brand-new guitar or a piece of crap, it did not matter to me - I was not going to do anything with it but put it in the corner of my bedroom. So, I met Carl that night at the show. There would not have been any serious connection other than that he was meeting a fan. A few years later, I began working at Shatter Records, and that is where I got to meet Carl professionally. I started at Shatter in March of 1987. I ran promotions for college radio. So, I was not involved in doing anything except promotion. I certainly was not talking to the producers, nor did I have anything to do with making a record. The only record that I actually had anything to do with was a new record that came in from a band called E-X-E called Stricken by Might. Carl produced that record. I am sure Carl has lots of stories about struggling to get paid from Shatter. There were at least two or three records that actually got shelved because they (Shatter) ran out of money. They were recorded and everything. But never seen the light of day. So, Shatter did not stick around very long. In December of '87, I went to work for Roadrunner Records. And pretty much worked there for the next 25 years. Early on in my Roadrunner days, I was interested in a band that Carl was co-managing - a band called Apollo Ra. I was interested in signing them to Roadrunner. Because of this, Carl and I spoke on the phone, and we met in person quite a few times. And I do not remember what happened. I just remember that we did not do the deal. Whether we pulled out of it or we could not close the deal, or my boss turned me down, I really do not remember but I know I wanted to sign the band.

"As for the guitar I won? I kept it in my room for a few years, and it disappeared when I moved. I have the date when I saw The Rods in my concert log - August 17$^{th}$, 1984. I had also seen The Rods with Vandenburg and Metallica as openers at The Paramount in 1983. [Note: Impressively, Monte kept a concert journal for his first 10 years of concert attendance in which he lists the dates, opening acts, venue, and rating.] I do not believe I have ever used Carl to make a record. But we have been friends since. Carl is just a great guy. And it is just amazing that he is still going, and that The Rods are making some crushingly heavy modern records - modern production, modern sound. Brotherhood of Metal is probably the heaviest thing they have ever done.

"It is just amazing to me that Carl still has the passion for this. Drumming is incredibly physically involved compared to other musicians, and he still has the power and the ability to just crush it. But here is a story to close - on LP records, they used to put numbers in the run-out groove. [Note, Run-out groove was the dead space between the label and the final grooves. Most record companies would list lot numbers, batch numbers or a plant matrix/number.] *I had the vinyl of In the Raw back then and sometimes people would put messages in the run-out groove. My buddy and I looked at the run-out groove to In the Raw and found a phone number. So, we called it. And who picked up? Peter Morticelli, the manager of The Rods at the time. Of course, we did not know he was their manager at the time. I did not connect the dots until many years later when I met Peter. I do not recall what we said, but we probably yelled 'The Rods rule!' or something similar."

# Rhett Forrester: Gone With the Wind

During the summer of '84, Jack's album was in the process of getting pressed when he received an offer to play at the Breaking Sound Festival, which was scheduled for late August in Paris, France. Keep in mind that there were very few heavy metal themed European festivals at the time. There was the extremely successful Monsters of Rock, but nothing to the amount that we see today, in which a band can tour solely on a festival circuit. With Breaking Sound, Ozzy was headlining the first night, Dio would be headlining the second, and Metallica, Gary Moore, Motley Crue, Accept and a host of others were scheduled to complete the lineup. This was not an event to miss. It was a great opportunity and Jack agreed to play.

Since he did not have a touring band, he asked Gary and me to join him. We were more than happy to do so. But since recording *Out of the Darkness,* some tension was beginning to sprout between Jack and Rhett. Rhett was a great guy, but he had a rapidly progressing drug and alcohol habit that was beginning to make things a bit difficult. Nothing was overly apparent during the recording process; I had heard rumors of drugs, but the less I knew the better. As we got closer to the festival, it was evident that Rhett had some serious problems. Rhett was extremely charismatic - when he walked into a room, he had a commanding presence. He was a true rock star. He had talent, and he had a magnificent aura... but there were times when he went overboard with the rock star thing. It was downright embarrassing at times. The first night in France, while having dinner, he had a bit too much to drink and was verbally abusive towards the waitstaff. He told one waiter to, "Get me another beer you fucking frog!" He could be verbally abusive when he was drinking. He would make the handlers/guides bend over backwards- he had them running in circles with demands. The airline staff even refused to serve Rhett more alcohol on our way over. Now, Jack is a smart guy - he could see the writing on the wall and knew what the future most likely held, should they continue. A few months prior Jack and Rhett were discussing a second album, but at this point - and I am not sure how Jack delivered the news - Rhett was informed that he would not be invited back for a second go. It is a good thing an entire tour was not booked. But there was the issue of the festival. Jack, seeing the possible train wreck, figured it would be good to have a plan B for the festival. Rhett was beginning to become unreliable, and he could not take the chance of Rhett deciding not to perform. So Jack invited Neil Turbin along. Neil had recently left Anthrax and was an extremely wise choice. He had the look, the presence, and the pipes. Knowing that Neil was waiting in the shadows, Rhett was not happy.

Oddly, we were billed as Virgin Steele – which we clearly were not. I assume that was because Virgin Steele had just broken up and had a good following in France. Jack Starr, as a solo artist, was just getting started and did not have a product on the market yet, so from a promotional standpoint I get it - but it was not accurate. Once we arrived in Paris, we met a local couple who had volunteered to host us. Christiane and Dan Terbeche were to be our handlers for the festival. After all these years, I cannot say enough good things about them. Their hospitality was unparalleled. They treated us like family and to this very day I consider them as such. (I went back a few years ago and took Dianne, Dianne's mother and Erin to meet them. It is amazing how one encounter, one moment in time will forge a lifelong friendship.)

We had a few days to enjoy ourselves in Paris and we did the typical sightseeing routine. One day, Jack's guitar tech, Lenny, and I decided to go visit the famed catacombs. I had heard of the catacombs but had no clue what they really were. The catacombs, unbeknownst to me at the time, were these endless caverns of skulls and bones. I knew there were to be some skulls and bones, but I did not know they were this vast. It went on for what seemed like forever - we were down there at least an hour and a half. At that point I was starting to worry where we were, because I had no clue. I felt we might be lost. There was no one else in the catacombs, just us. Suddenly we started seeing these shadowy figures trailing us in the distance. The figures remained far back enough that we could not make out the details, but they followed our every move. If we turned right, they turned right. If we went left, they went left. They were clearly not interested in the catacombs as they had their focus on us. We kept moving a little faster, and they ended up following us faster. This went on for 20 or 30 minutes and we realized that these guys were definitely following us. It had now officially breached scary territory. And so we were really getting concerned. And we walked fast. They walked fast. And then we started sprinting. Then they started sprinting. And then we really picked up the pace. We were really running now - just hauling ass through these catacombs. And now so were they. We were scared shitless. The thought of getting knifed, robbed, and left for dead in a cavern void of the living and full only of the dead was beyond frightening. We were pissing our pants. And finally, we saw an exit. We gave it all we had and booked through the exit and down the street - and once in civilization, we slowed down to catch our breath. And just then, the figures emerged. They had been running after us through the exit. There were two men. They began to get closer. And closer. And now we could see them clearly. Both very rugged and intimidating in appearance. They had a blank stare. These guys were fast, and not out of breath, unlike us. And when only a few feet away, one of the men said, "Excuse me... are you Carl Canedy?" Lenny and I started laughing hysterically. Most likely to cover our surprise and embarrassment. It turned out these guys were huge fans. We had a pleasant chat with them, and I gave them some autographs. Who would've thought?

The festival went off without a hitch. Unfortunately, Neil did not get to perform. I was really hoping to hear him on some of the songs. This is right off the heels of *Fistful of Metal* and Anthrax was really beginning to gain a following. Neil coming out for a few songs would've blown the crowd away. Not that Rhett did not do a great job. Rhett was such a natural and charismatic frontman. He took control of the audience. Problems aside, he was a total professional on stage and was a master of his craft. It was a great show and one of the most memorable live events I had participated in. Perhaps the most interesting facet of the festival was to see the rise that Metallica had accomplished. When I last saw them, they were four young newbies playing small clubs and crowds that were exclusively male. It was clear that they were going to go far, but this was much quicker than anticipated. At the festival, Metallica were clearly the most anticipated and the most discussed. I remember sitting offstage, watching Gary Moore with the guys in Metallica, and female concertgoers were flocking to them. They were quickly becoming the new kings. It was spectacular to witness such a grand transformation. I had never seen anything like it.

**Neil Turbin**; *Ex-Anthrax, Deathriders*
*"I went to France with Carl. I went there with Jack Starr's band. I had to get a passport in one day because the flight was leaving in the following two days. Friday, I was there at the embassy trying to get a damn passport and get it approved with a rush status and a 9080 – this was the week after I left Anthrax. I was supposed to replace Rhett Forrester or be a backup in case he fell through. I did not even know the songs on the album, but they brought me over there. But it was a great experience. I was kept in the shadows, and I had to kind of go my own way. But that did not have anything to do with Carl. That was due to the promoter. I really was not in the band. I was kind of like a third wheel. But Rhett did a fantastic job. I was just there for insurance. Because Jack, I think felt that Rhett was going to maybe bail out. But he looked great. He was great. And he did a great job."*

Rhett was a bit upset that he was not going to do Jack's second album. I recommended to him, "Rhett, why don't you do a solo album?" Rhett lit up immediately. He loved the idea. This was before the festival, when we had just gotten to France. Now, most artists would have put together a long-range plan, spent a few months writing, and then worked on booking some studio time and session players - but not us. I recommended we record in France. It made sense - he had a willing and capable rhythm section ready (Gary and myself). Paul Kayen was enlisted to do the guitars and help write. We spent a few days writing the album. We knocked 100% of the writing out in just a few short days, Rhett, Paul, Gary and myself. And disappointingly, I am not credited with any writing on the album, despite contributing quite a bit. Gary as well. I did get paper on some of the songs, but the entire thing was copyrighted without us, which I thought was a bit sneaky. Plus, I did all of the arrangements. I do not intend to sound egotistical, but that is the truth, and unfortunately, those things happen occasionally in the music business.

Dan and Christiane were able to find us a financier. We found a studio with availability: Max Waldberg Studios. The studio had only a single small room and we used electronic drums, which was a mistake. I should have used real drums. But I wanted a live sound that was like Music America, where there is a traditionally big sound. And as it turned out, it was such a small room that it was good for amps and vocals. But it was not a big win for drums. But that is not to say we could not have gotten a great sound. I opted for using Simmons drums, which were very expensive and took a lot of playing with to get the sound tight. I think, in retrospect, that was the biggest flaw. There is one song we needed a harp for, and we hooked Rhett's harp up to a Marshall stack, and it sounded absolutely amazing. With the vocals, Rhett was prepared and had some really good ideas. They came out great and with no issues. Paul was fantastic as well. Gary knocked his parts out quickly. We were all very efficient and the entire album went through without a hitch. It is a really good album overall and recording in France was a memorable experience. It is amazing how quickly we ran through the entire process of writing, arranging and recording - and we certainly did not cut any corners in the process. The title is a bit hokey, but the songs are great, and it was a fun experience.

Rhett, unfortunately, did not slow down with the partying, and that ultimately contributed to his early demise. Drugs tended to get him into trouble. He told me that once he had gotten stabbed on his way to the airport (apparently buying drugs before his flight, he got into a scuffle with a drug dealer) but was so out of it that he was not even aware that he had been stabbed, and as a result, had a collapsed lung. Halfway through the flight, the flight attendant saw the blood and they had to make an emergency landing!

After the recording sessions of *Gone With The Wind*, the entire project fell apart. I am not sure what happened with the mixes, but the end result was not cool. The mixing was atrocious. The mix did not translate from the studio. The guitars sounded horrid. And then the tapes disappeared. So we essentially had to remaster the album. The tapes were never found. To this day we are not completely sure where the tapes ended up. When I came back to America, I took it to Shatter Records. They released it sometime later. There was never a tour to support the album. The album never made it far into the public eye until a few years ago, when High Roller Records re-released it.

**Fabrice Saure;** *Engineer on Gone With The Wind*
"Rhett had an interesting way of warming up his voice. He would stuff a silk scarf in his mouth and do these vocal exercises, like 'la la la da da da'. I had never seen anything like that. I asked him why he warmed up with a scarf stuffed in his mouth and he told me he grew up in the city and could not warm up loud because he did not want to disturb his neighbors. Rhett did have a loud voice. Very strong. And he was very professional. He was serious, but in a good way. That project is a good memory for me. It was great working with Carl."

## Anthrax: Armed and Dangerous

Jonny Z reached out to me a few months after *Fistful of Metal* was released. Both Danny Lilker and Neil Turbin were now out of Anthrax. Jonny was in a tight spot - he really wanted to get the issue resolved while the momentum with Anthrax was still there. Danny was let go right before the album was released and Neil was let go two weeks into their first major tour. Losing a frontman during the middle of a band's first major tour can quickly decimate a band's rise. Anthrax was at a critical point - their first album was doing really well. Thrash metal was just beginning to germinate. Metallica had just released their second album, *Ride the Lightning*, and they were absolutely killing it. All with no radio airplay. And with no MTV videos. At this point in the '80s, it was nearly impossible to be massive without an MTV video on rotation. The demand was certainly there, and Anthrax had the potential, but they had just lost two key members.

Anthrax had found a prospective singer, and Jonny wanted to release an EP as an introduction to the new vocalist. The proposed singer was a young man by the name of Matt Fallon. Also new to the lineup was Frank Bello on bass. I really liked both Danny and Neil. I was sad to hear that they were no longer in Anthrax. Frank was a great guy. He was green, but clearly, he was very talented. He had the chops. He had the look. He was new to the recording process, but he was a smart guy, and he would be just fine. Matt, however, was a different subject. Jonny had his doubts and he asked that I work with them and give him my thoughts. So we booked time at Pyramid Studios. We spent five days in pre-production. Matt was young and I think he was partying a bit too much. He was a great singer but there was no chemistry with the band. He was just not a good fit for Anthrax. Nothing was clicking, and nothing was gelling with the band. So, at the end of the week, I pulled the rest of the band to one side and said, "I do not think this guy has major label potential." This EP aimed to solidify them with the major leagues. It really needed to happen to kick the door open for them. And I told the boys in the band, "I do not think that guy is going to get you to the next level." They said they would discuss it with Jonny; so we went into the conference room and called Jonny.

I began by telling Jonny that I did not have a good feeling about Matt. Jonny said, "Okay, let me talk to the guys." I left the room, and they spent a couple of minutes chatting with Jonny. It was all very brief. They walked out of the conference room and told me that Jonny wanted to talk to me. I picked up the phone and Jonny said, "Put Matt on a bus now and send him home." I have nothing but respect for Anthrax, because another band would not have made a choice that quickly - they clearly knew what they wanted. This time it was make it or break it. They had just lost their first singer and were not moving forward with their proposed second singer. Time was running out, and they had no back-up plan. I reached out to my good friend Andrew "Duck" MacDonald and asked him if he knew of anyone who might be a good fit. He told me about a singer by the name of Joey Belladonna who was in a band called Bible Black. I was familiar with Bible Black - Duck played guitar for them. Local legends Gary Driscoll and Craig Gruber were also members. With a lineup like that, you know their vocalist had to be world class. However, Bible Black was a traditional hard rock band. Joey had an amazing voice, but it was geared towards Journey type stuff. I was not sure if he would fit in with the guys. Andrew said, "Give Joey a call!" I got a hold of Joey immediately and he agreed to come down.

Now, Joey had never heard of Anthrax. He had never heard of thrash metal. He really did not know what to expect. Once Joey arrived at the studio, Jonny and I sat down with him and went through everything - we told him the concept, direction and gave him a rundown of the scene. This was very fascinating as this was the changing of the guard. This type of music was very new. Joey had never heard stuff like this. We were talking about a lot of different changes and tempo changes. Joey was used to the Steve Perry type stuff. Anthrax was a very different world. Very few vocalists could do both arenas well. So we brought Joey into the vocal booth for a trial. It took Joey only a few seconds to get acclimated. When he let it rip, everyone in the control booth dropped their jaws. He nailed it. It was very clear after the first song that this was it. It worked out well and the rest is history. Literally. The audition was quick. Right after they told Joey he had the gig, we started recording the EP. Which moved extremely quickly. We could all see what was going on. It was an exciting time because the band had turned the corner and we knew that they were going to be massive. And what a great guy Joey is. One of the nicest guys out there.

**Andrew "Duck" MacDonald;** *Bible Black, Thrasher, Ex-Blue Cheer*
*"Carl and I, we had not met formally. But we had met in passing a few times - we knew about each other from playing locally. We did not really have a relationship until 1984. We were both playing the clubs in upstate New York during the '70s. Just honing our skills. There was Joey DeMaio, me, and Carl, and we were all just working on our shit in the 1970s. So that is where we come from. Now Joe (Joey DeMaio) and I were good friends. And I remember when he asked Carl to do their (Manowar) demo. It was really early - which I think was 1980 or 1981. And I remember how good*

that demo was with Carl and Joe as a rhythm section. It was fantastic. And I told Joe, I said: 'This drummer (who I did not know really well) and you as a bass player, are amazing together.' I had a good ear for rhythm sections, and those two guys played so well together. I told Joe: 'You and him are perfect for each other. It is like a musical match made in heaven.'

"While it worked musically, it was not a personality match. They were both very ambitious guys, and Joe wanted to control his own thing. Carl did not want to be in someone else's band. Which I understand. Joe was ambitious and extremely talented. I worked with him for many years. I did all of his early demos. All of the vocals and all of the guitars. Right up until Manowar in the late 70s. A few years later, I was in Bible Black, and that was when I got to know Carl really well. Bible Black was my band with the rhythm section from Elf and, of course, Rainbow. After a couple of singers, we found a young singer from Syracuse named Joey Belladonna. He was really young. I think we were all a few years older, which at the time seemed like a lot. Carl talked to me about Anthrax because we were planning the Thrasher album at the time. And I thought of Joey because he was a good singer, but he was young. I thought he would be a good fit for Anthrax. I told Carl: 'I got this young guy singing for us now. I think he might work. He is a good singer.' So, Carl had him come to the studio and the rest is history. Was I bummed to lose Joey to Anthrax? No. I was happy for him. I knew he would be a great fit with those guys. Plus, you must understand where we were at the time. Bible Black, which I thought was the catalyst that was going to get me into the big time, as they say, folded.

"We were having financial issues and one of the guys was having marital issues. Craig Gruber left to tour with Gary Moore. In 1983, I was going to be 30 years old. And I was ready to make changes. I had an epiphany and had to meditate on rather. I really wanted to keep playing music for a living. Once you start getting older, you begin to consider if you still want to do this. I had been going at it for 15 years and nothing was really taking off. Carl really saved me at that point. He had this idea for a project called 'Thrasher' and he kept calling me. He insisted that I work with him on this project. He told me he would not consider anyone else. And of course, I kept saying, 'No, I'm not really able to right now.' I was not in a good space. And he would not take no for an answer. This went on for a couple of months. He hammered me so much that I agreed to it... reluctantly. So, we put a demo together with guitars and electronic drums. He sent it to a record company, and we ended up with a deal. And so, I was in. That was the Thrasher project. Carl took me off the edge of not wanting to play music anymore. I will always appreciate what he did for me. So that is the decision I had to make. And Carl helped me make that decision. Without Carl, I would not have done that album. I might very well have *retired from the music business at that point. But yes, it really did inspire me."*

**Joey Belladonna;** *Anthrax*
*"My father got the call. It was probably from Carl, but I cannot recall. I think Andrew Duck Macdonald told Carl about me, or he (Carl) had asked about me. And the message was 'So this band Anthrax wants you to audition.' Carl had started the conversation. They (Anthrax) were looking for somebody and he was the connection. I was in Bible Black at the time. It really was not going that far. We were kind of up in the air with everything. We just came in kind of late. So, I was open to exploring other things. I had gone off and did something else. I was doing a cover band thing - just to keep myself busy. And that is when I got the call. I had never heard of Anthrax – I really was not listening to a lot of metal. Maybe things like Priest and Scorpions, but mostly hard rock. So, I did not know what to expect. I almost feel like I did not even really try out. I mean, obviously, they had to hear me. I got there, and we started hammering away. They were like, 'Here are some songs. Here are the lyrics. Let's go.' I kind of threw out some classic rock stuff, like Journey or something. And they just were not expecting it. There were four or five people and management with the guys - and I did not know anybody. I think they asked me quite early - maybe that night. But as far as Carl, we were very much into digging into this stuff and really making the coolest record we could. Carl was so, so cool. He was on the same page as me, whether it was the harmonies and building a good chorus, or the effects and everything that really goes into play with a song. The cool thing about the early Anthrax stuff was that it was a little bit more straight up. So, it was still in my range, and I was able to absorb it in a way that I could grasp. I love Carl for that, because he was so patient, and that is the coolest thing. We had a lot of good times together. I remember going to his house. We went there quite a bit to eat and drink. One memory that I always laugh about, and I am not sure if he remembers, but I ended up offering to mow his lawn. With a push mower. I laugh when I think about that. We really have a good rapport, and he understands where I am coming from. We had some great times with Carl."*

# TT Quick

Once again, Jonny Z told me about this great band that he had signed. That band was TT Quick. I did not get any material from them before pre-production. I really did not know what I was getting into, but if Jonny said they were good, it was a sure thing. As with most of the early Megaforce albums, there was very little budget for this. This was in Megaforce's early days and money was in short supply. Rumor has it that Jonny told them that they could do a first album as long as it was "thrown together quick." Hence the name of the band, T.T. being short for "thrown together." Which it most certainly was. We did not have an option. They had five songs ready. We had to rehearse, record and mix - in less than four days. By this time, Jonny had helped both Metallica and Anthrax secure major label deals. Having one low-budget album on the market made it an affordable way to shop a band. Because once that first album gets out there, with time comes sales data. Not to mention, you have a finished product. It makes it easier for the record labels to understand what they were getting and what their return on investment could be. Keep in mind that this was in the early days of metal. Many record labels were still hesitant about signing a metal act. They did not understand metal. Major record labels depended upon radio hits (and later MTV). Like The Rods, most metal bands were not geared towards mainstream radio. But Iron Maiden and Metallica became proof that you can still get big sales without radio hits and without videos. Once record labels started seeing the success that Metallica was having, they slowly began jumping on the bandwagon.

I met TT Quick at Pyramid Sound. When we started pre-production, I was immediately blown away by the voice of lead vocalist Mark Tornillo. I was a bit taken aback. God, what a voice! Mark should have been a huge star in the 1980s, and I am really surprised TT Quick did not hit it big. Mark is currently vocalist for Accept, replacing the mighty Udo Dirkshneider. I am really happy for him. He is a great guy, and I am proud to call him a friend. TT Quick wrote some great songs. They were amazing musicians - all of them are pros. Guitarist Dave DiPietro was incredible. Glen Evans was a monster drummer. (Glen later went on to drum for Nuclear Assault.) Walt Fortune was on bass and he was an absolute badass. I have no bad memories, no gossip, and no crazy stories from this experience. Just pure pleasantry. It went beyond well. And I know that does not make for an exciting chapter, but it is the truth. These guys came extremely prepared.

They were, by far, one of the easiest bands to work with. I wish I could have done a full album with them. But a year later, Johnny had a major label lined up for them, so he was able to hire a big-money producer. I totally understood that, because back then, you were looking at it from the viewpoint that if a producer had a big name, the labels were more inclined to pump in additional recording and promo funds. Eddie Kramer produced some of their major label stuff. I am not sure why they did not break through in the '80s. They certainly should have. The end result of this session was their self-titled EP. It features a killer version of the Creedence Clearwater Revival classic "Fortunate Son". They were an absolute class act. I was ecstatic I got to work with Mark on a future project, which we will cover later in the book.

**Glenn Evans;** *TT Quick, Nuclear Assault*
*"Early on, I was very familiar with The Rods. They played Lamour's in Brooklyn and that was the first time that I saw them. I can still recall the cut-off Jack Daniel's t-shirt that Gary was wearing on stage, so I bought one and began wearing it on stage too with TT Quick. It was Jonny Z's idea to have Carl produce the first TT Quick record. The recording session for the TT Quick album was smooth. It was done in Ithaca, NY at Pyramid Sound. I brought my Rogers drum kit to track the drums, but Carl replaced them with a studio kit. The Rogers kit didn't have bottom drumheads on the tom toms, and the studio kit did, which made for a better drum sound. We were limited on recording time. I think we had a total of five days to record. Monday through Friday. It was during the middle of winter, and I can still recall Dave DiPietro recording his lead guitar tracks on the song 'Victims' with a leather jacket on as we were loading out in a snowstorm and the doors were wide open. We stayed at The Rock & Roll Hotel during the recording sessions. I recall I didn't sleep one bit because I was both excited and nervous about my first professional recording session. Exciter was also staying there while recording and they were just finishing up.*

*"I watched everything Carl did as a producer, from the way he tuned the drums to getting the different drum and guitar sounds. Carl was the first producer I've ever worked with, and he was quick on making decisions and his overall technique was very professional. With a limited budget for recording and studio time being very expensive, that was critical. Carl also suggested that I push the drum beat rather than lay back on it. That came in very handy when I joined Nuclear Assault and recorded the next handful of thrash albums with them. I have Carl to thank for giving me a launching pad for my drumming style."*

**Dave DiPietro**; *Ex-C.I.A., Ex-Nuclear Assault, T.T. Quick*

"I saw The Rods as a teenager in Wolcott, CT. They had a huge impact on my career. I was being dragged down the commercial pop road. I saw them and stood my ground and wrote heavy rock. That was around three years prior to the first TT Quick EP, which Carl produced. The whole album was completed in roughly four days. On the last day, as the band was packing up and the studio was beginning to prep for the next act, Carl turns to me and says, 'OK, let's bang out all of your guitar solos.' I had only hours to get every one of them done. It turned out to be a great thing though. I had to shoot from the hip and just go with gut instinct. Carl was masterful at getting the most out of me back then. It also became the way I did every record to follow - solos dead last. It was scary, but very beneficial. For the second album, using multiple producers was a Jonny Z idea. He wanted Michael Wagner for some songs and Eddie Kramer for others. He was looking to see which producer would get the most out of us. I think at the end of the session Johnny liked elements of what both producers did and loved Rob Hunter for arrangements and pre-production ideas.

"I love Carl. He was a super talent wrapped in a very caring individual. I would love to work with Carl again. I love him as a drummer and producer. The Rods were so cool and raw. They inspired me / us to go three piece and just keep the music real and street level. I am forever grateful that Carl was put in our path at that time. I really hope to work with him again."

## Overkill: Feel the Fire

I get asked about this one quite frequently. It started in the usual manner, by Jonny telling me, "Carl, I signed this great band named Overkill." I recall the Overkill guys showing up in the studio: DD Verni, Bobby "Blitz" Ellsworth, Rat Skates and Bobby Gustafson. They had that tough New York / New Jersey demeanor. They were very street smart, and they were no-nonsense fellas, despite a healthy appetite for partying. They had no issues with throwing fists during band disputes. Gustafson seemed to have quite a bit of friction with the others. While he was an accomplished guitarist, there was some tension, and he did not seem to gel with the rest of the band. It finally got to the point that I had to corral them and tell them that I did not really care what problems they had, as they had a limited budget and limited time, and they needed to get this thing done. And that is exactly what they did. They came through.

Of course, it was no surprise that they were immensely talented, even early on. I know I have said this about every band thus far, but it is true. Jonny had great picks. He did not get behind duds. I am sure, by this point in time, he was receiving a lot of demo tapes from bands seeking a record deal. Jonny was giving me the cream of the crop. Years later, major labels would snatch up the quality metal bands, but in the early and mid-80s, a new metal band did not have many options regarding suitable record companies. This is why Combat, Metal Blade and Megaforce were so crucial. The early bands on these labels were spectacular. Those record companies were a starting point for so many great bands. Major labels were not going to give an unknown band the time of day. Overkill was a perfect example. They were young men at the time. But it was evident that they had put their time in. They had definitely paid their dues. They were great guys. It should come as no surprise that DD, even then, was such a solid bass player. He knocked his parts out quite quickly. DD was unbelievably solid and had this really great tone. Blitz was a rock star. He would tell these great stories and have us all in stitches. He was very funny, yet he was also very professional. Rat Skates was a real sweetheart. He partied a bit much the first night and his legs were burnt out, so he was shot the first day of recording the drums. I gave him the lecture and sent him home to rest. He came back the next day and knocked it out of the park. I recall Bobby Gustafson was the outsider, and the tension was thick. He was easy to work with from a recording aspect, but his interaction with the other guys was distant and cold. It could have just been a bad time. He could have been unhappy with the process and did not want to say anything.

It should come as no surprise that their material was really strong. I did not really need to offer much in the way of production arrangements. Thank God, because we did not have much time to complete this. The entire thing was recorded and mixed in less than two weeks. Jonny and Marsha were flying by the seat of their pants. Megaforce was really starting to take off, and clearly, they could not devote the amount of time to Overkill that they had to Metallica and Anthrax, but it was overtly clear that Overkill was going to be huge. During the recording process, there was a lot of discussion about what to do for the album cover. Given the title of the album, *Feel the Fire*, they came up with an idea of getting photographed in front of a large fire. Kind of similar to the iconic Lynyrd Skynyrd album *Street Survivors*. But with more ferocity. Alex jumped on it. He had a photographer friend who lived out in the country by the name of Mark Callisto. The band went to the photographer's place a couple of days later. Mark had built this massive bonfire. For the album, you can see their silhouettes in front of this massive fire. That fire was real. There was no form of digital enhancement – which is all too common nowadays. They waited until dusk to get that much-needed darkness. If done today, that would have been an overlay. But this really was a raging fire, and it came out perfect. It really is a killer album cover – it perfectly conveys the tone for the entire album.

**Alex Kayne;** *Legendary DJ:*
*"I met Carl for the first time at a show with The Rods and Vandenburg - and Metallica were opening. I went to the show, and it was great! I met Carl the next night when I was DJing at Lamour's. Vandenburg had a date somewhere else that night, so it was just The Rods and Metallica. They played on April 9$^{th}$, 1983. And then I met them backstage. That's all that matters. I'm a drummer man and when I saw those chrome fives on the stage - I had never heard a drum kit sound like that. Fibes was a very different sounding drum than any other drum. And Carl was also using double skins back then - there were a lot of guys using only single skins. I noticed the smallest tom tom on the left side of his kit was bigger than my largest tom tom on the right side of my kit. The Rods were an amazing band - a three piece and they sounded like 100 guys. Marshall stacks up to the ceiling of the club and Dave and Gary were so tight. Very powerful performance. There was no clear sense of individuality there. At least not on the stage. They came on as a band - as a unit. What a night it was. They did a lot of stuff from Wild Dogs. It was one of my favorite albums. It was just a great set. And Metallica opened the show. I had a feeling that they were going to be around for a while, but I had no idea they were going to be this massive.*

*A lot of people did not have an idea of just how big they'd become. I went backstage and got to talk to Carl. It was such a good time. We talked about drums, and it escalated from there. We talked for two hours, without even realizing the time. I never really got to see him all that much again. Except for at shows here and there. Carl has this body of work that is pretty unbelievable. The list of achievements is vast. Also, what impressed me about Carl and his playing is that he is a big dude. You see a lot of big dudes playing drums. A lot of them - 80% or so of them, just pound away. They beat the crap out of the drum set. They often do not have any dynamic - just completely void of it. But not Carl. He understands dynamics. He understands timing. He understands a lot more than most drummers do. And Carl is such a nice guy. He is very humble."*

# Life in the Mid-80s

I was 16 or 17 when I went into the studio for the first time (with my high school band, Wadsworth Anthium). The studio was housed at Elmira College. Our guitar player's girlfriend was a student at Elmira College and was able to get us some free studio time. One of the first songs we recorded was "I'm Tired" by Savoy Brown. Kim Simmons was the guitarist in Savoy Brown. Years later, I was introduced to Kim by Arnie Goodman. Meeting Kim was a huge thrill for me. And because I had some rental units, Kim Simmons ended up staying with me for about three months. Kim was such a great guy, and sadly, he's no longer with us. I was a big Savoy Brown fan, so when Kim asked me to mix a live album for them, I was more than happy to do so. They had recorded material for a live album, which was to be *Live in Central Park*. They had the tapes – they only needed to mix it. I suggested that we go to a studio in Syracuse to mix the album. And that's what we did. *Live In Central Park* turned out great. You can really sense their greatness. And they had genuine chemistry. It was a fun project and something that I am proud of. I was proud to have become friends with Kim, and I was proud to be part of that album.

Meanwhile, The Rods had been put on hold. Not intentionally, mind you, but life got frantic, and we each had our own thing going on. David was busy with his restaurant. I was busy producing. We still saw each other regularly and I ate at The Hollywood every other day. But we had no dedicated management, outside of what little I was doing. It became extremely difficult for David and me to sync schedules. Plus, we had no booking agency. And that is why from 1985 on up, we played very few shows. I am not sure how we could have - it was a busy time for each of us. One year evolved into two years and before you know it, the '80s were almost over. But we always managed to write on our own, which came in handy later.

There was another hiatus in my life: my longtime girlfriend, Dianne, and I had split up. By the early '80s, we were both seeing other people and we were both doing our own thing. Which was not easy as we had been together for quite a few years by that point. She had tolerated all of the tours, the road time and the poverty that comes with a rising band. We survived all of that but agreed that it be for the better if we put things on hold. That period was not a good time for me personally, even though professionally it was booming. Once we split, I had nowhere to live. I really wanted to be close to Pyramid Sound, which was located in Ithaca. David recommended I try Cortland, which was only a few miles from Ithaca, and housing options were slightly more reasonable. Being close to David would be another benefit. I eventually found a property in Cortland with three rental units and a small house in the rear. The house was priced right, so I went with it, and as a result I became a landlord. I rented all three units. There were always landlord duties to attend to: repairs, maintenance, and day to day upkeep. That property kept me busy on any off time that I was fortunate enough to have. While it was eating up my free time, the properties were paying for my mortgage, so it was quite necessary. I made money on that property. It also meant I was able to house any visiting musicians, so it was to come in handy during some of the projects later in the decade.

One of the renters, an older lady named Agnes who used to own the property, used to call me Johnny Cash. One day, I had done some laundry and put all my shirts on the clothesline to dry. Every single one of them was black - so she named me after the original man in black, Johnny Cash. Sometimes Agnes would take pity on me and do the stack of dishes that I always seemed to have piled up. She must not have slept much, because often I would come home at two or three in the morning and she would stick her head out of the window and say, "Hey Johnny Cash, do you want to play euchre?" So, we would play euchre until the sun came up. Even though it was more on my plate, having rental properties was a good introduction, and eventually led me to jump full time into real estate.

If you cannot tell by now, this was a very hectic time period. Looking back, I should have hired an assistant. And that would have made everything much better. Not having an assistant really hurt me later in the decade. I was trying to do too much at once. It was tough because I would be in the studio, and I would get calls for upcoming or potential projects. It is difficult not to take those calls - but nobody in the studio wants to see you on the phone. That was not fair to the others in the studio, but I thought I could handle it. I really should have hired someone to help. That was one of my big regrets. The other big regret is that I did not get a manager. I did not have anyone in my corner. I did not have somebody pushing to escalate things, to get bigger and better projects. I missed out on a lot of projects. Jonny Zazula asked to manage me initially. I should have gone with it, but I did not. Jonny and I were tight, and I did not want to create a possible rift in our friendship. I knew his world was chaotic. I thought it may be best not to be involved in it. But that was a mistake, because he was one of the few people who would have been looking out for my best interests. If I only knew then what I know now. It was not all craziness. It was a very productive time. All of these metal artists started coming to Pyramid as a result of me bringing the first few bands there. Pyramid was soon to be a mecca for thrash metal. The Rock & Roll Hotel was also flourishing. Almost every metal band that came to town to record, to do pre-production, to write, or take some R&R before touring, wound up staying there. I was happy to see the local scene doing well. This little pocket of the northeast certainly seemed to be thriving. It was an interesting time.

For those who may not be familiar, "The Metal Rap" by The Lone Rager was a single released by Megaforce records in the early '80s. It was one of the first heavy metal rap songs. Keep in mind that in 1984, rap had yet to reach mainstream. Rap was rarely played on MTV at that time. It was not on the radio and few metalheads had any idea of awareness of it. The Lone Rager was an idea by none other than Jonny Zazula. I was in Rochester at Music America Studios at the time. The Rods had just finished recording *In the Raw*. Jonny wanted me to help him with a project, as we were nearing completion on the album and had all of our equipment set up. Jonny said, "I have an idea for a metal rap! It has never been done before!" Of course, we agreed to it. It was completely novel, and no one was quite sure how it would turn out. Gary, David and I started jamming, and eventually, we laid down a very basic track. It was a very simple arrangement. Now, the identity of The Lone Rager, who was later pictured on the cover donning a white hood, a western buckskin jacket and studded leather bracelets and gloves, was intended to remain a mystery. The Lone Rager was in fact Jonny Z. He did the entire rap. We recorded his rap separately. For the chorus, Jonny's wife, Marsha, brought in a children's choir. She directed them and was absolutely fantastic with those kids. We then brought in Andrew Duck MacDonald and had him lay down a solo, as David had to leave. Basically, we recorded the song as an instrumental and then laid Jonny's rap over it. So that is how The Lone Rager came to be. A few years ago, I helped Johnny get it online. It had been out of print for over 30 years by that point. We added it to all of the platforms, and I am glad it is finally seeing the light of day. It is a bit hokey, but it is a fun addition to the Megaforce catalog.

## Blue Cheer: The Beast is Back

In the 1960s, I was into top 40 music like all of the other kids. This was when I first started playing drums. I was only buying 45s at the time. More often than not, the only artists you could see on TV were top 40 artists. Ed Sullivan and Dick Clark hosted many of the top 40 bands. I would watch those shows primarily to see other drummers. After all, that was the only outlet at the time. It was all very fleeting and quite difficult to see. The camera was mostly focused on the frontman and guitar player, and they had very direct camera shots that did not give you a linear view, unlike today. On the rare occasions they would show the drummer, if you were lucky, you could get a rough overview of their setup. Or you could discern their style. There was no VCR at the time, so you had to be focused and alert. You had one chance to catch it. Blink and you would miss it. For a young, hungry drummer, this stuff was important. On one notable occasion, I was watching Dick Clark and Blue Cheer came on. I was not familiar with them before that point. They absolutely blew me away. When they played, the little speaker in my black and white TV set began rattling. They were heavier than anyone else at the time. They were playing their hit song, "Summertime Blues". I had never seen anything like it. It was life changing and it made a big impression on me. I had never seen anyone drum like that. That very day, I decided to tailor my drum style. Those few minutes impacted my life and my style.

In 1985, Jonny reached out to me and asked me to co-produce the latest Blue Cheer album with Paul Curcio. I jumped at the opportunity. This was a dream come true. Blue Cheer hadn't released an album since 1971. To be able to produce their comeback album was a true honor. Paul had produced *Kill 'Em All* only a few years earlier, so he was gaining some notoriety. He was not there when we started pre-production. I immediately began working with Blue Cheer on the material. Their new material was great, but there were a few things we needed to tighten up. Paul Whaley, their drummer, would get really tired and he would easily get discouraged. Once he put his head down, it took a lot to get him back up. I had to convince him, "Paul, you are an originator! A lot of drummers out there look up to you! You need to go with that!" He was very insecure, and he lacked self-confidence. He really was a great drummer, and he was somebody that I respected. We had one song that was really giving us difficulty. It was "Ride with Me". They were having trouble getting it down. We spent a lot of time on that one song. Paul Curcio came into the control room, and unbeknownst to him, Chris Bubacz had the talkback mic on. Paul told me to "just let it go." He said, "That's good enough, they cannot play it any better. Do not waste any more time on it." Well, the guys in Blue Cheer heard every word. They heard Paul badmouthing them and boy, were they pissed! They ended up locking Paul out of the control room. At that point, Paul was not allowed back into the studio. He was not there much to begin with. Even though he got co-production credit on it, he did not do anything in terms of arrangements or any of the actual recording.

Dickie, the vocalist and bass player, was not one to mess with. He was an easygoing guy, but man was he a badass. He came up in a rough part of San Francisco. He was a biker type guy. I absolutely loved him. One night, we were scheduled to record vocals at 7pm. Dickey showed up with a bottle of gin. There were approximately two inches of gin left in the bottle. Dickie was talking like he had a mouthful of marbles. He could not pronounce a single word. We could not understand anything he was saying. At first, I was a little upset. And then I just started laughing. I laughed because he was adamant that we record his vocals. I had to laugh because it was absolutely comical, as he could not even talk, let alone sing. So I said, "Dickie, please... let's do it tomorrow." After some begging, he agreed to postpone the vocals to the following day. Other than that, they were real easy guys to work with. I'm glad I got to work with my heroes. That was a big honor. Jonny had rented a house for us. We stayed there with my friend Victoria. She took care of the band. She made food for everybody and made sure we all had really healthy meals. She was a great cook. Overall, it was a great experience. I am proud of that album. It was a blast, and it got some really great reviews. But sadly, at that period, Blue Cheer never got the love that they did in the '60s and '70s. By the mid-80s, they were seen as a classic rock act. They were pioneers, they were true innovators, and during my youth, they were the closest thing to heavy metal that we had.

**Maria Ferrara**: *Megaforce Records / CraZed Management, 1982-1996*
*"How did I start with Megaforce? I was just a girl from Old Bridge, New Jersey. I was friends with this guy named Gary Johnson, who lived next door to John and Marsha. I would go to his house, and we would hang out in his bedroom listening to Black Sabbath and Judas Priest. I think we had just started listening to Iron Maiden. And, of course, Van Halen. We were massive Van Halen fans. So, I would just hang out in his bedroom listening to music. And one day he said, "Did you know my neighbor next door sells heavy metal records?" Of course, I walked next door, knocked on the door, and Jonny Zazula opens the door. Jonny goes out front and opens his garage. He had all of these records sitting in his garage. God, I*

*might have been 15 at the time, and Johnny was probably like, 27 or 28. I bought a Motorhead record on clear vinyl from him. I still have it to this day! That is how it began. I became friends with Jonny and Marsha after that. Of course, that led to me working at Megaforce. But early on when they were operating out of a flea market, it really was not work - it was considered more along the lines of hanging out with my friends who had a record store. And sometimes I would babysit for them. I also worked at Roy Rogers. They would come in and I would give them food. We were friends and we really had that camaraderie. As a friend, I was supportive of them, and I was an extra hand. It developed and grew from there. As the business grew, so did my duties. At first, they did not know what they were doing – that is when they started the label. Nobody did. They were so young. And they were not from that industry. It was new to all of us. We all kind of learned and grew into what became Megaforce records. We became a company, and then I became a publicist, and then I became someone who signed bands. But it all started out with being friends and supporting each other. I was still in high school at the time. It was crazy!*

*"I met Carl for the first time at Lamour's. The Rods played there. It was my very first concert. I believe it was 1982. And then I got to know Carl more through Jonny. Carl is one of the nicest people in the music business. And that's fucking rare. I so appreciate that about him. Just a very, very nice guy and he is very generous with his time and with his heart. And what a talent! He is an amazing drummer and incredibly talented person. Everyone loves Carl. He is just one of the best humans. Heavy metal would not be what it is if he did not lay the groundwork. And let's not forget Jonny Z. What do I have to say about him? He was my best friend. Thank God for Jon and Marsha. None of this would have happened without Jon and Marsha. Absolutely none of this shit. You would not exist. You do not even know who you would be. If there was not a Jonny and Marsha Zazula who put heavy fucking metal on the map, who stabbed us in the heart, and infected us for the rest of our lives with such an incredible love for music, you would not be who you are now. You better quote me on that. I had no idea who I would be when I was young. I posted a picture the other day on my Instagram. It was when I was like 13 years old - I was super, super fat. Really, really fat. Awkward. I was a 13-year-old girl who's dressed like shit. I had no fucking style. And I looked at that picture. I'm like, that does not even look like me. Who the fuck is that? And then I realized that it was before I met John and Marsha. I had no identity. No identity. Before I met John and Marsha, I had not discovered this deep fucking passion for heavy metal. And we all owe it to them. In 1997, I was on my honeymoon in Bora Bora, riding bicycles around the island with my husband. On the ground, nothing is built higher than a fucking palm tree. Right? It is a small island*

*in the Pacific Ocean. It is very remote. And we were riding our bikes, and on the asphalt, there was graffiti that said 'Metallica'. I'm like, Wow! It really has taken over the world... and it is fucking great! We all marched to make it happen. Johnny did not do it alone. Johnny and Marsha did not do it alone. Johnny and Marsha did not do it alone with me and with Eddie Trunk and the rest of the staff at Megaforce. It was everybody. All of us. We all made it happen and it is awesome."*

## Anthrax: Spreading the Disease

While *Armed and Dangerous* was simply meant to be an introduction to the record-buying public and industry, showcasing the new lineup (and most importantly the new vocalist), Jonny had high hopes for the next Anthrax album to be explosive. Jonny said there would be a lot riding on this album. Metallica was getting insanely popular with each consecutive album, and he was expecting Anthrax to follow suit. It is clear they were quite capable, but with two new members, including a new frontman, they had to convince the old fans and win a legion of new and developing metal fans. *Armed and Dangerous* had just finished recording when Jonny Z booked studio time for what was to become *Spreading the Disease*. We took a bit more time with this one. Though we still did not have a large budget. By this time, we had a great working relationship. The boys had plenty of studio experience, and the process went very smoothly. I recall there was a great synergy, and it made the entire process flow really well. Joey Belladonna was and is an absolute talent. For a newcomer, he really nailed it. Everyone came in and killed it. They were a very serious and dedicated bunch, and by this point, they were stellar musicians, in and out of the studio. I am sure some of you are expecting some inside gossip or tales of craziness/excess during the sessions, but the guys really were professional. And as a result, the entire project was drama free. They were well rehearsed, had written some strong material, and they were extremely focused. The only area of concern was during the mixing of the album, when I began to see some changes in some members. There were some developing egos from newfound fame, which is quite common in this industry - and understandable. Overall, I was proud to be part of this project and am proud to see the guys have become so successful. Interesting note - this was when Scott started saying "NOT". It caught on in the studio and it was funny at the time, but I never would've imagined it becoming what it is today. It was interesting to watch it catch fire.

**Dan Spitz:** *Anthrax, Red Lamb, Master Watchmaker*
*"I'm the only one back then that could drive a clutch, so I was always the one driving the rental trucks. Jonny put Scott (Ian) and me in a box van with our gear and sent us upstate New York to a studio. Now Scott and I are New Yorkers, but we have never been that far upstate. You know, where you have to shovel the snow off the roof of your fucking house? The first*

studio, we walked up these rickety stairs that took us into this so-called studio. The head guy had this little eight track mixing board - and he claims he did all the local bands in that area. Scott and I look at each other and we were like, 'We are not recording in this shithole.' Though this was interesting - he played us a demo from a local band called Bible Black. And of course, we later got Joey - who had come from Bible Black. We quickly left the studio and went to the first phone booth we could find. Remember there were no cell phones and there was no internet back then. So we actually went to a phone booth that had a phonebook hanging in it. And we started looking for a studio in the Yellow Pages. We found this place called Pyramid Studios. It was a big fancy ad. So we called the guy, and he told us to come on in. Pyramid had an amazing mixing board. His (Alex Perialis) father was running his real estate agency out of the studio. We wanted to record there! So, we call Jonny Z and tell him, 'So, I do not know where you will find the fucking money, but we are not leaving. We need to record here.' From there we met Carl.

"In the '80s, when we were sitting in the studio, we knew what we were listening to, we knew what we had, but the world had not heard it yet. We were years ahead of anything else that might have come out at that time. We knew what we had behind the scenes. We just needed help - how do we reach people with this new ship? Who is going to put up money to put us in a van and get us on the road? Because the regular record companies are not going to understand this fast music. We were just fans of music, and we were making music. So, we knew what our friends would like. We knew those people were out there. But getting a major label deal? It is not Bon Jovi style music. We were doing something completely different – and new. They'll (major record labels) see no way to make big money off it, so it is not worth their investment. But sitting in the studio, we knew what we fucking had. We knew this was precision music, just like my watchmaking.

"It was beyond normal playing. You had to get shit right the first time. We always blew away producers when we did that because they expected us to be like fucking cripples. The objective was to take over the world. When you're young, and with that mindset, the word 'no' did not exist. That was the way Scott and I were bought up. If we were going to do something, we were going to fucking do it better than anyone else on planet Earth. And that's the goal. And then Joey was added into that mix. We had something that did not sound like anybody else. So, it was not repeatable. You know, we created a movement, and we changed music, forevermore.

"Now, we all knew of The Rods. We needed someone besides the engineer who knew how to run all that crazy shit. Because anyone reading this needs to understand there was no laptop recording studios - anything of the sort did not even exist. None of that shit existed. You needed big money to go into a studio and go in with someone who went to school to be trained to run those big mixing boards and those tape machines and all the outboard gear. And we needed someone who is somewhat metal to be sitting there translating this to the engineer. Because no one knew what the fuck to do with our music. How do you get the sounds you wanted? We were creating new sounds. We were inventing. What you're playing through your amp - you're feeling that in your chest. That was power. And we wanted to make that happen in the recording studio. We had sounds and tones and frequencies in our head that hadn't been invented yet. We were all inventors – back then you could not buy that shit in the music store. We had to find a way to get it through the speakers and then another way to get that sound on tape. And you cannot because it was new and no one at that time knew how to translate that in studio. Like there was some recording studio law that forbade it. Scott and I were both good at breaking laws. We were like 'fuck the laws', like figure out a fucking way. Metallica had the same problem. That's why if you listen to our first album, and you listen to their first album, they almost sound weak in the low end, as opposed to the current stuff. Back then no one could understand what we were trying to do. That's why there were fights in the studio with every producer and every engineer because they would sit there trying to figure out how to make the bass and the guitars work.

"We had the same fights with Eddie Kramer years and years later. And he invented fucking everything with Jimmy Page. Because we listened to the album, and we were like, 'No that's not my guitar. My guitar has way more low-end than this.' It was always the same response, 'You cannot have that low-end guitar and the bass.' We were like, 'fuck the bass!' It was always, 'Can you turn the bass down in your guitar?' Our answer was 'No mother fucker, that's the sound of my guitar.' That was what we wanted. This sound was new. It was in our heads and then we had to mess with the guitars and amps to get that sound. Then we had to do the same in the studio to get this 'new' sound. I'm doing the same thing in watchmaking. I mean, I am inventing new mechanisms, new ways to tell time, and helping everyone else around the world to see America and Americans as badass watchmakers. We saw the British making music back then, and we were like, well, fucking Americans can make kickass music. Let's show the world what America can do. Apply that to whatever you do in your life, and you'll never really work a day in your life.

"Now, Carl was there in the beginning. He helped us find Joey, right after we went through that little turmoil with singers. Carl helped to catapult the name Anthrax into what it is today, because without him, we would never have found Joey Belladonna. Joey filled the connection of who we were, who we are, and how we can mold the singer to fit our music.

*What Scott and I had in our bloodstreams - and the riffs we were inventing and all that stuff. There was no one out there. It is not like we could say, 'Band seeking a thrash metal singer.' Because thrash metal had not even been invented yet. Scott and I, after Neil, were determined to find someone we could teach. And Joey was perfect. The first day he came in - Carl was there. And Jonny was there and sitting in front of the mixing board. He was in one of those chairs with the big springs – you know the office chairs, that if you lean too far back it feels like it is going to tip over? So, Joey comes in and goes right into the control room. It was like you see in the movies. Like 'Let's see what you got kid.' And Joey went in there. Now, Joey is a Journey freak. Like he could jump on stage and sing better than the singer Journey has now. That is all he knows is Journey. He starts to sing and he was like, 'Ohhhhhhhh Sherrryyy' and Jonny Z is rocking back and forth in the chair - he absolutely loved it! I think he even hit the floor. He had dollar signs rolling in his fucking head! We were like, 'Shit, he is too good!' So, Carl really helped us catapult history and change the planets. Joey's singing is on planet fucking Mars. Carl is the man. You know, I will reiterate before we close up here... that without Carl, Fistful of Metal would be a different album, and it is just perfect the way it is. People should know the struggles we had - all of us, even Carl, who had struggles behind the board. Hearing this new and foreign thing and trying to figure out what the hell we were doing. It was not easy."*

# Thrasher

At 16, I discovered the Al Kooper album *Super Session*. It was a double album, which was really cool. Mike Bloomfield was tapped to do the whole album, but somehow, he flaked out after the first day. Since the studio had been booked for two days, Kooper enlisted the help of Stephen Stills to complete the album. That album was part Bloomfield and part Stills, which gave it a very different feel. I did not think it was a particularly great album, but I loved the concept of bringing in different players, and consequently having different styles. This album in particular really stuck with me. By the mid-80s, I was producing a lot of bands, and a lot of the musicians were still in the area. There was a lot of talent in upstate New York during that era. I figured it would be cool to do my own *Super Session* - but with more players and more variation. I pitched the idea to Barry Kobrin at Combat Records, and he loved the concept. Combat eagerly gave it the green light. At this point, I only had a rough concept. I did not have a plan as to what, how and with who. I could have worked with a number of guitarists, which I considered initially, but I knew that I needed a strong partner. I needed a skilled lead guitar player who could also write songs, who could arrange, and who knew his way around a studio.

Andrew Duck McDonald fit those parameters perfectly. After working with him on a few smaller projects, I knew he would be a good fit. I wanted to do the project with Duck - I really liked the guy and he was super talented. I wanted it to be our project – a team project. Duck was at a low point with Bible Black, his upstate New York supergroup. They were head and shoulders above many of the newly signed bands and they just could not catch a break. So, understandably, he was a bit bummed out with the industry. Consequently, it took some convincing. But I persisted. I had made up my mind that Duck was the only option. I really had to push him on this. With some nudging, Duck finally agreed, and we quickly booked some time at Music America. When we started, I had some ideas and he had some ideas, and we found the collaboration came together quite easily.

We worked really well together. More often than not, I had a song that was partially finished and then Duck took it to the next level. We went back and forth for a few days, and finally, I began reaching out to some guest musicians: Brad Sinsel of TKO, Rhett Forrester, Maryann Scandiffio of Blacklace, James Rivera from Helstar, Dan Beehler of Exciter, Dan Spitz from Anthrax, Kim Simmonds of Savoy Brown, Jack Starr, Billy Sheehan,

Gary Driscoll of Elf/Rainbow and a host of others. Many of the players I had worked with before. Others were recommended by friends in the industry. Barry recommended Billy Sheehan. Billy, at the time, was in an upstate New York band by the name of Talas. They were the first band to be signed by Combat Records. Billy was a local legend. Even before Talas got signed, Billy was very much revered. Only a year or so after the Thrasher project, Billy was to join David lee Roth's solo band with Steve Vai and Greg Bisonette. Barry also recommended MaryAnn Scandifio, who was the vocalist for the NYC band Blacklace. Blacklace was one of those bands that had it all - great players, great songs, and a killer frontwoman. To fill in some gaps, Duck placed an ad in the *Village Voice*, which was how we landed Rick Caudle (who was later to do an album with The Rods). We had a lot of talent signed up for this. As we approached the dates of the recording session, Duck and I holed up in the Sheraton that was across the street from the studio.

Once we started recording, things very quickly turned chaotic. To write, produce, play, record, and organize the large number of musicians was not an easy task. I thought I had it under control, but looking back, I did not. I had no clue what I was doing. While it was fun, it was also frantic. I bit off way more than I could chew. Just to coordinate all the musicians was extremely difficult. All because I did not really plan it out the way I should have. This was long before you could send digital clips to someone. No one knew what they were doing until they walked into the studio. We were bringing them in, and they were learning things cold. It is tough to get the feel of a song that quickly. We chewed up a lot of studio time working with musicians. I learned a major lesson – that pre-production is key. Pre-production is king for everything you do. The other difficult thing was scheduling. Some musicians were not getting into the control room on time because the person before them was taking longer to learn the material. That was when I learned that not all musicians learn at the same rate. But it was a different time. That was what you were dealing with back then. You did not have a lot of options to contact somebody – no email, no cell phones. You had to call them and hope they picked up. Messages could go days without being checked or returned. Multiple times we overbooked ourselves. On the other hand, you cannot space it out too much either, because the studio is booked by time. The longer you went, the more you paid. It could get expensive.

When you have that many young guys in the studio, things tend to get a bit rowdy as well. There were always attractive girls around during these sessions. Always. They would just be hanging out. Multiple times I had to pull a musician out of the arms of a partially naked woman in the lounge because it was time to record their part. There was a lot of, "Sorry, but we need you to play now!" James Rivera and I were laughing about this recently. Because there were quite a few times that I had to pull him away from a woman (or two). I had to tell him, "Do not worry - you can come back to her, but right now I need you to sing!" Luckily the control room was closed to all female visitors. We had to, or we would not have gotten anything done. It was the only way that we could finish our tasks. It was pure craziness. Duck was fantastic. And I loved working with Duck. He took all of my songs to a better place than what I had originally written. Duck was the first one up in the morning and the last one to bed. He is that guy. He was the hardest working guy in the studio. Duck was the perfect partner for this. He was rehearsing all the time. He has one of the best work ethics. There were some difficult logistics along the way. Renting amplifiers was where I made the biggest mistake. We rented twin reverbs for Duck. We really wanted more of a Marshall sound, but our budget was not big enough to secure Marshalls. Later, I realized that we did not need to rent a Marshall. I could have bought a Marshall with our budget and then turned around and sold it after the album was finished. We would have recouped much of the cost. Lesson learned. As a result of using the wrong amps, the guitar sound is a bit discouraging. It really was not up to the standard of Duck's playing. He was such a great player, but the sound did not translate as well as it could have.

    I recall when Billy Sheehan came in. I was really excited to work with Billy. We occasionally played in each other's territory (Talas ruled the Buffalo area and we were primarily in the southern tier) but somehow, we never met the guys in Talas. Billy showed up with a bass rig that contained more equipment than the entire Rods PA system. Chris Bubacz, the engineer, looked at me and said, "What do I do with that? How am I supposed to mic that?" referring to the massive rig. Because it was a *huge* stack. He figured out a way to make it work, but honestly, I do not think we did Billy's sound justice either. We did the best we could, but I do not think we were able to deliver. Billy and Duck basically had dogfights with guitar and bass - they were going note for note with each other. You can hear it on the album. It was just unbelievable playing by Billy and Duck.

    **Brad Sinsel;** *TKO, War Babies, Angels of Dresden*
    *"Well, TKO was signed to Combat Records. It was bought to my attention through Combat that Carl was interested in using my voice for some tracks on the Thrasher project. I jumped at it when I saw who was on the roster, especially when I saw Billy Sheehan - and I was already a big fan of Carl's. So they flew me out to Rochester. And that was the first time I met Carl. I believe the music tracks were done. They just needed vocals on them. Carl at the time was producing Blue Cheer, which was kind of an*

*interesting dilemma. He was kind of juggling that and we did not have much time to hang out. But what I learned about him in those sessions is that he knows his way around both sides of the glass. Because you can always spot a pro drummer - once they sit down on that kit, they lock in the snare, the top floor, the kick, and usually bring out a drum key and make two twists - and boom, it is in the pocket. Carl had that same approach in the control booth. He was very comfortable behind the board. It only took a day or two and we had all the vocals that we needed for the two songs.*

"*I was staying in the same hotel as Blue Cheer. I had a lady friend join me for drinks in my room. And about one o'clock in the morning, there's a heavy pounding on the door. And I cannot remember which guy from Blue Cheer it was, but he was hammered! And he was screaming, 'Open up! I know you got liquor and women in there!' He was just pounding the shit out of the door. I was such a fan as a teenager of those guys - I wanted to be those guys. But you know, they had fallen on hard times. They had an in-store appearance booked. It was an in-store scheduled the same day as a live interview on a Rochester FM rock station. I tuned in to the radio station. Blue Cheer was having a 'Shave That Thang' contest (Shave That Thang was a popular radio contest of that era in which the guests shave the winning listener's head in exchange for a prize, usually concert tickets.). So, at that time I was in the engineering room with Carl and his phone rang. It is the record store guy who was hosting the in-store, and he says 'Carl, I think you should cancel because there's nobody here.' Hearing that, Carl hangs up, shakes his head, looks at me and says, 'Spinal Tap.' Carl then asked, 'Would you mind going down and tell them their in-store is cancelled?' I was like, 'Oh come on man.' But finally, I went and told Blue Cheer that no one was at their in-store appearance. I think I spotted the guy that was banging on my door because there was one in particular that looked really rough. To this day, when I shut the door in a hotel room, I think of that.*

"*So, TKO recorded 'In Your Face' in '81 but it failed to sell until 1985. We were behind the game on that one. But Carl was on the first wave of things getting heavier and darker. All those bands were gritty where ours was more mainstream, or R&B - with some power behind it. What caught me about him is just his sonic presence on the drums – it was just unbelievable. I cannot say enough about that. But he was early on the game - and more than once. First during the rock to metal transition, and then when metal started breaking up into sub genres. I did not have contact with Carl until much later on, when I was doing a project called Angels of Dresden. I had a great lineup. Mike McCready from Pearl Jam was on it! I had painted myself into a corner in metal and I wanted to get out of it. So I just started writing songs. They were all rock songs, but they were not metal by any means. On a whim, I called Carl and said, 'Hey, let's do a tribute to Lemmy.' And Carl said 'Definitely. We can give the proceeds to Stand Up and Shout, the Ronnie James Dio cancer fund.' So, we did 'Ace of Spades' and an original called 'The Criminal'. We did that all through file sharing. Carl produced that and also played drums on it. That is when I first started working with Carl in the present tense. He is not limited, as I found out later - he has an R&B band on the side. He is a total pro."*

# Attila: Rolling Thunder

I was made aware of Attila through David Carpin. David was an attorney who wanted me to produce some projects he was working on. He had started a new label called Shatter Records and wanted me to work with the band Attila. I had never heard them, but David was not going to hand me junk. Attila was a three piece, so that made it all the more interesting. We booked a few weeks at Pyramid Sound, and they started rehearsal at the go-to place - upstairs at Al Falso music. The guys were professional. They were very well rehearsed and super easy to work with. They were young but they were really enthusiastic. They did not waste time partying - they were very serious. It was a great couple of weeks. There are some really fun songs on this album: "Thermonuclear War", "Urban Commandoes", and a killer cover of the Alice Cooper hit "School's Out".

I did not expect *Rolling Thunder* to become a hit - Shatter was a small label and there were already rumblings of brewing financial issues. I knew they would not get a lot of PR or media. A video was impossible with small labels. Things were different then. Videos were reserved for the major league bands and video production was expensive. 1986 was the MTV age, and a video was a necessary thing to build a large base. But it was a great album, and I am glad to see it has a small cult fan base currently. I wish they had done a second album - who knows what would've happened?

**John DeLeon**; *Attila*
*"Living on Long Island, everyone was playing covers in bars. So, to get a gig you had to you had to play covers, and I put together a cover band. It took a couple of years to get a solid lineup - I believe it was '83 or '84. We had recorded some stuff, but the other guys had left the band because of the typical 'musical differences.' I eventually got in touch with Vinny (Vincent Paul) and A.T. Soldier, and we started jamming - we rehearsed for about three months. And then we started playing out and within a year, we landed a record deal. For Attila, I had an image in mind. So, when we were playing out, we played some covers, but we also played our own stuff. We were really heavy. We were head and shoulders above some of the other local bands. We were serious and we had a different mindset. Dave Carpin signed us, and we were the first band on his new label. Dave actually worked with Clive Davis at one point, and David left because Clive would not sign the bands that David thought had potential. He was missing out on*

*these bands, and as he could not get approval to sign them, they were picked up by other record companies. Some of those bands went on to be very successful. So he got frustrated and began Shatter. Dave was really open to our input. I had a vision. And, you know, I threw all my ideas at him. And he went along with 99% of them. I suggested Carl as a producer. I looked on the back of the albums from similar bands - bands that had gotten a deal like a year or two before us, like the Megaforce stuff - and Carl's name was on the back. So, it made sense to get the guy that produced those other albums. And I was already a fan of The Rods. I had seen The Rods live a couple of years prior. I thought they were great. We had X amount of dollars to work with. It turned out that we could afford him, so David set it up.*

*"In September we went upstate to start the album. We rehearsed for a week above this music store in Cortland (Al Falso Music). One day we go to rehearse, and Al (Falso) comes up to see us. He said, 'I have someone here I want you to meet.' It was Joey DeMaio from Manowar! He came up and introduced himself. He wanted to listen to us. So, we played a song or two for him and afterward, he deemed us, 'non-false metal.' How cool is that? We were blessed by Joey. Eventually, he left, and we stood around for a couple of minutes and said, 'Wow! Did that just happen?' Because Joey was the most intense character we had ever met. He was definitely a unique individual. We stayed at a big house with Victoria (Rock and Roll Hotel). I did not party a lot. I did not do a lot of drugs. So I can remember almost everything. We had a lot of laughs at that house. There were really nice people out there. There were no attitudes.*

*"Carl was really easy to work with it. Here's the funny thing - I was a fan before I met him, and he looked tough and intimidating sitting behind the drum set. He looked like a guy that would tear your head off. And then you meet him, and he is actually a mild-mannered guy. He was really nice. One night, after a session, we were finishing up and we asked him, "Carl, what are you going to do tonight?" And then he told us he had to go to the hardware store to get some modular shelving. We laughed. We were thinking he would be chasing women and running amuck, and here Carl is going to look at fucking modular shelving. We rehearsed for one week, and then we recorded for two weeks. We took off a week and then we went home. I think most of us came back to mix for a week. The entire process was maybe five weeks altogether. I'm pretty happy with the finished album. The issue that we had was the record label was starting to spread itself thin. We never went on tour. We never had management. We played out of state on weekends, but never a tour. By the late '80s, I was out of music because the whole scene had changed. I had to fucking eat, you know? I had to pay rent. I had to put gas in my car. So I could not devote 100% to a band. I just*

*could not do it. Vinnie, who was our bass player, and I really did not see eye to eye on a lot of things. We made up later on, but by then we had missed the window. I was not aware until the last couple of years that it was on the Internet. The majority of the reviews are great. I really get a kick out of that. It was a good debut record on an independent label. So that's kind of the way it went. The big caveat is that Vinnie died about three or four years ago."*

# Hollywood

During the making of Jack Starr's solo album, I had met a few guys from Passport Records. This laid the conversation for what would eventually become a two-album deal with Passport Records. Technically, The Rods were on hiatus. David had the restaurant, which was doing very well and occupied much of his time. Gary was touring with Savoy Brown. As the earlier chapters detail, I was busy with production work. But officially, we were still looking to do what we do best - and that was play hard rock and roll. Between David and I, we had quite a few songs and ideas in the tank. Most were in their infancy but getting them album ready was an easy task.

Also, during our last record, *Let Them Eat Metal*, we laid down some parts for songs to be used in the near future. Studio time was expensive, so we had worked overtime to get some extra material. Even though we had our own projects, and life was keeping us busy, getting an album worth of solid material was quite painless. There was just one issue: a large amount of the material we did have, while really good, did not fit the format of the typical Rods catalog. Much of it was quite a bit more melodic than our standard material. It was a bit more commercial - at least according to 1986 standards. And that is why we had not used it previously. We had two main concerns.

The biggest concern was that releasing the material in the Rods format would be disingenuous to our fans. Not that it was of poor caliber - there were some solid songs in the pipeline. But it would make for a different album. And we did not want to piss any fans off. The second concern was that these songs needed a different approach. They were not ideal for a balls-to-the-wall three-piece. These songs needed harmonies and a bit more finesse. David and I agreed that we would need a different vocal approach to make it work. So we made the decision to bring in another singer and approach this as a 'project', and not under the 'Rods' designation. We were in David's restaurant, The Hollywood, when we were discussing the potential album. David had just acquired a new logo for his restaurant, which was done quite well. So we made the decision to use the exact same title and the same logo. Now we just had to find the right vocalist.

We really needed someone with a wide vocal range. We wanted a voice that was versatile. As the Thrasher album was wrapping up, I thought Rick Caudle would be ideal. He had the most amazing voice, and he was a true pleasure to work with in the studio, so when David and I were discussing potential singers, I threw Rick's name in the hat. I knew he would be absolutely perfect for the material. David liked what he heard on the Thrasher tracks, so we decided to give him a shot. Rick was obviously the right choice for the material. His vocal tracks were recorded in only four days, which, given the material, was quite amazing.

We also decided to add a keyboardist. I had worked with a very talented singer, songwriter and keyboardist by the name of Emma Zale. I first met Emma Zale right before the Breaking Sound Festival in France. Emma was a graduate of the famed Juilliard Institute and was a truly talented pianist. She even showed me some scales and chord structures that became beneficial to me as a musician. We became great friends. We used her for the Thrasher project for a couple of songs. She became an attorney shortly after I had met her and was practicing law. I would see her whenever I went to New York City. So Emma was the immediate choice for keyboards. We loved working with her in the studio. She was super professional and one of the nicest people in the industry. After Hollywood, we stayed in touch and would talk from time to time. In 2012, quite sadly, Emma passed away. I was stunned, because we had been in communication, and her passing was not expected. It was very out of the blue. I still do not know what happened. But God, what a talent she was. She was fantastic on *Hollywood*. She helped us nail that "wall of sound" we were aiming for.

We mixed the album at Pyramid Sound and Passport released it shortly after. Passport had their own issues, mostly financial, and it was clear they were not going to pump a ton of money into promoting the album. Mostly because they did not have the money. We did not know what to expect with this one. It was different than our previous efforts and we were worried the fans might have a hard time digesting it. Passport was worried about this as well, which is why they begged us to release it under the moniker "The Rods." But we insisted it could not be sold and merchandised under that name. We insisted upon *Hollywood: Canedy, Feinstein, Bordonaro, Caudle*. We compromised with Passport and ended up with a small circle in the upper right corner of the album that said: "A Rods Project". The album was very era-appropriate, but it did not do well. It was not promoted, and we did almost no press, no PR work, and we did not tour behind it. We did play one show with the material. However, it was just Rock, Gary, and me. Rick had returned to the city by that point. We performed most of the songs from *Hollywood* at that show, and it did not go over well. In fact, it was a disaster. For starters, the songs did not lend themselves to a three-piece. They needed extra layering and a more developed sound. The audience did not know what to make of it. It was not a good show by any means, and it was the first and last time that we played those songs live. I really like some of the songs on there, though - there are some strong moments.

**Rick Caudle:** *Vocalist on Hollywood*
"When I was living in New York, I answered an ad in The Village Voice. I think it was Andrew Duck MacDonald that put the ad out. Duck and Carl were looking for singers for an album that was in the works. They listed some of the people who had signed up to participate. At the time, I was performing in an off-Broadway feature. I was singing as Christ for Jesus Christ Superstar. I loved that music. So, I sent Duck a tape, and later, Duck and Carl called me. They said, 'Hey, we love your voice, man. Would come up to Upstate?' I went and did the Thrasher project. It was really kind of amazing. I flew there from New York City. It was recorded in Rochester. I got there that night and I just listened to the tunes on a little cassette player in the hotel room. The next day I went and did the songs for that album. I opened my mouth the first time and sang, and they all about fell off their stools - their jaws dropped. I knew then I had found my niche. You know, Duck and Carl both got amazing things out of me. They really guided me because I was a bit all over the place. They were the two forces.

"They told me what they wanted, and I did the best I could. I think it was during those sessions when Carl mentioned something about playing on another project that he and David were putting together. Which I quickly agreed to. That happened but a few months later. My only regret was that I did not meet them a lot sooner. I regret that we did not get to tour - that would have been a blast. At the time, I started writing and playing with Kim Simmons, from Savoy Brown. I met him doing the Thrasher album. Kim actually came and stayed at my house for three weeks and slept on my couch. We wrote a lot of music together, but nothing ever came of it. And the Hollywood album? I think it was done at Pyramid for the most part. I think the Thrasher album was in Rochester. I did all of the tracks for Hollywood in four days. We did not have much time. It went very quickly. I did not know if the Rods fans were going to accept me. It is kind of like when Steve Perry joined Journey, I mean, I loved Journey before Steve Perry joined. Because I really liked their progressive side. When Steve joined, I thought, this is way different from their past albums, are people going to accept it? The early Journey fans were hardcore. I thought about that a lot. But they needed a different approach.

"I tried to use vocal dynamics as much as possible on Hollywood. You will notice in some sections that it is soft and pretty. And then later in the same song, it may be hard, gritty and high. I tried to cover a lot of different ranges when I did the album. Carl and Rock gave me the opportunity to cut loose - yet they gave me guidance. I think we gelled quite well. I got along great with both of those guys. Well, I was not sure what was going to happen. Like I said, I was down in the city. And of course, they were up in the Cortland area. It just never went any further. Now here is a story - it was around 1989 or 1990 and I got a message on my machine asking me to try out for this new band that was being put together. Rock knew some of the people involved in the project, so I asked him for his advice. He said, 'Nah, I do not think they are your type of music. Definitely not your thing.' So, I never contacted them in return. That band was Dream Theater. Who knows how that would have turned out. Eventually, I stopped singing and focused on martial arts training and teaching, which I had been taking since my early 20s. I'm 70 years old now. I still teach martial arts three days a week. I do private lessons. I train Special Forces teams, airline pilots, sheriff's departments, customs agents and all kinds of police and law enforcement."

**Rob "Wacko" Hunter:** *Ex-Raven, Recording Professional*
"I was a drummer in a band called Raven. We had some success in England – in an underground heavy metal way. Johnny Z wanted to bring us over to the United States to do some gigs. We gladly accepted and we came over - and he eventually became our manager. We started working more and more over here. Eventually, we built up our following Stateside, which led to us pretty much moving to upstate NY in the 1980s. And this is where I met my wife, so basically, I relocated here from England. Initially, we stayed at the Rock & Roll Hotel. It was kind of crazy. I mean, we were young guys - we were in our 20s. At the time, Cortland was a rock and roll college town.

"We did not have much money, so we stayed at the Rock & Roll Hotel in between gigs or recording. Then we would go back to England for a little while and come back to Cortland. It was wild. It was crazy. I mean, all kinds of parties and just everything that comes along with being in a heavy metal group. As for Carl, I'm going to give you a little bit of background. When Raven was in its infancy, we knew of all of the bands that were in our genre (and that could be considered competition) - The Rods was one of those bands. I remember I used to live in a small apartment with my parents. I had the first Rods album. I remember I had this makeshift drum set with pieces of wood on it and rubber and stuff. And I used to practice along to that album. That was one of the records that I used to listen to and I really admired it. When I came over to the States, I would bump into Carl and Rock frequently. And Gary (Bordonaro) and I actually ended up playing together for a brief while. There was a lot of admiration for them, as they were a three-piece like us. Metallica and Anthrax were there when we first came over. Metallica was the opening act for our first tour, which was called the 'Kill Em All For One' tour because they had just released Kill Em All and we released All For One. I think it was about 32 days.

"We played with Anthrax also, when Neil was still in the band. Overall, it was very accepting. It was very vibrant. And it was pretty crazy. Not the kind of crazy that we have these days. Today, people are just insane. But back then it was fun - it was crazy in a good way. We made a lot of friends. That is why I stayed here. It was just a great party atmosphere. The Rock & Roll Hotel was, at the time, perfect for us. Being in a band really was (and probably still is) a young man's game. Living in vans and sleeping on people's floors and stuff like that. Yeah, that is not a lifestyle for married guys. I still miss it to this day. It never leaves you. It is always part of you."

# Heavier Than Thou

1986 was a hectic year. We had a two-album deal with Passport Records, and we owed them a second album. Luckily, we had plenty of material in the can. We had saved a lot of material from the *Hollywood* sessions and there was even still some leftover material from the recording of *Let Them Eat Metal*. We had saved all of this material. We just needed to sweeten it. We had the drums, bass and guitars laid down - they were all pretty much done. Many of the tracks leftover from the *Hollywood* sessions were a bit harder than the material that actually ended up on *Hollywood*. These "leftover" tracks were traditional rockers, a bit more in range of standard Rods material. Sometimes a song might not work when you write it, but later it can be reworked and used on another album or as a bonus track. For instance, we had some songs, like "Angels Never Run", that were written years ago but we never got around to finishing. And years later, we were able to approach those songs differently than originally intended - and it worked out well.

For this album, we decided to bring in vocalist Shmoulik Avigal. Jack Starr had introduced me to Shmoulik. Jack had used him for his side project, Guardians of the Flame. Shmoulik started out with a Dutch heavy metal band by the name of Picture. They released a really cool album in 1982 called *Diamond Dreamer*. Shmoulik was an amazing vocalist, so much so that I had started a side project with him early on. Accompanied by Andrew Duck McDonald, Craig Gruber, and guitarist Tom Innamorato, we wrote and rehearsed for a few months. We named the project Paris, but unfortunately it never panned out. We rehearsed weekly, but I was not happy with the songs. Paris had all of the right players, but it just did not gel, though because of the project, Shmoulik (and Tom) were living with me. So, when we were working on some demo tracks for Paris, I called David and let him hear Shmoulik's vocal tracks over the phone. David was really impressed. Shmoulik made perfect sense for the new material. He was a monster vocalist. Plus, it was convenient. He was staying at my place and was readily available. We did have one issue, and that was Gary. He was on tour with Savoy Brown. So we enlisted Craig Gruber to help us complete the bass tracks. Craig, thankfully, had been helping us out since we started. He had been there since our formation, and he was always there to pull us out of a jam.

We booked time at Pyramid Sound to finish up the pieces. We had two songs from the *Live* album, "Cold Sweat and Blood" and "Born to Rock", that we felt would benefit from a studio treatment, so we included them in the set. David and I felt the *Live* album did not do those songs justice and we wanted to get a cleaner studio version. Plus, Shmoulik's vocals gave those tracks a different feel. We also included a Led Zeppelin cover, "Communication Breakdown", which was the perfect outlet for Shmoulik's vocals. David and I frequently used that song as a warmup, and occasionally we performed it live, so it made perfect sense to include it. "Angels Never Run" was a song that David had written years prior. It was originally titled "Angels on the Run", but I recommended a change to "Angels Never Run" as it sounded tougher. "Make Me A Believer" is another fan favorite. I also played rhythm guitars on "She is Trouble". This was at the end of the sessions, and we really needed to lay down the guitars. David was so busy with the restaurant that he told me to go ahead and lay down the rhythms. This album also included Al Falso on harmonica for the track "Music Man". It was so cool to have him on the record. Not only was it great for us, but it meant so much to him. He was so happy that we included him. We finished a few of the songs at Music America. Much like *Hollywood*, this album was completed in pieces. Essentially, we were salvaging our old material. This was great material, but with everything we had done in the past decade, there was a lot that was forgotten about or not included for one reason or another; so this album really forced us to finish that material.

When *Heavier Than Thou* was released, Passport pushed the song "Crossfire" as a single. "Crossfire" was starting to get traction around the country on radio. But Passport Records invested in a deal with Sony that quickly went sideways. Passport had run out of money and the Sony money never came in. By late 1988, Passport Records was out of business. It was a shame because "Crossfire" was really starting to take off. I thought this was a great album. The songs are fantastic and the album as a whole is really cohesive; though, looking back, I think we could have done better with the mix. Sonically, I do not think *Hollywood* or *Heavier Than Thou* are great sounding albums, but I love the material. I think the biggest compliment came from Johnny Z. He called me up to tell me how much he loved this album. That meant the world to me. We actually played a couple of shows with Shmoulik. As for The Rods, we would not release another album for over 20 years. Though that was never our intention. Sadly, Shmoulik passed away in 2006 from cancer.

**Tom Innamorato:** *Warhead, Tung, American Mafia*
*"I had started my own band, which was called Warhead. Over time, we had an issue with the the vocalist. So, that was when I spoke to my friend*

*Jack Starr (who was then the guitar player for Virgin Steele). Jack told me about Shmoulik Avigail. I sent a demo tape to Shmoulik, who lived in Holland at the time. Shortly after, he flew to New York. After trying out, he told me he was not very impressed with the other guys. He did not feel they were up to his level of perfection. So, we were at a crossroads. Shmoulik said, 'I'm not crazy about the rhythm section,' and I immediately listened to him. Looking back, I think it was the biggest mistake I made as far as my music career went. Warhead were on a good path. We did four or five shows and got a great response from those shows. The owner of Lamour's, George Parenti, who was also managing White Lion, wanted to manage us. There were seven labels that wanted to sign us - all decent independent labels. It was the right time also: Anthrax rehearsed down the hall from us in the Queen's music building. And Metallica came from California, and they were there as well. So, at one point, all three bands were on the same floor, all playing the same style of music.*

"At the time, nobody else was playing that type of music in the building - it was Warhead, Anthrax, and Metallica. So, my mistake was not sticking with my band, and not sticking with the other members. And this brings us to Vision (later called Paris). Jack Starr tells me Carl and Craig were playing together and were trying to put something together. When he mentioned those two names, I was like, 'Dude, I want to play with them!' And that is how it started. Basically, Shmoulik and I drove up to Cortland. Then we started the band. We just started recording ideas. Shmoulik and I were living with Carl for a short period of time and then we got our own place. We rehearsed at Al Falso's and David "Rock" Feinstein let me borrow his gear. Which was really nice because we had no income, and I had no gear. I had to sell my rig so that we could afford to live. We practiced for four or five months – a good portion of the year. But we were not coming up with many ideas that we were happy with. Eventually it just fizzled out. We had some partial songs, but we were never able to finish one. So that was it. We each went our separate ways."

## Possessed: Beyond the Gates

Steve Sinclair, who worked with Combat records, hired me to produce the second album from the band Possessed. Possessed were arguably the first death metal band, and released their first album *Seven Churches* for Combat Records in 1985. Of course, in 1987, "death metal" was not yet a household term. I certainly was not aware of it. Thrash had just started to hit the big time, so this was a very interesting time when sub genres were being created out of a very new genre. Coming off of the Overkill and Exciter sessions, I was certainly familiar with speed metal, but these guys were unbelievably heavy. They were intense and I absolutely loved that.

Possessed were young. Very young. Larry Lalonde, who later played in Primus, was their guitar player. He was only 16 or so at the time. They were still in high school, so we had to schedule pre-production and the recording of the album around their school schedule. It was recorded on Easter break for that reason. We were booked to record in California, at Prairie Sun Studios, which was in the Bay Area. This would be my first time producing on the West Coast. I stayed at their manager's house, which is also where we were scheduled to do pre-production. And during pre-production, the guys were absolutely tight - very impressive for such a young bunch. But interestingly enough, they had a sort of ebb and flow in the tempo. They would ride it together and speed up and slow it down in very subtle ways; but they would all do it together. That was a new challenge for me. They were really dialed in as a unit. When we recorded, as this was the standard, I had them play to click tracks, but looking back, I should have had them play live and record them that way. Because they had this great synergy.

They were really tied into each other musically. That was one of their strengths and I wish I had taken advantage of that. I think it would have made for a better product, and ultimately, a much easier experience. Their material had some really cool elements. Their sound was dark and leathery. I loved it. I decided to focus on the vocals foremost. I wanted to make sure that they had some depth and body and that the vocals did not get lost in the heaviness. Remember, death metal was not yet a thing. The Cookie Monster-style vocals did not yet exist. Like Anthrax, Possessed was doing something very new. It needed a new approach. Frontman Jeff Becerra has such a great voice and it translated well to tape. It was a fun experience, but it was tough trying to get everything done in the minimal amount of time that we had. It was crazy, working around a high school schedule.

While the boys were in school, I had some free time and went out with Cliff Cultreri from Combat Records. Cliff said, "Let's get something to eat and stop by Dickie Peterson's place." Which I was cool with. Dickie was the bass player and lead vocalist for Blue Cheer. I had just produced Blue Cheer's comeback album, so I was eager to see Dickie again. Instead of a restaurant, Cliff took me to the store, and he bought a bunch of deli meats, cheese, snacks, and condiments. He filled the cart. I really did not think much of it - I just assumed he wanted something easy that we could take there instead of meeting up at a restaurant. But Cliff bought a lot of stuff.

He loaded up and I thought that was a bit strange. Once we got to Dickie's house, I was a bit taken aback. Dickie and his girlfriend were living in absolute poverty. They were extremely poor. That was certainly not what one would expect from the frontman of a band as important as Blue Cheer. Blue Cheer had the massive hit "Summertime Blues"! It was not at all what I expected. Proof, folks, that rock and roll doesn't always pay. Dickie and his girlfriend were total hippies. I think his girlfriend's name was Moonflower (or something equally hippyish). Moonflower and I became good friends during the next few days. She was really cool. But anyway, they were living out of a rundown trailer that had a shed in the back, which is where Blue Cheer practiced. And that is why Cliff brought all that food over. I do not think they had much at the time.

At the time, record deals were the same as they were in the '60s and '70s, pretty much; record labels are not designed to make money for the artist. Occasionally there is a big advance, but expenses are so numerous – the costs of recording, touring and promoting are excessive and it is very easy to piss away anything you are lucky enough to get. And I think that's what happened - they just ran out of money. They probably did not have good management. As a result, they wound up having only small offers here and there. Most likely, they signed some deals that were not favorable. Once you go down that rabbit hole, it is tough to get out, because now you've diluted your value and your brand. But I do not know for sure. I do know there were some rather unfavorable deals that they had made. When you are a young rock band and you are getting some success, you often do not think about the future. Very few have a retirement plan. That was very sad to see. Blue Cheer were a huge inspiration to me, and I felt they deserved so much better.

The following day we finished up the album. Overall, it was an enjoyable experience. The guys in Possessed were really talented and they were very easy to work with. The mastering was set to take place on April 15th in New York City, so, with a few days off, I had time to check in at home, do some laundry, and run a few errands. I left Cortland on the 14th and of all things a massive snowstorm hit! In April! It rarely snows in April on the East Coast. That's upstate New York for you – you never know what you are going to get during those months. The snowstorm came on fast and furious. It was evident that there was no way I was going to make it to the city. It is typically a six or seven hour drive. And that is not a drive you want to make in a snowstorm. I still attempted the drive; however, I only made it to northern PA - close to Dianne's mother's house. Thankfully, I was able to bunker down there. As a result, I never made it to mastering it. Which is something that bothers me to this very day. The record got slagged by the bigger press, but it has been one of their biggest-selling albums. Fans love it, and overall, it has stood the test of time. Steve Sinclair was really happy with the album and that made me happy. The best part about this project was it led to a friendship with frontman Jeff Becerra. Jeff has been very kind to me over the years. He is one hell of a great guy. I also became good friends with their manager, Debbie Abono. I stayed at her place when we were recording the album. Debbie was so cool. For those not familiar with Debbie Abono, she was the "mom" of the Bay Area metal scene. She managed a lot of the bands, and she really took care of them. Not at all what you would expect from a grey-haired grandma. She was an amazing person. The early thrash bands of that era really respected her. She managed most of them I believe. Debbie contributed greatly to the thrash movement.

I had a great time out there. It was a much different vibe from the East Coast scene, but it was still very cool. East Coast musicians have a totally different feel than West Coast musicians. It was interesting to see the difference in attitude and the different approach to music. Steve Hager was the engineer on that project. And Steve was a really good guy. In fact, we drove down the coast together – I was blown away by how beautiful it was.

**Jeff Becerra:** *Possessed*
*"I met Carl when we started working on the second album. Combat offered Carl to us. We were like, 'The guy from The Rods and who just did Anthrax? Hell yeah!' We did not know shit - we had done our first demo at a tweakers house for 110 bucks. So, to get a big time producer was amazing. We recorded it at Prairie Sound Studios in Cook County, California. I do not think Carl understood just how noisy it was supposed to be at first. But he very quickly grasped that. He understood what was going on. He was super helpful. In fact, he helped with the intro. He helped with the drums. He helped pull us together and gave us a lot of great input. He was just a really fine producer. I think we were at the studio for a total of two weeks. That was one of our highest grossing albums. I think it sounds good. Carl shot himself in the foot because he said (publicly) that something went wrong in the mastering - he should never have said that. Because once you say something, once you ring that bell, some people will run with it. I think*

*all artists do that - we're super hard on ourselves. But it was great. Carl asked us, 'Hey, do you guys like Blue Cheer?' And then he took us over to party with Blue Cheer!"*

# Roxx Gang: Love 'Em and Leave 'Em

Early 1987, a young man by the name of Brett Steele reached out to me. He asked if I was interested in producing a band by the name of Roxx Gang. Brett was not only their manager, he was also the younger brother of frontman Kevin Steele. Brett was very young, I believe only 19 or so at the time, but he showed a lot of promise as a new manager. Management is a tough business and even more so when you are young and fresh faced. Most of the folks on that side of the industry are older, have amassed years of experience and have a fat rolodex of necessary contacts. But Brett was persistent and focused, which is exactly what you need when trying to corral a young rock band. Roxx Gang, as a band, also showed promise. After listening to the demo Brett had sent me, I agreed to work with them. While very rough around the edges, there was some potential. They definitely needed some polish. They did not have any deals on the table yet, but they were hoping that an independent album (or polished demo) would help get them there. They had some strong songs and they also had the look, two things that were crucial for the hard rock genre. So I agreed, and booked a flight to Tampa, Florida.

Roxx Gang were to be a slight departure from the bands I typically produced. They were a straight up hard rock band. They had a glam (or 'hair metal') look. I had been doing so much thrash, speed, and heavy metal that I was afraid of painting myself into a corner. I wanted to spread my wings, as they say. I was really enthused about this project. But the day before I was to depart, their lead guitarist (and one of the primary songwriters), founding member Eric Carrell, died. I do not recall the specifics, but his death was unexpected and controversial. In an instant, everything was in limbo. I really was not sure if they were going to move forward as a unit or not. But I went with my gut feeling and carried through with the trip. I spoke with Brett after arriving, and after some discussion, it was agreed that the band would carry on. I was to help them get back into fighting shape. Eric would not be easy to replace. He had written most of the songs that they had planned for the album. He was also an amazing guitar player.

Once in Florida, Brett set me up with lodging at a parolee's house (unbeknownst to me). The guy who owned the house was nowhere to be found, so I was there alone. I unpacked and arranged myself to be there for a few weeks. The next morning, while I was waiting for Brett to pick me up, all of a sudden someone busted through the window, and at the same time, the front door. It was the local police department, and they were storming the house. It turned out they were looking for the parolee, who had apparently violated his probation. I had to do some fast talking to convince the police that I was not the person they were looking for. They wanted to know if I had seen him. And of course, I had not – I did not even know the guy. Thankfully, Brett moved me to a hotel, where I felt much safer.

After a brief period of mourning, I urged the three remaining members to hold tryouts, not for one, but for two new guitarists. Having two guitarists would allow for a broader and more pronounced sound. It is also a good way to add another dynamic to the songwriting and performance, especially if the two guitar players have different styles and strengths. After a few weeks of trials, the band was able to find two new guitarists: Jeff Taylor Blanchard and Wade Hayes. Both were accomplished guitar players with differing styles. The improvement on the existing material was immediate. We wasted no time, and I got them into pre-production right away. From day one, it was abundantly clear that Kevin Steele was a total rock star. He dressed the part. He had the look and the attitude. And he was very talented. Though, as a singer, he did not have a great range and was limited vocally, the band was able to adjust the tone and tempo to fit his vocal style. We had to rearrange the songs to fit his voice. And although he did not really play an instrument, he communicated the songs by singing melodies - he was very hands on. He did all of the lyrics as well. All of the guys were talented. They all had huge rock star potential. And they were all great looking. It was bewildering to see the vast number of girls that were chasing after these guys. I had never seen anything like it. Every time we went out to eat, beautiful women would approach them suggestively. They really nailed the rock star thing. That was not something you typically see on the thrash metal side.

In the studio, Roxx Gang were great. I did a lot of arranging on the album, and I was proud of that. I still am. I thought it turned out great, though I do not think the band was happy with me during the sessions. Kevin Dubrow of Quiet Riot was also producing a band in town. I believe that band was Julliette. Word quickly reached the guys that Julliette's session was a balls-to-the-wall party with a buffet of drugs, booze, and women. It was a legendary party, so the word spread quickly. A few of the guys wanted to go check it out. But I had a very strict no partying and no drugs policy in the studio. The boys were not happy that they were missing out on the fun. I was very strict about making it a closed session. It was tough on the guys, because we were isolated, and we were working long days. It could get difficult and there was no outlet for them to blow off some steam. But we knocked the album out and it was well worth it. This album (or demo) was what got them signed to Virgin Records. Getting signed happened rather quickly - so I am really proud of this album. It accomplished exactly what we had wanted it to.

I was a bit disappointed in one aspect though. I knew these guys had major-league potential and could make it with some fine-tuning, which we did during the three months I spent with them. I took this project on hoping they would bring me in to produce their first major label effort. I felt that, in all honesty, if I was able to take them to a good studio, we could give them a fantastic major-label album. But the record company wanted a big name behind the board, so they executed a clause and bought me out, and went with producer Beau Hill. Beau produced Ratt, Kix, Alice Copper, Winger, and a lot of the hair metal bands of the era. He was (and still is) one of the most well-known of the genre. Now, I thought Beau did a good job, but there were some things he did that made them sound a bit too much like Ratt. I thought they ended up sounding a bit over-processed. Having Beau produce them automatically put them in the hair metal category, which was also the reason for their fall, as hair metal was soon to face a rapid demise. These guys were anything but Ratt, but they immediately got lumped into the hair metal genre.

By the time they got signed, that genre was getting a bit crowded. And while they had that look, they were very much a standard hard rock band. I really believe I would have been a better fit for the band, but that's only my opinion. There is no doubt that all of the guys in the band were talented. Wade Hayes was a phenomenal guitarist. A virtuoso. And Jeff Taylor, the other guitarist, was such a great showman. Roby "Strychnine" Strine, their bass player, was a great player and a great guy. David James Blackshire was their drummer and really knew his shit. He was an incredibly hard worker and uber focused. And they had a killer visual with Kevin upfront. The band should have done way more than they did. But as is the story with so many great bands from this late in the decade, some made it, and some didn't. There are so many from this time frame that released a stellar album only to come and go with little fanfare, effectively driving the band apart. Virgin really dropped the ball on the band. The label should have supported them more than they did, in my opinion. There was no reason for Roxx Gang to not take off. But anyway, I had a great time working with them. Brett's been a great manager for them. They are lucky to have someone like Brett in their corner. Right after the turn of the decade, Virgin dropped them; but that was not the last time I was to see them.

**David James Blackshire**: *Ex-Roxx Gang*
"In the '80s, I was the drummer for a band called Bad Attitude. We played mostly throughout Maryland, Pennsylvania and a lot of the Northeast. We played often with Kix and Wrathchild AD – the Hammerjacks type bands. (**Note:** Hammerjacks was a legendary rock club in Baltimore, Maryland. Arguably, throughout the 1980s, Hammerjacks was one of the most renowned venues on the East Coast. What Lamour's was to thrash, Hammerjacks was to hard rock and hair metal. Hammerjacks was also ground zero for the Baltimore scene, which gifted us great bands like Kix and Childs Play.) I knew of The Rods because my band used to cover a couple of their songs. We used to play 'Hot to Trot' a lot. We were young kids, like 17 - but we were total pros. We were doing the circuit, from Maine all the way to North Carolina. So, we were doing really good. We played a lot of gigs and as a band, we were great. We had an amazing singer. But I left to join the Roxx Gang, and that was actually all because of Carl.

"I had gotten a phone call from an old friend: Roby Strine. Roby had moved from PA to Florida and had been playing in a band there. 'I have been trying to get a hold of you. We need a drummer, and you would be perfect,' Roby said. Now Roby knew of my style, which I was chasing a Tommy Lee vibe. I was a hungry fucking show-drummer. And I guess that is what he was looking for. He told me he was with this great band in Florida called Roxx Gang. 'They have financial backing,' he told me. 'And Carl Canedy is going to work with us!' By this time, Carl was gaining a reputation as a producer, plus he is one of the best drummers out there - so that got my attention. I did not really know anything about Roxx Gang. I did not know much about their music or what they were doing. But I knew Carl Canedy. And I'm a drummer. And I'm like, well if they've got Carl on board, then there's something real going on here. And I was thinking to myself, if I go down and join this band and it does not work, at the end of the day, I would at least get the opportunity to work with Carl. So, that was my reason to explore this opportunity. Roby sent me a package - it was a demo. A very bad demo of Roxx Gang. Honestly, I thought the band was pretty awful. Except for their guitar player, Eric. There was something about his playing that I really liked. He had a little bit of a Mick Mars thing going on. But the singer was not very good. Lyrically, he was not bad – there were some pretty good lyrics. But his voice was not very good. But Carl was working with them, so there must be something there. And I really wanted to work with Carl.

"So, I went to Florida. The band was not so great. I had left a fully functional touring band. The band I left; we were playing some really great rooms. We were getting some great opening slots. We opened for Kix a lot.

Pat Travers, Uli Jon Roth and more. Quite frankly, in the beginning, I thought that it (Roxx Gang) is not going to work. At first there was some good camaraderie. But the band was not that great, and I just could not see them making it. But I stuck it out and then Eric died. He died in a tragic way - he fell off a bridge. Kevin and Brett were best friends with this guy. But everything with Carl was planned already. I think this happened a week before Carl was scheduled to come. And then Carl stepped in. He was like, 'Listen, why don't we do this - why not audition some guitar players and I will come down, and we will continue? I will produce the band. We will go into the studio with two different guitar players.' And that is exactly what we did. We ended up getting a guy named Wade Hayes, who was this young Japanese American kid. He was 18 or 19. He was a fucking wizard. Wade was Zakk Wylde on steroids. This guy was incredible. He was absolutely one of the most undiscovered talents in metal guitar, and the work that he did is probably the only reason anyone really knows Roxx Gang. So, Carl comes down, and he's kind of the guy who regroups the whole thing. He is the rock that everyone is leaning on. He was like, 'Okay, we're going to reassemble this band. You guys are going to work. I'm going to take you guys into pre-production.' He came in with an agenda and with a schedule. I stayed because of Carl. I was a mercenary. I also noticed that this was Kevin's project. You know, it is Kevin and his brother. They're the team.

"Carl was one of the most organized people. He organized us. Nothing would have happened after Eric's death if it was not for Carl. He assembled us. He focused us into a functioning band, and it turned out to be amazing the way it came together. And the weakest link at the end of the day was Kevin. Though he had some decent lyrics, he just was not a vocalist. And that really limited us musically. We were lucky to get that record deal. Carl did a lot for free, and he put so much heart into it. And I think that he expected that if we got signed, they were going to use him (for the major label album). I knew that they were not going to use him. When we got signed, Carl handed those guys the blueprint. He gave them a how-to book. The process of recording with Carl was eye opening.

"So, it was a miracle we got signed. Because we really were not playing out a lot. No tours. No touring up and down the state. There were only local shows. And very few at that. So outside of the area, no one knew of Roxx Gang. So, prior to Carl, I thought they were unprofessional. Maybe it is because of my previous band - we were a traveling band. We worked hard on the road. We had our own road crew. We were making money. Roxx Gang did not have any of that. And it felt like a step back. Now, they had some strengths. Kevin was a prolific lyric writer. So, he did write some pretty fucking good songs - lyrically. He relied on us to get the music done. And we did. We wrote all that shit. The band wrote all that shit. Carl, like I *said, he was the linchpin in the survival of this band. He made it work. And all of a sudden, we went from this sort of mediocre kind of fucking thing to a band with promise. Thanks to Wade and Carl. That's really what elevated the band. For 'Love 'Em and Leave Em', I think at the time, in metal, you had some bands that had gotten signed, like Ratt and Motley Crue, that had put out an independent record and that caught the record label's attention. They had this product that was produced pretty well and then they shot up to a major record label, right? There were a lot of demos that were albums, I would say even Kill 'Em All was like a demo. It was a fucking really good demo. But it worked. So, we thought we should produce something that has polish to it, something that a label is going to notice. And they're going to drop some money on us, which has happened to many bands. Like 'Too Fast for Love' from Motley Crue. That is exactly what we wanted to do. There was nothing before that record (Love 'Em and Leave 'Em). There was barely a band before that record. There was no scene there. There was maybe three clubs down there. They were playing the local strip club. But there was no giant rock scene there. Now there was a build. Right after finishing the record - things started happening and a fanbase was emerging. Again, I did not join the band because of Roxx Gang.*

"*I joined because of Carl, and he made something happen. He produced the fuck out of us. He made lemonade out of lemons. And I knew that when I had that cassette in my hand that I was going to be okay. Because I was like, 'Okay, if I leave this band, I'm going to have something to shop somewhere else.' And I can get another gig. So, lo and behold, with Carl's guidance, and with Carl's input and his support, we did get signed. All because he was working behind the scenes to help get the band signed. He wanted us to get signed, so he could record the next record with a bigger budget. That was the whole plan. 'I'm producing this. So that you guys can land a deal. And I can be the next producer for an album with a bigger budget. And with a bigger budget, we can really make something happen here,' Carl had told us. Now, I knew that that was never going to happen. Because those guys never really even considered it. We ended up working with Beau Hill. And I do not regret working with Beau Hill. Who would not want to work with Beau, right? But nobody could have done what Carl did. He worked magic. And he really put in a lot of work. The only reason I have a musical work ethic today is because of Carl. He came in and he had a sheet with 20 rules on it. He is like, 'This is what I expect. I do not want anyone arguing back and forth. We are going to do this in a democratic way and get the ideas out.' He was very democratic in the way that he went about. I would say that he made it clear that he was in charge, and he has the final say. And that's because he had a lot riding on it.*

*"So, after getting signed we started to have to do things – like a first tour. I am sure Virgin was shooting themselves in the fucking foot for signing us. They put us on tour with Warrant. We ended up going to Montclair, New Jersey, which is right outside of the city. Well, Kevin got pissed for some reason and threw a bottle against the wall in Warrant's dressing room. He sprayed beer all over their wardrobe. And the guys in Warrant could not have been nicer, so I am not sure why he had a hissy fit, but it was embarrassing. Their album (Cherry Pie) was doing really good. This was a great slot. Well, the next day we were kicked off the tour. We had to go out on our own. He just blew a massive tour. Well, in addition to that, the scene started to change. I was 20. We had a fucking MTV video. We had an album on Virgin Records. But music was changing. And these guys were not changing. They expected the red carpet to be rolled out. They think that everything's happening for them. And when we went out to LA, that was when I really understood that this is going to be over soon. Because being in LA at that time, you started to feel something happening.*

*"I remember thinking that we were on the tail end of this. I could feel it. The very tail end. There were a lot of bands that fucking sounded and looked just like us and they were huge. But some of these bands were so much better. I mean, I do not want to say better, but they had a more cohesive philosophy. We were not super tight. And Virgin dropped the band. When they dropped the band, they were so happy to get rid of us that they forgave our debt. They wrote us off. They cut the fucking cord. Then I had to make some choices. Because the band was getting dropped. I've spent too much time fucking backing this horse that isn't going to get through the finish line. I figured I had to get the fuck out of Florida. When we were working on the record with Carl, he recommended that we move to LA. He said, 'You need to be where the industry is.' I absolutely, 100% wanted that. Fuck this hot ass state. And at that time, there was a lot of bad blood that was already happening in the band. Plenty of negative things started popping up. I did not want to stay there. I was not going to stay there. And of course, I fucking stayed there."*

**Brett Steele**: *Steele Management, Manager of Roxx Gang*
*"We were young kids, and we did not know anybody in the music business. We did not have any relatives or anybody that had ties to the business. We just had a lot of drive, and fortunately, I had a band with a lot of talent, and Carl was one of the first to recognize that. Initially, I had no understanding of how the business really worked. I just kind of loved the promotion and marketing side of it because it tied into what I was doing in college. Kevin had the ideas, and I would just run with them. I do not think Tampa Bay, Florida had ever seen anything like Roxx Gang. This was*

before original bands were playing in bars. Back then, you would go into a bar in Tampa Bay, and it was only bands playing cover songs. No one hired original bands. And I had to sell a then-unknown band that played originals to these venues. Back then you had to bring your own PA and light show in as well. That was a tough sell at first, but we marketed the band so heavily that we had a good fan base. So, wherever we played, people would come out and it just kind of started snowballing. We were guerrilla marketing guys. I had friends, girlfriends and fans out there - putting up flyers and posters everywhere that we could. We were coming up with these really creative flyers. I would go to all the major concerts with a team of people and flyer the whole fucking coliseum parking lot. And eventually we started having some success. It was tough to win those crowds over, but the band did it because Kevin could sell a song. And the band was so good. It was not easy at first. The beaches were filled with beautiful women, but that's not where we were playing. I was definitely persistent. There was a $99 JetBlue flight from Tampa to LaGuardia. Round trip. And this is the mid-80s, long before the internet or anything. So, I would fly up to New York. I did not know anyone in the industry. You could not look it up on the internet and find out who the A&R rep was. So, I used to just go to the record labels' headquarters and walk into the lobby and say, 'Hey, I need five minutes with your A&R guy.' A lot of times I'd sit there all day, and then they'd finally let me talk to somebody.

"Sometimes they would not let me talk to anybody. And these flights were like red eye flights. So, I'd get in at some god-awful hour and I would have to sit in a coffee shop until the labels opened. And luckily, I had a good product. One of the first A&R people that kind of took me under their wing and respected what I was doing was Jason Flom at Atlantic Records. Jason eventually came to Tampa and saw the band do a showcase, and he also introduced me to an entertainment lawyer named Robert Urban. And that helped a lot. And then Carl helped us out. There was a record company called Combat Records and they listened to the demo. They said, 'Hey, this is really good! You should work with this producer named Carl Canedy.' So, I met Carl. He also introduced us to an attorney who we still work with to this very day! And as a result of this recording that we did with Carl, and with Jonathan Blanc and I shopping the band, within a year we had Epic Records came down to check out the band. Atlantic came down. Virgin came down. Even Gene Simmons' label came to check out our showcase.

"Now, Roxx Gang had the look down to a T. Kevin grew up with Mott the Hoople, T Rex, The New York Dolls, the Stooges - and he just took that street-glam punk look and made it his own thing. He was doing it before Motley Crue were big - really before the LA scene took off. But we were in Florida, so people did not hear about us until we made this recording with

Carl. And Carl, hats off to him, recognized not only Kevin's songwriting talent, but also that he had this flair for the style and also how to present that. It is not just having it, but also knowing how to present it to a mass audience as well. The things that stand out to me the most, all these years later, is that the band was very good, but they were also very raw, and I think Carl brought discipline to the band. Carl brought a different type of professionalism. The band was professional, but Carl had a way of doing things that I think was very good for the band - a very disciplined approach to rehearsing and recording. At that particular time, that's exactly what the band needed, and it was really a good fit. As a result, I think they made a really good record.

"What made things difficult was that our guitar player, Eric Carrell, passed away right before Carl started working with us. Eric was an amazing guy and an amazing talent. We all loved and missed Eric Carrell, but Kevin was driven. This was his life dream, and nothing was going to stop him. He immediately reached out to Jeff Taylor, who had played with us before. Wade Hayes actually played bass in Roxx Gang for a while, which is pretty amazing when you consider what a talented guitar player he was. So, we knew Jeff and we knew Wade. And I think there was some consultation with Carl about bringing Wade in, and we decided that was the best route to go, with the two guitar players. They had to learn all the parts and get ready to record. Now, Carl, besides producing the record, had by then became a good friend. He also mixed the band live for some of the showcases and stuff. And as soon as the labels got involved, they were like, 'Well, you got to record with a different producer.' The labels tend to have their own people/producers picked out. They said it the first night (the Virgin executives) - right there in front of Carl, perhaps not realizing who he was. It put us in a very uncomfortable situation. But we were all in our early 20s and it was our first record deal.

"We listened to what the label had to say. They made a list of producers that we had to pick from. I think a couple of them came down and saw the band. Beau had just done the Kix album Midnight Dynamite. So that's how that relationship started. Some people like Carl's record better, some people like Beau's record better. Beau's is more polished. Carl's album captured a great moment in time. It was rawer and plenty of people prefer that. But they're both fantastic records and we were always grateful to Carl for being one of the first people to recognize the band's talent and for everything he did for the band's career in the early stages. We really hit it off with Virgin - they threw a ton of money at the band - but they did not know what they were doing with a rock band. There were some good people there, but they made some mistakes with us, and they did not always listen to our ideas because they thought they knew better."

# E-X-E: Stricken By Might

Chances are, you have not heard of this band or this album. Which is a shame, because it is a true heavy metal masterpiece. E-X-E had the unfortunate luck of getting signed to a fledgling label and coming on the scene a year or two too late. If they had gotten signed in the early '80s, then their luck might have been different. By late 1987, when this was released, heavy metal was fractioned into multiple sub-genres. And this is an album that really does not fit into a specific sub-genre. It has elements of speed, thrash, and early black metal. It is a great, traditional heavy metal album. What I remember most about this was that I really liked the guys. E-X-E were a really tight metal band from New York City. They were signed to Shatter Records, a very small record label with emerging financial troubles. That did not leave a lot of hope for the guys, but a small record label is better than no record label. This was in 1987, and the first wave of thrash and speed was ushered in around 1985, so they had just missed the initial rush. I think if they had emerged a year or two earlier, things would have worked out much differently for them. This album has been out of print for some time, but I highly recommend you get your hands on a copy and give it a listen. It is a really solid album. And it is kind of hard to place in a sub-genre. But it is definitely balls-to-the-wall heavy metal.

Recording wise, it was quite enjoyable. We did pre-production at Al Falso's store, which was a lot of fun. They were well rehearsed, and they had some great songs. They were on top of their game. I had just gotten back from Florida, having finished the Roxx Gang demo. We recorded this at Pyramid Sound and the sessions were fun - and overall, quite easy. Who knew they were having internal problems? They were professional – they came in and did their jobs, so any band drama was certainly not on display. Given their record label, I did not expect much to happen. Shatter did not have the money or the means to get them an opening slot with a bigger band. I occasionally hear from a few of the members. It turns out this album has a small cult following. I am glad to see it is getting some appreciation. I just wish it would have sold better out of the gate for them.

**R.H. Boeckel;** *Ex-EXE, Bile:*
"*It amazes me people still write to me and ask about it. It was the early '80s when we started. So, as far as we're concerned, the album is over 40 years old for us. I'm 59 so if I was going to put that shit (spikes and make-*

up) on again, I'd look like somebody's fucking grandmother in fucking spikes. That isn't going to happen. But recording wise, everything that Carl and Alex did to help us get to that point was amazing. Carl worked with us for weeks beforehand, just tweaking things in the songs, and he really helped to make them better. He was definitely a great producer. He knows exactly what he is doing, and he was great with us.

"I believe it was David Karpen who owned Shatter Records. I think Carl actually was the only name that came up as far as producing us. I think David had some sort of connection to Carl - if I can remember that. Now, I had all of their (The Rods) stuff beforehand. Plus, I had seen them (The Rods) play at the Palladium in New York. So it was exciting for us. Well, we went upstate and there was a music store up there called Al Falso Music. We went up into the attic and that's where we practiced and worked with Carl. That's where he tweaked the songs. That music store had a huge history. There was all this equipment up there from David "Rock" Feinstein. Rainbow was storing their equipment at Al's. I was running around playing with Richie Blackmore's wah-wah pedals and Craig Gruber's keyboards – there was a lot of history up there. And it was all Carl. So, for two or three weeks, all we did was tweak the songs. And then we came back home. And then we went back up there after a short break. Carl took us in to do all the click tracks for the album. That took days and that sucked, having to play to a click track, because we never did that. But that's the way he did it. We took another break and then we came back again – to Pyramid Sound. And that's where we worked with Carl and Alex. And that was definitely an interesting recording process, because none of us had ever worked with a producer before. And just like I said, Carl knew exactly what he wanted.

"We had a lot of fun doing it because we got to hang out with Raven. Raven lived up there and Wacko was in the studio. I really love Raven. So that was the coolest part for me. I was a New Wave of British Heavy Metal fan. So, when I met them, I was like 'Holy shit! I am hanging out with Raven in their house, and I am recording an album with Carl!' That was fucking great to me. We hung out with Carl almost every night. He became a very good friend. He introduced us to a whole different world of how it would be in the studio. He was in control all the way. Carl gave us the best groundwork to work with - everything was there. He always made sure that everything was there, and he was all about multiple takes – we did it over and over and over and over until we got it right. He is a taskmaster and he definitely tortured us.

"As soon as the album was done, and it was getting ready to come out - that's when they decided to get rid of Jose (vocals) and Charlie (drums). Can you believe that? I understood getting rid of Charlie because he was not the type of drummer that we really wanted. Now getting rid of Jose's voice was a big mistake. Nobody tried to talk us out of it. And that was a bad thing for us. We definitely made mistakes. We did all of those interviews, and we had a number one indie album in the UK and ultimately, we shot ourselves in the foot. All of the good work that Carl did and all the good stuff that we tried to do - we definitely shot ourselves in the foot. You could tell that we were definitely not a unit by the time we finished recording that album. Everybody had their own distinct styles. Just like I said, Carl definitely made us a unit while we were recording and playing, but as far as the personalities go, I do not think anybody had a choice in that. Because it was usually Carl, Adam and me hanging out. Everybody else did their own thing. So, we did not tour or anything. We just went right into salvaging the band with a second album. I was already gone though. I was there for all the demos, I was there for the writing, and putting it together and everything like that. And they did not like the idea of me going off and doing other bands (which I wanted to do, because they did not want to tour, they did not want to do anything). I would not have quit on my own. They decided to go to New Jersey and record it on their own. If we had toured, I'm sure we would have done a lot more. We could have toured Europe. We wasted a perfectly good, well produced album. We did not do what we were meant to do. I will continue to do what I was meant to do (play metal). Carl is still putting out stuff and he looks exactly the same. He is still wearing the jeans and the fucking leather jacket and The Rods stuff - and good for him. I fucking hope he continues forever."

**Adam Marigiliano**: *E-X-E*:
"We would always play Lamour's East. It was close to where we lived, so we also hung out there. It was a cool situation we had there. We got to play there. We hung out there. And we knew everyone there. We were playing one night, and we had about 90 – 100 people there. We were just having fun with the show. We were goofing off with the audience and they were throwing stuff on stage. And we did not know that this record company guy was in the audience watching us. After the show, someone told us, 'There is this guy out there who wants to give you a record deal.' I was only 18 years old. And I'm like, 'Yeah, that sounds good.' Like, to me, it seemed perfectly normal. And looking back, it was fantastic. I was very happy. We more or less just went along with whatever David Carpin (of Shatter Records) said. And that was fine. At that age, my attitude was, 'Let's see what happens. Let's do this.' He set us up with a great house. A great studio, a producer and a engineer. It all seemed normal. This was when Ozzy came out with the Ultimate Sin album. And that's probably the best way of dating it because I remember that album had just come out. And the girl whose

house we were renting, she had it and I just remember playing that again and again because it was new at that time. We had a blast. And it really was a fantastic experience. Even if I had to make up something negative, I couldn't, because it really was so great. We did a lot of work. I think it was seven hours of rehearsal a day. Before Carl would even let us start to record, we had to do pre-production. All day. That's the kind of producer he is. He has a very hands-on approach. And I think for a young band with their first album coming out, you need little bit of expertise and Carl definitely helped us with that.

"Alex (Perialis) and Carl both play solos on the song 'Autopsy'. At the end of it. That's how much fun we were having. Chill dudes to hang out with. So, you know, there was a little bit of an age difference. And it never came out. Everybody was just hanging out. I'm like, how cool would it be to put the guy who is engineering the album and the producer on the song? In fact, you could tell which solos were from Alex, because he doesn't know how to play guitar. It was still salty, and I liked it. And when Carl did a solo, I remember him saying, 'Man, I missed that last note. Let me do it again.' I'm like, 'No, it sounds great Carl - leave it.' But he was so concerned with hitting the very last note on his solo.

"For the cover, someone knew of an artist. And he had wanted to do it, so we let him. When it came out, I kind of liked it. I also thought it might be a little hokey. But I think for that time period, it is perfect. Because it is strong. No mama's boys are going to pick up that album. And it is exactly that inside. I think we had some type of tour that the record company was planning along with the manager we had at that time. Honestly, I do not remember his name. He used to manage Al Green and the SOS band. But we had a nickname for him. We called him 'The Thumb' because he had this really weird thumb fingernail. So, I only remember him as The Thumb. But in any case, I think the record company had very limited resources. And that was part of the problem. And then we got rid of the drummer. He was not a bad drummer - for a Kiss style band he would have been great. But we needed something a little harder. We really were not his style of music. As far as the singer goes, getting rid of Jose is something I really regret. I think that he has a great voice and wrote some really great vocal lines - I love his lyrics. I think it came down to that we needed a little bit more time commitment. And we were not getting that from him. So maybe that was a mistake that we made as a band. But at that point, we were showing up to practice. And we would not have our singer a lot of the time. I really did not see any recourse at that point.

"But I am glad people still have an interest in the album. I am proud of both albums we released. We were getting a lot of different companies that were coming to us. They wanted to rerelease it. I did not really think the *time was right. I always thought that if we were going to rerelease it, we got to put something else on there. As a band, we never made a penny from anything off those albums. But I'm happy to see it out there. I see this company making E-X-E shirts, right? Never contacted us. I'm happy to let them get that out. It was cool to see E-X-E out there - 35 years later."*

## Apollo Ra: Ra Pariah

I nicknamed this "the album that will not die" as this album has been reissued a number of times. It has obtained a loyal cult following. Better late than never, I suppose. I am happy that it is finally getting some love, because initially, this project ran into plenty of bad luck. Coupled with bad timing, Apollo Ra was constantly teetering between breaking big or breaking up.

Apollo Ra was something that David Carpin came to me with. David had just started Shatter Records. David was a lawyer and had some very bad habits (mainly drugs), so what was to happen shouldn't have surprised me. Apollo Ra were a great power metal outfit out of Baltimore. Their music had a really cool progressive feel, and the band and their lyrical themes were centered around ancient Egypt and Egyptian mythology. I headed out to Baltimore to check them out. They were managed by Elena Rudolph, who I soon got to know, and we became fast friends. The band was very talented. While they were not a strong live act, they had some very solid material, and they were accomplished musicians for the most part. They were also doing something very different, which was going with a Egyptology theme. They certainly were unique. We started pre-production in Cortland to work the material out. We spent a lot of time tweaking and arranging the songs. The songs were great. As a band, they were really tight. But one of their guitarists was lacking. He just could not play the parts. He was actually one of the primary songwriters, but he would never have been able to record the needed tracks, so I had to have an uncomfortable conversation with the band and let them know that, with this particular guitarist, they would never make it to the major leagues. And he was such a great guy. I felt terrible about it. But at the end of the day, my job was to give them the best record possible, and being that we had a small budget, we did not have time to waste in the studio. The guys did not seem to vibe with him all that much, which made things a lot easier. That always seems to be the case: the weakest links usually have some animosity with the band. So they fired him.

By this time, I had my own studio in Utica, NY, and we were to record there. Unfortunately, since we had started pre-production, I had not heard a peep from David Carpin. He had totally disappeared. And he still owed me money from a previous project. That led me to open up a case against him. Shatter Records was done. It somehow had ceased to exist - and I was not kept up to date on the details. David had my money. He had a promising band very close to putting out a record. He had the financing for the band. And he was gone. Well, I never got my money. But, as part of the case, I was awarded the rights to Apollo Ra - which was great, but unfortunately, I did not have enough cash to finance a full album. These guys were ready to do an album. They needed to do one. So we agreed to do an album - a low budget album, or essentially a polished demo, something that we could shop around to the major labels. Just like that, my role began to change for this project. Now, without a record company, and with limited backing, we had to work to find these guys a better deal.

To finish the album, we needed a second guitarist who could knock out the parts, so I brought in Andrew "Duck" McDonald. As usual, he was the first one there and the last one to leave. He is a total pro. Duck and the other guitarist, Bill McKeown, were amazing together. They really pushed each other. Duck told me, "Bill gave me a run for my money." The vocalist, Danny Miller, had such a strong voice. The guys were a talented bunch, so I wanted to work hard and find them a rightful place in the major leagues. With the album complete, I was really happy with the finished product. It was not perfect, but for what we needed, and with no budget, we had a pretty good product. At this point, I had begun to take on more of a managerial role with them. Their manager Elena stepped back. While she was really nice, she had no clue how to get them to the next level. We did a video to add a visual element to the press kit. I had a lot of fun directing it. Now that we had a polished demo, a video, and a full press kit, we were ready to get them a deal.

Gary Dalaire was my partner at the time. Gary and I were not always on the same page. Gary had wanted them to showcase in New York City at the Cat Club. I felt that New York City was a terrible choice for a showcase. It has always been a tough spot, which I learned throughout the years attempting shows there with Kelakos and The Rods. But I conceded, and Apollo Ra were booked to showcase at the Cat Club. I believe it was on a Tuesday night – which is traditionally a terrible night to play. And of course, hardly anyone came. The band was off that night as well. For whatever reason, they were having a difficult show. Quite a few record industry executives showed up. I wish they had not, because overall, it was a disaster. With poor attendance and with the band's subpar performance, any interest that was on the table quickly disappeared. Nothing came of the showcase. The poor performance and attendance killed all offers on the table. If you do not have a strong live act, you will be hard pressed to get signed. Back then, bands made their money from album sales. To get album sales, you had to tour. Lots of gigs, if done right, often translate into strong album sales. But the band were not on their game. They were really struggling. Factor in a sparsely attended venue and it is hard to coax thousands and thousands of dollars out of a label. The only offer came from Metal Blade Records. However, they only wanted to offer $10,000 or so up front. Maybe I was being a bit overconfident, but I really thought we could get more. Ten grand was not much. I've always regretted not taking the Metal Blade deal. That would have been a perfect label for the band. I had financed the entirety of the album, so I was really looking for a home for it – and I wanted to recoup everything I had invested. That showcase killed Apollo Ra. It was not immediate, but it was clear that the end was within sight. The band slowly drifted apart. The music scene changed. And nothing ever happened with that album until decades later. Thanks to the internet, the band gained a massive cult following. There was also plenty of mystique behind this album. And it was a great album, so I am glad people are slowly discovering it. As a result, it has been reissued multiple times. People love it. It is a draw to this very day.

**Danny Miller:** *Apollo Ra, Museum of Fear*
*"I was listening to a lot of Black Sabbath, as were my friends. We were into Iron Maiden - all of that metal stuff was just starting to happen. I hung out with this girl and her brother (Steve Albinek) was a drummer for a local band called Child's Play. They were pretty big locally. I was playing in some pick-up bands. We really were not that close early on. We certainly did not talk that much. Then I got an opportunity when he had left Child's Play. He was starting a band and that gave me the opportunity to try out. It had some different people in the band, including Chris Murphy - who later came up with the name Apollo Ra. He was an Egyptology major, and he played guitar. We got together, played a few small shows, and ultimately went through different members. Nothing really clicked. We made a demo tape, which we bounced around for a little while. Eventually, we got a manager, Elaine Rudolph. She somehow got in touch with Carl, and we got to meet with him. Carl said, 'I think I'm interested in working with you guys. Let's go ahead and arrange a time. Let's get you up here and get you working.' We basically had that entire first record written. We were playing those songs live, and at this point the band was Todd Weaver, Steve Albinek, Bill McEwen, Chris Murphy and myself. We went up to Cortland and met with Carl and we started working on pre-production. We did pre-production at Al Falso Music in Cortland. If I remember correctly, we were using some of Richie Blackmore's cabinets! The guys from Manowar stopped by. Carl really put us through the ranks. We had never been tasked by a producer like that, so when Carl came in, he started looking at things like the meter of the songs and when the changes were taking place. He worked with us on some modifications to the compositions - things that he*

thought were going to make the songs a little stronger, a little better. I do not disagree. I think the way that it came out was pretty much as good as we could have gotten it for that collection of music. Not to mention, while in Cortland, we ended up letting go of Chris Murphy. We had a dilemma. We were getting ready to go record an album in Utica, New York, and now we needed a second guitar player. Carl knew Andrew Duck McDonald, who had played with Blue Cheer. Andy ended up playing on the album - he was the second guitar player on that record.

"We spent a month getting the record finished in Utica. One of the things that Carl did, which I thought was a great idea, is he would put the rough draft of the recording on cassette (at the time we mainly used cassettes), and then play it in a boombox, and then play it in the car, and finally play it in the studio. He would test it in various formats to make sure it translated well to each medium. Pat Kenyon, our engineer, was pretty incredible. He ran around, tabled everything, and worked with everything that Carl was trying to achieve. Once we got the record done, we went about the business of shopping for a label. We did a show opening up for Danzig. I believe it was one of the first shows they did as a signed band. We were getting a lot of great opening slots. We opened for Cycle Sluts from Hell, Overkill – lots of great bands. We started doing a lot of press and magazine interviews. A lot of the effort was geared to Europe as the response from Europe was very strong. But Carl was there the whole time lobbying on our behalf. Every one of these deals to rerelease the record has come through Carl negotiating. He has believed in us for a very long time. As for our first manager, I think the perception was that, ultimately, she was not going to be able to get us where we needed to go. She did a great job and lobbied for us while she was there. I just think we reached a point where we needed something a little bit more, and I think Carl took the reins to try and move that all forward. So, Ra Pariah was originally recorded as an album, but it was an album quality demo. The hope was that if we were able to get this finished (with little budget), then we wanted it to be in a condition that it could be remastered or remixed, and then rereleased as a professional album. If we had a little more money and a little more time, then we could have done some extra fine tuning on the overall recording. It was done as a sellable demo, which is why we did pre-production. As for Chris (the original guitarist), he had a different vision for Apollo Ra, and that's really where we parted ways. Now, Chris is a friend of mine. I do not really see him much, but I still talk to him from time to time. I'm glad he was there. We kind of grew to a point where something else was needed.

"By 1989, going on 1990, it was a perfect storm. Slowly we started to get frustrated - and that's eventually what took the band apart. Everybody was kind of going in different directions in life. The end came kind of quietly. I think at one point, I put a stake in the ground when we were officially done. Some of the guys did not want to do certain shows, because the night the show fell, or they had other things going on. But nobody walked away from playing. Bill still plays. I still play and I still sing. It is just that we never really reached any kind of fruition. And then time goes by, and we get released, and then we get released again, and then the boxset comes out. We even saw the boxset on eBay for $90 for a vinyl copy! Now that is pretty fascinating. It is really cool to hear that people are discovering it. They seem to be digging it! There is even an Apollo Ra cover band in Europe called Ra Pariah! I could not believe it when I heard it. That blew my mind."

# Dianne

I was 17 when my friend Ed Styles asked me to attend a mixer at Elmira College with him. At the time, I was still in high school. Ed had just started seeing an Elmira College student by the name of Dianne. "She is going to bring one of her friends for you," he insisted. Ed had met Dianne at a previous mixer, and things seemed to be going well for them. Dianne was beautiful, educated, and she seemed easygoing, so maybe there was something to these mixers after all? Keep in mind I was in my junior year of high school. And for a high school kid at the time, there was nothing cooler than to be able to date a college girl. So we crammed into Ed's Volkswagen Beetle and went to Elmira College. And this one worked out well. Dianne's friend was nice enough (and quite attractive), and we began to date. It never progressed into a serious relationship, but because of that connection, and because Ed was bringing her to the house constantly, I eventually became good friends with Dianne. Dianne was classy. She was smart, studying a double major of Psychology and Social Work. And she was very pretty. She became a great friend.

After a few months, Dianne and Ed split up. I do not recall who left who, but Dianne and I maintained our friendship. That friendship slowly progressed and before either of us knew it, we began dating. It was very organic. It evolved quite naturally and we kind of fell into it. Eventually we upgraded into sharing an apartment; not a small step, but I loved living with Dianne. Dianne was extremely understanding. It is not easy to date a young musician. We tend to be gone... a lot. We come home late. We keep erratic schedules and earn erratic paychecks; though during the early part of our relationship, I was mostly playing locally, so I was home most nights. However, once The Rods took off, "home" became a foreign word. We were on the road constantly. And I did not think that was fair to Dianne: Here she was maintaining a career and going home each afternoon - to an empty house. She was not one to complain, but I did not foresee things getting easier anytime soon. The Rods were very close to getting signed. It was not fair to have her wait for me, to have her put her life on hold while I was out on the road. And she did not think it fair to ask me to give up my dream and my goals - especially when we were so very close to making it. So, agreeably, we split up. It was far from your standard break up. It was peaceful. It was amicable. There was an intense amount of understanding between us, and we both agreed that we should maintain our friendship.

And that is exactly what we did. When my mother's health was failing and I was in England, it was Dianne who took care of Mom. My friend Greg helped out a lot also. That speaks volumes.

During the '80s, we both dated other people. But I think we both knew deep down that we would get back together. I certainly did not want to spend my life on the road. While the studio was much better than touring in terms of maintaining a home, it was still hectic. It still required long absences. I wanted to get married and have children one day. That was always a goal of mine. Dianne wanted that as well. Somewhere in the late '80s, Dianne had just got out of a relationship. It was a month or so later when I became single, after the demise of a short-lived relationship. Here we were - friends, both newly single and both at a point in our lives at which we were looking to start a family. I always thought that Dianne would make an amazing mother. She had all of the qualities one would look for in such a role. She felt the same way about me – that I would make a good father. We both wanted to have a baby, and that was really the impetus for the whole thing. Now that I was off the road, it was time to start a family. I did not want to be an absentee father, so the timing was perfect. I went to visit Dianne's mother to get her blessing, which she eagerly gave me. We did not have a grand plan, but we wanted to get pregnant as soon as possible. By this point we were both nearing 40, so we made this our priority. Of course, marriage was a part of this. That was always a part of this.

Dianne got pregnant. Mission accomplished. At this time, we were living in upstate New York, but we realized that Dianne's mother, Dorothy, who lived in rural Pennsylvania, was not doing well. Dorothy was showing early signs of dementia, so we agreed to move there and take care of her. This came at a time when the music scene was changing rapidly. I was getting less work production wise, and I presumed that The Rods were defunct, so I was not opposed to the move. Not that I was keen on living in such a small town, especially one located hours from a major recording studio, but with Dianne pregnant and her mother declining in health, we both thought it best. Plus, her mother's house was quite large. It was the very house Dianne grew up in, and it was a great area to raise a child. The school system was pretty good. So we made the move. For our wedding, we skipped any extravagant ceremony. We wanted something simple. We simply wanted something legal for the impending baby. We ended up getting married at Dianne's mother's house. It was only her mother, the justice of the peace, and Dianne and me. She was pregnant, so technically my daughter was there as well. It was perfect.

We knew something was wrong with Dorothy in Paris. I had such a good time at the Breaking Sound Festival in Paris in 1984 that I wanted to take Dianne and her mother there. Dianne did not think her mother would want to go, but Dorothy agreed without hesitation. We flew there and did the usual tourist thing: saw the sights, ate the food, and I got to see some old friends. But that was when we began to notice some cognitive issues with Dorothy. It was small things at first. Forgetting people. Not recognizing places. From there, it only got worse. Confusion and paranoia soon became commonplace. As mentioned, Dianne had taken care of my mother and I felt it was fair that I repay the favor. So once Dianne had our daughter, Erin, she resumed her career as a director of social work and went to work each day. I had a studio by that point (more on that later), but there was not a lot going on, so I took care of Erin and Dianne's mother when Dianne was at work. It was not easy. Newborns are a lot of work, but a person in late-stage dementia requires even more attention. There were some days when her mind seemed good, when she was smart and sharp. And then some were some when it was extremely difficult. Dementia brings paranoia, forgetfulness, and absent mindedness to the point of forgetting the most basic of habits. We had no family in the area, plus Dianne was an only child, so we were doing it alone. There were no siblings to share the load with. It was a rough road for two and a half years, but we got through it and were able to keep her home until the very end. That was important to us. Now I see the same issues with some of my friends' parents: there are certain patterns, certain things - they lash out at people close to them. It can be unpleasant because you take it personally. I've passed this advice on to many of my friends: do not take it personally. I hear it from other people, what they are going through - they're all identical, all of the symptoms. It is what happens when people start to lose control. It can be scary. And it must be terrifying for the people who are going through it. They become confused, they get scared, and they tend to get angry. I sympathize with anyone who had or has a loved one going through that. What is amazing is that her dementia never affected her maternal instincts. Even at her worst, she knew how to handle Erin. It was amazing. That part of her never left.

By the time Dorothy passed, we had been living in the house for three years. Dianne had a good job locally and I was getting adjusted to the area. Erin would be starting school in a couple of years, plus we had the house and wanted to keep it in the family, so we agreed to settle there. Initially, I kept my two rental properties in Cortland. I kept them for a year and a half or so, and then I sold them, because an absentee landlord doesn't work. My accountant warned me. I said, "I have the best tenants in the world. When I'm on the road and something happens – they handle it." They would call the plumber, the carpenter, whatever the case may be, if I was out of town; they took care of any issues that arose. I had the absolute best tenants. But of course, I had lived in the unit behind the tenants. Ultimately, he was right. Once I moved, it was mind blowing the numbers of issues that began to pop up. It was always stupid stuff like someone flushing a corn cob down the toilet. So after a year and a half of running back and forth, I sold the rental units. With the rental units gone, we did not have much of a reason to move back to Cortland. Carbondale was going to be our home for a long time.

I did not love the area at first. It was a very small town, and it was a very tight knit community. I really did not have any friends in the area. At first, the locals did not seem very friendly, but the postman, who seemed to be warming up to me, told me, "We are a small community with a deep history - chances are if they did not know your grandfather then they do not want to know you." And no one knew me as being from The Rods. I do not think any of the locals were metal fans. But one day I had to rent a car in Carbondale, and the lady at the counter asked me what I was doing in the area. I replied, "My wife is from here, as was her mother." She said, "You married a local girl, huh?" And that was all it took. From there the word spread and I was accepted into the community. So, I have been here since around 1990, and now I love it and I am happy to call it home. It is a great community and I have made many friends and acquaintances in the vicinity.

### Dianne Canedy: *Carl's Wife*

*"Carl and I met because I was dating a friend of his. And at that time, everybody kind of hung out together. So, we knew each other for a while before we started dating. I was very much into rock music. I had been all my life. I grew up in the 60s and had my own folk group at the time. I played piano and guitar. And that was a lot of fun. So, we are a very musical family. And his playing in bands constantly never bothered me. There were so many bands during the early years that I lost track. There were too many to count. But I had no doubt that he would make it. He was obviously extremely talented. And he was very, very dedicated. Now, my father died when I was very young and I had no siblings, so it was just my mother and me. Initially, she was not really thrilled with the idea of me dating a struggling musician. She did not like it one bit. But I stood my ground. And as time went on, and as she really got to know Carl, she fell in love with him. She would not have had it any other way! He had that effect on people. But Carl was always very good to her. Even at first when she really was not sure about him. And Carl did not drink, he did not or do drugs... he was not your typical rock guy. But I do not think my mom realized any of that at first. He was always very sensitive and very caring. And he was very dedicated. The thing that was more important to him than all the other stuff was just playing music and being able to play it well.*

*"Well, the lifestyle got tiring. It was fun initially. It was enjoyable for a brief period of time. At first, I went everywhere with them. I recall many times they had a gig in Buffalo or another place way up there, and we would*

be driving home at 2 AM in a terrible snowstorm. And I usually had classes the next day. I would catch sleep wherever and whenever I could. I've been known to sleep right in front of very loud amplifiers. It was definitely fun. But I had school and just could not be gone all the time like that. I will never forget when they got signed (to Arista). It was a big event. His mother was so happy. I am not sure about my mom though. But once they started putting out albums he was gone constantly. And we kept in touch during those years. Eventually, when he started producing, he was in Ithaca a lot. And then he bought a building and turned it into a recording studio. I have a lot of memories from that time. I remember Young Turk and St. James a lot. It was a good time. My mom experienced all of that as well. She knew all of the bands that would stop by. There was an apartment at the studio, so if he had to record, he would often take Erin with him. She had a lot of exposure to that side. My mom got used to it and she actually really enjoyed it."

**Greg Bubacz;** *Longtime Friend*
"My father died when I was 15, and like a lot of people at that age, I was not dealing with it properly. That came back to haunt me many years later and I started drinking pretty heavily. Long story short, at the time, I did not think I really had a problem, but Carl, Dianne, and some other people certainly thought I did. And I finally got to the point where I realized that it was a bigger problem than all the problems I was drinking to escape from. I think it was at the Golden Calf, if I am not mistaken, on Green Street and we were sitting in the car. I said, 'Carl, I've got to do something about this.' Then he said, 'If you're going to drink tonight, call me first.' Now, I do not know if he actually knew what he was doing psychologically, but it mentally set up some sort of challenge for me. I thought, I'm not calling him, that's ridiculous, so I'm not going to drink. And it worked. That led me to realize that you cannot do it by yourself – you need a support system. With that, I figured I should go to AA, but I was really nervous about going. I was terrified. And Carl told me that he would go with me. He did not have a problem and most of the guys there did not know that he did not have a problem, but he was there for me. I find this incredibly moving. He came, he hung out and got me through it, because I do not like crowds. I'm not a group type of person. I do not enjoy being in groups or talking in front of groups or any of that. So that's something he did. And then he hooked me up with his friend, who happened to have a connection with the Alcohol Abuse Council in Ithaca. That was his part in trying to help me get out of the mess I was in. That's the kind of friend he is.

"My association with Carl's mother got pretty close when she was sick. Because he was in England and I went to see her every day while he was on tour, she ended up calling me her surrogate son. And it was just so tragic *that she was going, we knew that it was near. But it happened so quickly. We could not get him on a plane fast enough to get back here. Both of his parents died when he was on a plane. But I want to tell you about the relationship with my mother that Carl had. Growing up, I had a lot of friends along the way and my mother's place was a great place to hang out. We had a lot of people hanging around there. But there was something about Carl. And she really loved the guy. When his mom died, my mom took it upon herself to have the dinner at her house for a bunch of people she did not even know. That's how much she saw Carl. She used to make a dish called kibbeh. It is a Lebanese dish. And Carl loved kibbeh. So, every time I would go to Carl's house, my mom would make a big tray of kibbeh especially for Carl. That was the kind of thing I will never forget. He loved her just as much back.*

"*I remember him telling me that he was selling his house in Cortland and moving to Pennsylvania. It is no secret that Dianne and he had known each other since he was in high school. They always were connected somehow. There was always a connection there, even if they were not physically in the same place or even if they were not really involved at that particular moment. But he said to me, 'I just told Dianne, I'm just a little concerned I'm moving down there and what if this doesn't work out?' And Dianne's reply was, 'Well, then at least you'll have a really good friend in Pennsylvania!' It kind of put his mind at ease. That took the pressure off. If it did not work, it was not going to be the end of the world. Now, I got married here. Meaning the house I live in now. Carl was with Dianne at this point, so of course they were invited. When the wedding was about to begin, everybody's here and everybody is waiting, and of course Carl is operating on Carl time - which is usually about half an hour behind everybody else. Even the Justice of Peace was here - and here we were waiting for Carl. I refused to start the ceremony without him. Well, then I hear my sister-in-law at the front door. She started shouting at someone. She was saying, 'Carl Canedy you get your ass in here right now!' Carl comes in, we have a good laugh, and then we start the ceremony.*

*He was late because he was trying to rent a camcorder (back then camcorders were expensive - it was more efficient to rent them). And he ended up having to go to a few stores to find one that was available. That turned out to be a good decision - we filmed the entire wedding. For the wedding, there was one thing that really broke my heart – and I think Carl was a bit hurt as well. So, when my older brother got married, I was his best man. For my wedding, I was going to ask Carl to be my best man. And my mother got ahold of me. She was a wonderful woman, do not get me wrong. I cannot say enough good about that woman, but she got a hold of me, and she said, 'Your brother is really hoping you are going to ask him.'*

*So, I did that for Mom. I always thought it would be Carl and so did he, so understandingly he was a bit upset. He said, 'I will probably never have a chance to be anybody else's best man.' I said, 'Carl, I know, but what am I going to do?' He understood it, but I know it really hurt him. He was really looking forward to it. So that's something I've always regretted having to do because he was my best man. I mean, there was no way around it. Now, the funny thing is, when they got married, they had a ceremony, but they did not have anybody there. But by then we were both doing our own thing. Back in the day when we were living in the same house, I was playing in a band, he was playing in a band and our paths crossed constantly. We were always together at one point - usually every day. In the last few years, it seems we've kind of gotten back to that."*

# Becoming Erin's Dad

For the majority of my youth, it was mostly just my mother and me. As a result, I was always worried about losing my mother, because then I would not have anybody in my life. And then she passed away. I was alone, and it was very hard. Sure, I had some great friends and some distant family – but there was no one with the security and warmth that only a parent could provide. I had a tough time with that. But once Erin was born and I held her for the first time, at that point everything became clear. At that instance, I saw my mother. I saw that whole circle of life thing and it was so emotional for me. In my daughter, I saw my mother. And it was a truly beautiful moment. That was the moment that I went from "Carl" to "Erin's dad", which was the best thing that ever happened to me. I always wanted to be a father. During the pregnancy, I went to every doctor's appointment. It is common nowadays for the male to be involved with every appointment, but back then it was not common. I made every single appointment. As Dianne's pregnancy progressed, I began gaining weight. I started getting heartburn. I had every symptom that Dianne had. I even asked the doctor, "What the hell is going on?" He laughed and told me it was something called "sympathy pains." I had never heard of that. So that was me. I was all in.

Once Erin was born things fell into place a little bit and we began getting the hang of it. But we were taking care of Dianne's mother, and so that ruled out having a second child. We had a healthy, beautiful girl, so we could not be happier. There was so much we did not know and there was so much we had to learn. All of the books in the world cannot prepare you for raising a baby the first time. Dianne, initially, knew a lot about children. She either read it from books or she just knew. Motherly instinct, I guess. She is much brighter than I am, so she had a handle on it, but there was a learning curve for sure. We took turns taking care of the baby, and I changed a lot of diapers over the years. We were new parents, and while it was challenging, there was nothing like it. It was a beautiful time. I was really focused on being a father. I devoted everything to that role. Once Erin started school, I became the homeroom dad. A homeroom dad is a parent who is assigned to assist in class events and is the go-between for the teachers and the parents. I was the only male in the bunch. But those were some of the best and most memorable years of my life. I was there for the entirety of her youth. I was not interested in touring or being away for long periods at the time. I did not want to miss a thing.

I think, early on, Dianne felt that I was too strict, but I did not agree with that. I was positive. Personally, I always tended to look for the good in a situation. Negativity can be mentally poisonous. And when it came to my daughter, of course I'd wanted her to approach life with a positive mindset. You learn a lot when you are a new parent. You make mistakes. It is not easy. There are a lot of books but never a manual on raising a child. And what works for one child might not work for another. So there was a lot we had to figure out as new parents. And children, no matter how perfect, will test your patience. It is easy to say things like "You are grounded until you are 16" and mean it at the time, but I found it was best to cool down and then re-approach it. Then I would say to Erin, "I overreacted. I am sorry. This is why I was upset." And then perhaps scale the punishment down a bit. Because I wanted her to understand that in this life, you are going to get angry. You are bound to get upset. And sometimes you need to step back and think. If I was wrong, which happened frequently, I would apologize to her and show her respect as a child. I would apologize that I overreacted, or I was wrong. Because instead of blowing it off, I thought it was important for her to see an adult reverse themselves and apologize and show them the respect they deserved as a human being.

I never hit my child. Not once. Erin was never punished that way. It was always time out. I did not let her walk over me either. I've seen many parents that are ruled by their 6-year-olds. They run in circles for their kids. When they're young, you control everything about their lives. And so, if something needed to be done, I would shut it down. I tried not to say "no" so much but instead to explain possible consequences and provide options. One was, "I can't stop you from swearing when you're not with me and I can't control your behavior when you're not with me. However, if you choose to swear or misbehave, it could make things very unpleasant. Maybe you have a friend you really like and you enjoy playing with them – when a parent hears you swearing or sees you conducting yourself poorly, they will remove their child from your life." I really tried to approach things with her so that she had a more complete understanding of what the consequences were, and where poor behavior can lead. I did not get to experience things other children did. I did not have older brothers or sisters, so I decided that I would try to run interference for Erin wherever I could. Once, Erin was invited to a birthday party at an indoor fun park. She had never been to one, and I wanted her to be familiar with it in advance of the party. She was young and had never been exposed to that, so I took her a few days before the party. They had slides and ball pits and things of that nature. She and I went into this big slide, and I remember being stuck in the tunnel, and consequently getting claustrophobic while dozens of little kids were going crazy around me. I was panicked about being stuck in this thing, but I did not want her to get scared. I wanted her to have a positive experience; so I toughed it out. But that's the kind of thing you need to do as a parent. Nobody explained things to me growing up, and so I did not want to be that kind of dad. I wanted to be able to explain things to her, give her a heads up, and most of all - let her enjoy her childhood.

Validating my parenting choices, when Erin was 16 or so, she said, "Dad, all of my friends are rebelling, but I do not have anything to rebel against." At that moment, I felt I had done a good job as a parent. But Erin was a smart kid and she learned quickly. Overall, Dianne and I pretty much parented on the same page. I thought Dianne was a great mother, a great role model, and I took my lead from her many times. But I was glad that I was able to bring some things to the table. I also have to say that Erin has been my hero forever, because at some point when she was a teenager, she would never speak in anger. I was always surprised at that. Even if she was hurt by something that would typically make somebody angry, she would be very calm. One day I asked her, "Erin, why do you never say anything in anger? How do you do that?" Because I can never take the anger back. And once I reach a certain point, and the angrier I get, the further my IQ drops. Erin told me she doesn't speak in anger because she can never take it back. And that blew me away. Because that's the truth. Certainly, none of us can take it back. Once it is out in the universe, it is out there. But the fact that as a teenager, maybe 15 or 16, she recognized that getting pissed was not a good way to go - that was remarkable to me. Because I do not have strengths to that degree. I aspire to be that level-headed and calm. I really do. And because of that, to this day, she is my hero. I do not know of anyone who really can pull that off.

From age six until she was in college, Erin participated in a local acting company. A gentleman named Alan Benson, who had some success on Broadway previously, was in charge of the group. Alan had done very well for himself over the years. He was a great guy, and we became close friends with him. Erin adored him. When Alan passed away, she sang at his funeral. They were very close. But anyway, Alan was gay. When I would see him, I would give him a big hug and he would give me a little peck on the lips, and I never thought anything of it. Anyway, one day – I believe she was 15 at the time, Erin asked Dianne and me, "How come you did not tell me Alan was gay?" (Obviously she had just found out.) And I said, "Because it doesn't matter." Just last year, I heard her telling her husband about that. She said that simple response was ultimately very powerful - she carried that with her ever since and said she will take that thought to her children one day. I had forgotten I said it. It certainly was not a novel concept. It was just who Dianne and I were as people. So those small words and actions - they matter. Kids remember stuff like that – the good and the bad.

# Neon City

By late 1988, it was clear that production work was going to be my bread and butter for the foreseeable future. That was perfectly fine with me. I loved producing. David was going full blast with his restaurant career. I was busy with producing. So, obviously, nothing was happening in the Rods camp. I still frequented David's restaurant, The Hollywood, and spoke with David every so often, but another Rods album was not mentioned nor discussed. I had done the Thrasher project and David was soon to release an album with his side project, A'La Rock. So we were both still playing, but it was more for fun. With The Rods in intermission, and the production side picking up, the next logical step was to get my own studio. Over the years I had gathered a lot of clients for Music America and Pyramid Sound. It made sense, financially and logistically, for me to have my own place and host clients - on my own terms. Initially, I found a space in Utica. It was a great location - the space had great potential, as well as living quarters upstairs. Essentially, I was to partner with another gentleman. Partnering helped to ease the pain of operating costs, making it a much more feasible purchase initially. The studio was named UCA. I wound up buying a Trident 80 series board. This particular Trident 80 series console was rumored to have been used by both Fleetwood Mac and Queen. I am not sure if there was any truth to that, but it was a great 32-channel board. We quickly got up and running, and the studio was immediately put to use. I recorded a lot of music there. Apollo Ra were the first. I recorded St. James, Young Turk, Broken Dolls, Violent Playground, and a host of others.

Once I moved to Carbondale with Dianne, Utica ceased to be to be a convenient location. With Dianne expecting, I did not want to be gone for extended periods, which would have been the case if I stayed in Utica, so I asked Dianne to keep an eye out in Carbondale for a property that could be converted to a studio. I told her what I needed and asked her to do some scouting for me. One day she called me and said, "I think I found a building that might work." It was a former dress factory, and it was very much run down. It also had been a bar at one point in time, so there was a wide-open section which had been the dance floor. There were also a few rooms upstairs which had been rental units. The layout was great. But it was old, and it was beat up. The floors were warped. It needed a lot of work. We bought it. The price was right, and we were able to renovate it to a certain degree so that it was livable for bands. It turned out to be a great studio once we got up and running. We named it Neon City. Thank God for my friend John Rekus, who did all of the renovations and handled all of the many repairs that were needed. There is no way I could have gotten Neon City up and running without him.

The main room at Neon City sounded huge. It allowed for a massive sound - very much like Music America. We recorded the second Young Turk album at Neon City. When we went to The Record Plant to mix it, the team there asked how big the room was. "The room sounds massive. It must be huge." When I told them the dimensions were 24'x18', they were stunned. They were impressed we could pull a sound that big from such a standard space. It was definitely interesting, and building a studio from the ground up was an educational experience. Especially since the property was in such rough shape initially; it required a lot more work to get it compliant than if I was building one from the ground up. I definitely learned a lot throughout the process. There were always issues popping up – all unexpected. There were times when the local CB guy was transmitting, and it would blast through the control room speakers. We had a lot of outboard gear. A lot of it was vintage gear. Seven or eight years later, when I had to sell it, we made money, as vintage gear was skyrocketing. Once digital recording came about, some dedicated rock bands began chasing vintage gear to get that earthy vintage sound. It was in high demand, so surprisingly it worked out well in the long run; although when I purchased it, I did not know that was on the horizon. I was just trying to get the best sound for the lowest investment. Overall, it was a great studio and the bands really seemed to love Neon City. Because of the lodging we had, bands could work in the studio until late at night and then crash in the rooms. They did not need to wait for a ride to the hotel.

In Memphis, when we were recording *Tired of Laughing* by Young Turk (more on that later) I met an intern by the name of Pat Kenyon. We were there for three months, so we got to know Pat very well. I really liked the guy, so when I got Neon City up and running, I invited Pat to come and work in Carbondale. Pat agreed and he stayed the entire time we had the studio. I really liked Pat. He became part of the family over the years. He was there to watch Erin grow up. Dianne, Erin and I really got attached to him. We had a lot of fun and we had a lot of laughs. In the end, he was a far better engineer than I was. He learned quickly and he was extremely skilled in his craft. It was a case of "the student becomes the teacher" and it was a case of me learning from him most of the time. We were a good team. He did great work. Everyone loved Pat. I think of all of the bands that came through the studio and they are all friends with Pat to this very day.

Some thought the studio was haunted. One guy refused to stay there. He insisted that doors kept opening and shutting by themselves. Which they did, but only because Neon City was an old building and it had been built on soft ground. It was close to the river, so the foundation was a bit lopsided, which caused occasional door openings. But we could not convince him.

Carbondale turned out to be a great location in the long run. Carbondale was not easy for newcomers, but we settled in, and eventually they embraced us, even the visiting bands. One day, one of the guys (I will abstain from identifying the band) brought a local woman back from the bar. She had slept with him, and an argument soon followed. I do not recall what they were arguing about, but he called her a "stupid cunt". Without missing a beat, the local gal gets in his face and says, "I am not stupid!" and then added "And don't ever call me the K-word!" When the rest of the band heard her say that, they burst out in hysterics. The "K-Word" became a running joke for many years. That woman's sister actually ended up working for me in the office. On her first day, I was showing her how to use the fax machine and I explained it to her, "If you put the sheet in the top, type in the number and hit transmit - it will go through the scanner and the other person will receive the message." She quickly said, "So if I put money in there and send it to my sister in Scranton, she will get the money?" It took everything in me to not burst out laughing. Every time I see a fax machine I smile.

Overall, I have so many great memories from Neon City. We had done so many renovations that I thought I would have the studio forever. But the scene changed. Technology had changed. A funeral parlor occupied the unit next to ours. Eventually, the owner wanted to expand, and he made me an offer on the property. It was a fantastic offer, which ultimately I could not refuse. The deal was too good to pass up. It was also the perfect time, because this was when everyone was switching to digital. Neon City was still analog, and it would have cost quite a bit to switch out the board and equipment. To upgrade, it would have been a $60,000 dollar investment. The deal took about six months to go through, and in that time, I was able to sell most of the equipment and gear. I sold Neon City when Erin was six, so I had it for about seven years. We had a good run. It was a relief in a way because it was eating up a lot of time. I was there almost every day. I raised Erin in that studio. But it was a no-brainer selling it rather than investing in a upgrade. The only regret was that I sold some vintage microphones. I had no clue that I would one day need them, recording at home. It never occurred to me that being able to get a studio-quality sound from home would be the future.

**Pat Kenyon;** *Engineer and Studio Manager for Neon City*
"I was doing my internship at Ardent Studios in Memphis, Tennessee. Carl was recording the first Young Turks album there. And since I was an intern there, I was there late at night doing all the grunt work – the stuff that none of the engineers or assistant engineers wanted to do. So, Carl and I started talking and we just hit it off. He is a personable guy, and I was young and hungry. So, I mentioned to him that my internship is ending soon. I was not sure what I was going to do, but I wanted to start putting the word out. Carl told me he had his own studio called Neon City, which was in a small town called Simpson. Which was right next to Carbondale - I had never heard of it. He gave me his contact information and told me to look him up. When my internship was up and I was back home, I looked him up. He was recording with St. James at the time. They were doing a demo, and he told me to come check out the studio. So, I went there and just kind of hung out. I did not do much, mainly just got to know Carl and the guys from St. James. We all hit it off. And then slowly but surely it turned into a full-time gig, and I literally lived in the studio. The nice thing about it was the studio had an apartment that was attached to it, and bands would come and stay in that apartment. Sometimes I would stay at the apartment, but a lot of times I just lived in the lounge. It was a great opportunity for me.

"Carl had all of the old vintage gear. It is funny when I look back at it now, because I went to school for recording at Full Sail Center for the Recording Arts, and they had all the latest and greatest gear of the time. When I got to Carl's studio, I did not realize the gold mine he was actually sitting on. If you look back at it today, he had all this vintage gear. Like a Trident Series 80 console. Which was what Tom Petty, Queen, Led Zeppelin and all of the other great bands recorded on. They were not recording on these new consoles. They use all this old vintage gear – of course it was new then. And I did not see it that way when I was there. I look back on it now and it is like, man, you were stupid. Because the sound, that vintage sound that it gives off is amazing. And that sound was captured on that Young Turk album (NE $2^{nd}$ Ave). Right? That vintage sound was very different than the Geffen album recorded at Ardent. I go back time to time, and I listen to both. They both have their place, but I like the NE 2nd Ave album for the sound. It has that vintage "big sound." Eventually the pendulum swung back. At the time, everything was going digital. Everything. That was the new craze. But what was lacking with digital was the colorization that everything brought, right? Transformers, tubes, all of these things brought this warmth. And depending on who you talk to as an engineer, warmth is a different thing. But it is colorization. It is a warm sound. As opposed to digital, which was what you put in is exactly what you get out. And by the way, do not record it too hot, because if you do, it is going to clip, and that can be ugly. Whereas in the analog world, if you push things really hard, you get this nice, distorted, warm, compressed sound, right? So, it is funny how things switch back. And now, depending on who you talk to, you have people in two different worlds. You have people recording with these digital audio workstations - everything's digitized. But now they have these plugins that are trying to get the analog sounds that we were getting in Carl's studio back in the day.

"I worked a lot of hours. My day would start at 8:00 AM. I worked in the office in the morning. Paying bills, trying to get local bands in the studio - any kind of business we could drum up. At 6 PM I would start recording bands. And then wake up and do it all over again. It was difficult to get local bands in. There were not a lot of bands in the area. I know there were some polka bands that came in - and that was not always the fun gig. I was a rock and roll guy, I had long hair, and there I was recording polka bands. And then you would get some bands in that truly thought they had talent, but they really didn't. Some we really struggled to complete. And you would try and help the band as much as you could, but you could only do so much.

"Now, I will say this because I've said it to Carl a hundred times: Carl was really hard to work for. And what I mean by hard to work for is he really sought perfection. Whether that was from an artist, somebody he was working with, or from me as an engineer - even in the office, he knew what he wanted. And you needed to get it for him. But that's what made him so great. It is funny because he even said to me, 'God, I was an asshole to you.' And I was like, 'Not at all. Dude, you knew what you wanted.' Was it hard? Was the message delivered a little rough sometimes and not sugar coated? Yeah, but I always knew where I stood. But he was quick to praise, too. So, if you did something well and he praised you for it, it felt even better. But I never saw him scream or turn red with spit flying out of his mouth. Nothing like that. Now, I have seen those types of producers, but Carl was not like that. But boy, he could say some cutting things to get somebody motivated. I do not know if he remembers this one or not, but one time we had a band in, and the guitar player spent every single day reading guitar magazines. He had all of the guitar magazines. He wanted to be in the magazines. I remember Carl telling him, 'You need to put in the work, and you need to practice. You really have to put in the work.' And that player, while he did not suck, he thought he was better than Carl thought he was, right? So, I remember at one point, this guy was trying to lay down a track and Carl was getting frustrated. It was probably like the 12th take trying to get this track right. And Carl just stood up and basically told him he sucked. Carl said, 'You need to go practice.' And he goes, 'No, no, I can get it.' Carl replies, 'No, you are sucking. Go practice your part.' And the guitar player once again said, 'No, no, no, I can get it.' So, Carl picked up the guitar magazine and threw it at him, and said, 'The only way you're going to get in that fucking magazine is if you cut a picture of your face off and paste it on the cover!' And let me tell you, that guitar player went home and the next day he had all of his parts down. So, he'll challenge you. And he did that with me. And he'd throw that gauntlet down, and either you just walk away from it and give up, or you step up to the challenge. He did not do that for you to stop. He did that to build. I look back on it now, and I understand why he did that stuff. He wanted me to be better.

"Was there any truth to the studio being haunted? I'd like to say yeah, I mean, there were some weird things that happened. There were definitely some weird things that happened that I can't dismiss easily. And I do not know if I really saw it or if it was just a lack of sleep kind of thing. But at one point, I was doing something at the board, and I could have sworn I saw an old guy walk through the studio - on the left of me. I turned to look and he was gone. But I could have sworn there was an old guy there – wearing a pair of old denim overalls. But again, that happened at probably 2:30 in the morning after a long day. Was it because I was tired or was it real? I do not know. I wrote it off as 'tired'. But there were plenty of band members that say they either saw something or heard something. The studio was right next to a funeral home, so who knows.

"In the mid-90s, I started thinking that one day I might want to have a family. I knew a lot of engineers that never got to see their kids. They were often on their fourth marriage or whatever. I was like, is this industry conducive to marriage? Is this conducive to a relationship? So, I began thinking about taking a break. I wanted to step back. I told Carl, 'Look, I can't do this to the state that I'm doing it anymore, so I'm going to stop. If you still want to do projects here and there, I'm happy to figure it all out.' And then he came back, and he said, 'I think I'm going to sell the studio.' I think at that time, the funeral parlor might have made him an offer on the building. But I remember him saying, 'I'm going to get rid of my gear. I want to do a closed bid auction. You run it.' And I said, okay. So basically, it was putting ads in magazines for this auction with a gear list, and then we'd get these sealed bids that would come in. He sold a lot of the gear. I remember people coming in to look at the console, which by the way, breaks my heart to this day. I wish I could have that console back. That thing was amazing. I think if he had held on to some of those microphones, like he had some old Neumann KM84s, U87s and some of the Neumann tube mics – so much great equipment."

# Young Turk

I had spent more than three months in Tampa working with Roxx Gang. While I was there, a young man by the name of Rhett Perez reached out to me seeking a meeting. I really wanted to spend some time at home, but Rhett was insistent. "Just give me a few minutes. It will be worth your while." He was only 18 or so but he was a real hustler. I had met Rhett at the 1988 New Music Conference that was being held in New York City. He approached me at the show, and we exchanged numbers. Rhett was the frontman for a Miami band called Young Turk. They had released a demo/EP called *Do You Know Where Your Daughters Are?* At the time, they were doing the typical glam party rock that was found everywhere. Rhett wanted me to do with Young Turk what I had done for Roxx Gang - to get them in shape and hopefully help them land a major label deal.

    I met Rhett at the Tampa airport, and we sat down to chat. It was not a long meeting - I probably was not there more than an hour, but I was really impressed with his sales pitch. For a kid not even old enough to buy alcohol, he had quite the delivery. Much like Roxx Gang, Young Turk showed promise, but they needed to work on a few things. They were great musicians. They were hungry, and they were willing to work hard. They had also written some decent songs but needed some finesse and some coaching. Aside from Rhett, there was Rick Diaz on drums, Monte Hess on guitar, and Billy McElvy on bass. I signed them to my management company. At this point in time, I had the studio in Utica, so I asked them to come up to Utica and we would start pre-production. The goal was to record a full-length album that we could shop to major labels.

    We set a date. A couple of weeks before they were scheduled to arrive, someone poked their head in the studio and said, "Young Turk are here. They are outside." We were not scheduled to meet until the following week. Not only were they early, they were also very drunk. The drummer, Rick Diaz, was vomiting in the bushes profusely. He eventually passed out outside - on the ground. I had no clue what to do with them. Another band was using the upstairs apartment. So I told them, "I am finishing up another project. Can you hang out a few days more? Do you guys have any money to get through a few days?" One of them replied, "No. We are broke, but our girlfriends have money. They got jobs stripping locally." They all showed up with their girlfriends. Well, I am not sure if they were "girlfriends"... but they were definitely strippers who were supporting the band. Even more interesting is that the girls had already found jobs in the area. They began moonlighting at some local clubs so that they could support the boys in the band while they were recording. Thank God for those ladies – those girls drove them everywhere. Fed them. Clothed them. If it were not for them, I do not think they could have made the journey. So that was my first impression of the guys. And they were Miami guys. Miami guys are a lot like Brooklyn guys. They're tough. They grew up in an environment that's aggressive. They learned to hustle. They were no-bullshit guys – they were very blunt and very straightforward. But anyway, there was something endearing about these guys.

Once we started recording, it evolved into a good session. I was really impressed, so it was agreed that I would produce and manage them. These guys definitely had potential. But they were not easy to handle, nor were they easy to manage. They were young and they were troublemakers. I definitely had my hands full. They always had beautiful women around them. Women of all ages were chasing after these guys. I constantly had to kick women out who were marginally of age. If I did not think they were close enough to eighteen, they were gone. And that was a constant battle because for some reason, Young Turk was charismatic with all ages – older ladies, young women, all walks of life. They were super lovable guys. They had a charisma that came naturally. Everyone who met them adored them. They were great with the elderly.

Billy had long blonde hair and a full sleeve tattoo, which at that time was not very common and considered pretty extreme tattoo wise. He was loud and energetic. But we'd be at a restaurant, and I'd look around and there'd be Billy sitting with an elderly couple, in deep conversation, telling stories and laughing. He would meet these old people and they would be absolutely enthralled with him. That was the joy of working with them. Everybody loved the guys in Young Turk - they were fun and had so much personality. They were just like magnets for women. One time I was in the studio mixing and they brought in a woman who was a dancer. And I'm trying to work, and they say, "Hey Carl, come feel these." I told them I was busy. I did not even look up because I was used to those guys trying to fuck with me. Plus, nothing really threw me off course. I was focused. I'd been in a band my whole life. There was nothing I hadn't seen. They nudged me again, telling me to feel this woman's breasts. And I'm trying my best to ignore them and focus on the board. So, she takes her breasts out - she had massive implants and they really trying to get me to look at them. "I'm busy. I'm working here." And they come back with "Carl, come on, come on, check these out. Feel them." I'm like, "I'm good. I felt boobs before guys." And that made them even crazier. They would not leave me alone until I felt them. So, I reach and over and touch them and tell the lady,

"Good. Nice. They [plastic surgeons] did great work." And her reply was one that I would never forget: "Well, I'm retaining water." Lady, I do not care if you're retaining water. I was working and trying to get the album mixed. I had to kick them out. Only a few days later, after a grueling session, I was working on the board when they called me upstairs. I then noticed that it was dark. Oddly dark. All of the upstairs lights were off. Strange indeed. So I walk up the stairs and as I reach the top of the stairs, someone flicks on the light - and there's an orgy going on. It must have been eight people, naked and writhing on every piece of available furniture. Those guys were nonstop. They were always into something, and I always had to be on my toes.

When it came time to record, they sent their girlfriends back to Florida. They would occasionally call them from the studio. One day Rick was in the control room speaking with his girl when he accidentally called her another girl's name. I think he was seeing a few women at that time, so of course it caught up with him. It did not go over well, and she exploded. Since it was in the control room, you could hear everything – you could hear her screaming on the other end of the phone. Rick had a solution. He said into the receiver, "I'm going to call you bitch, and I'm going to call her bitch, and I'm going to call the other one bitch. That way I will not get confused and will not have to hear your shit." And that was his solution. The band and I had heard all of this, so we were on the floor in hysterics. We were all cracking up. Plus, Rick has a really great accent. It made everything he said that much funnier. He is a very funny guy. And just an absolutely great guy. Though early on, he was out of control, and was constantly partying and drinking. They all were. They all played hard - perhaps more than any other band I worked with. But they worked extremely hard. They were serious about the music, and if you listen to all of their material, there was a massive musical evolution that took place. Initially, they were not the best musicians. But they quickly became pros. They worked hard at that. They were determined.

I insisted they add another guitarist, which they gladly did. I knew adding another player would add a different layer to their sound. The band decided on Michael Alexander. He was a great addition. He added a different component to their songwriting and overall sound. We did a full length demo, which was released as *Train to Nowhere*. This is what we sent to record labels and the A&R reps. *Train to Nowhere* is their heaviest offering, as subsequent albums are more melodic. What impressed me is that they wrote the majority of the material for *Train to Nowhere* in upstate New York - shortly after arriving here. They certainly were developing a knack for writing. *Train to Nowhere* was a huge improvement over their earlier demo. It is a good album, and it served its purpose, as you will see.

The guys were a handful at times, but they were total pros in the studio. They took it very seriously. They were easy to work with in the studio.

Outside of the studio was a different story. Susan Henderson from MCA was looking to sign the band, so she took us to dinner at a nice restaurant. We were trying to get MCA to raise their offer to $125,000, which, at the time, was a lot of money, It still is, but even more so in 1990. I had to give the guys 'the talk' about being on their best behavior and being gentlemen. So, they made it through the dinner with no problems. Susan and the guys decided that they were going to go to a club. When it came time to go, Susan asked Rick, "Are you going to come to the club with us?" Rick told us no, he would not be joining us. Susan said, "Well, it was nice meeting you, Rick." Rick replied, "Thank you. Now I'm going to go home and take a great big shit." What do you even say to that? I mean, it was so embarrassing. Thankfully, she just started laughing. We were all laughing because that's how Rick is. You can't help but love those guys, but God they were a handful.

Through the demo, I was able to get them some very strong interest with numerous major labels. We wound up doing a showcase in Miami, in a very small but charming club. This was their home turf, where they were very popular. We really needed a packed and enthusiastic crowd, so Miami made perfect sense. We could not have done this in LA or NY. Always showcase the band in their hometown if possible. Most every major player came out for this show. An hour before showtime, there was a line of people down the block waiting to get in the venue. This was shaping up to be a promising night. However, the opening band would not leave the stage. They knew there were some A&R reps in the audience and they thought if they kept playing that they might get their attention. I do not think it worked but it certainly pissed me off. We did not want to unplug them, but it was looking like that was the only option. I think someone actually threatened to do just that and they finally left the stage. A&R reps aren't known for spending great lengths of time at shows. They usually come late, watch a few songs and take off if nothing catches their interest, so the opening act doing this definitely pissed me off. But that aside, the showcase was a huge success.

Young Turk played an amazing set. They were formidable showmen and great at their craft. The audience went nuts. In the end, they were approached by a few different labels. They got multiple offers. Michael Alago, who was then an A&R rep for Geffen records, loved the band and wanted to sign them. They offered us a great deal. Ultimately, Young Turk went with Geffen and Michael became our A&R guy. He was fantastic. He made sure we had everything we needed. Michael was hands on, yet he was hands off. He knew what he wanted from the band, and he knew we could deliver it. We would send him recordings all the time, and we kept him up to date as we progressed. Michael, in the early '80s, when he was with Elektra Records, signed Metallica after their famous Roseland Ballroom show. And only a few days before he signed Metallica, he came to Rochester to watch The Rods. There was some interest in signing us and there was some discussion, but he ultimately signed Metallica. Which in hindsight, certainly seemed like the better move for all parties. Michael was a great A&R guy. It is clear why Michael has been a great A&R person to so many bands. He has the ear, he has the energy, and he has the talent.

Young Turk quickly went about writing material for their first album on Geffen Records. They were very prolific writers. There was no shortage of good material. Getting a major label deal is a huge deal, especially at that time, so they were all ecstatic, as was I. At this point, the scene had not changed much, just the typical changes that come with time. Grunge hadn't quite hit yet, though it was right around the corner. But nobody knew that. By this time, we had Neon City up and running, so we did pre-production there. They quickly ran through the chosen songs and spent a few weeks polishing them up. Thanks to Michael Alago, we were booked to record in Memphis at Ardent Studios. Ardent was a world class facility. Some big names have recorded there, such as ZZ Top, George Thorogood, Joe Walsh, Stevie Ray Vaughn, and many other greats, so I was really looking forward to the experience. We had a few months before the studio was ready, so Young Turk scheduled some dates throughout the States, the idea being that this mini tour would get them in shape for their upcoming session. It would give them a great chance to nail down the new material.

Now, I have a strict 'no underage girls' policy: I know the kind of trouble that could bring. But I was not on this leg. I was at home at the time as Dianne was very pregnant and I was helping her. So my partner, Gary, accompanied them. He was far more lenient than me. Well, I got a phone call from my local sheriff, who I was good friends with. It turned out that after a gig in Wisconsin, a female fan followed the band to their hotel room and slept with the majority of the band. Gary carded her, but it turned out that her ID was fake. She was underage. Only sixteen, and not eighteen like her ID had said. It also turned out that this girl had lied to her parents – she told her mother that she was staying the night at a friend's house. But somehow, the mother found out she was hours away, and hanging out with a young rock band. The day after, she was forced to come clean and that is when warrants were issued by Wisconsin authorities. It's no secret that this happens in the industry. Unfortunately, at the time it was far too common. But if the band was big time, someone would show up with a suitcase full of cash and make the thing disappear. I did not operate that way. They were in a tough place. They were getting to record their first major album, and a few of them had warrants out for their arrest.

Rick and I were in Memphis finishing up the drum tracks and he had a warrant out for his arrest. But Rick was determined to finish his drum tracks. We tried to hide him until we got the drum tracks done. One day, we were walking out of a restaurant, and he saw a helicopter hovering over. He said, "They found me!" He was joking, but we each had an uneasy laugh given the absurdity of the situation. We even sent him to Pennsylvania, and he stayed at Neon City for a while. He laid low until we got the album done, and then he turned himself in. Ultimately, everything was cleared up. But it was a very rough time. This was not done – the band would have to face this for the rest of their time together.

Ardent was great. It was a top-notch facility. John Fry, the owner, was really cool. I learned a lot from John. He had some interesting management techniques. One day he was walking around and just kind of looking and listening, not saying anything. For a guy who had his hands full, he sure did seem to do a lot of wandering. I asked him if he needed anything because he was just kind of hovering over us. Finally, he told me it was a Japanese management technique, which is to walk around your facility and absorb the details. You look, you listen, and you observe with an open mind. I always thought that was brilliant. You take things in, you observe, and then you learn how to make it better by adding, altering, or removing people, procedures, or processes. I loved working there because the vibe was so cool.

Pinnacle Management, a booking agent, took on Young Turk. Their rep's name was Susan, and she was the absolute sweetest person. She was very polite, a bit reserved, and she seemed a bit innocent. She was very professional. Susan came to Ardent to check in on us. She was sitting on the couch - it was maybe 10 AM - when Rick burst through the doors. He had been out all night and had his Ray-Bans on to cover up his bloodshot eyes. "You guys would not believe what I did last night," he said. Rick came in and sat down and put his arm around Susan. "Oh, dude, I've been out all night partying. I was with Jim Dandy [frontman for Black Oak Arkansas] the entire night!" Rick proceeded to tell us how he was out with Jim Dandy. They went bar hopping, got drunk, and did coke all night. They ended up meeting these two biker chicks who they took back to Jim's hotel.

At this point, Rick began to describe their escapades in detail - which included a dildo, anal sex, and a host of other depravities. Rick was really getting into this story, and it was getting more detailed by the minute. I am talking about minutia – just pure down-and-dirty details. Susan was turning red - I think it was the explicit description of anal sex that was a bit much for her - so I gave him the eyes - you know, the stare of death. I was hoping that he would notice that Susan was next to me. Well apparently, he had, and kept going into the nasty details, when he became distracted and jumped to a different subject. I asked sarcastically, "Rick, finish your story, what happened?" To which Rick replied, "Oh no, not in front of Susan. I cannot tell you that. She is a lady" and then he proceeded to scold me. We started laughing. With his voice (envision early Cheech from Cheech and Chong), it made it that much funnier. He had spent ten minutes talking about every sexual detail, only to refrain from the modest part of the story. Rick was an endless source of fun and comedy, some of it intentional, some not. But Susan took it in her stride because she loved Rick like we all did. You just could not get mad at him. He was so harmless and so sweet. Another memorable event is when we went to a strip club and of course Rick had no money, so he tipped the girls with a handful of change. Even the strippers thought it was funny. He is a riot. To this day, Rick and I are really close. I love him like a brother.

We wrapped up at Ardent and the album was sent off to be mixed at Kiva Studios. The album was to be titled *Tired of Laughing,* and it had some stellar tracks. Songs like "Death of a Salesman", "Disinauguration Day" and the title track were stand outs, but all twelve songs were absolutely fantastic. They used only two songs from the *Train to Nowhere* demo: "Love Me Like a Suicide" and "Biscayne Boogie". They were very skilled writers. As soon as the tapes were sent out to be mixed, we went to Miami to record a video for the song "Death of a Salesman". It was 1991 - a video, and more importantly, a video that received repeat airplay, was absolutely crucial to a newly signed band. A steady rotation on MTV translated to massive record sales. And that meant the difference between a club act, a theater act and a coliseum act. By this time, MTV was slowly peppering in non-musical programs, but the bulk of their material was still videos. It was still the video age. On the other hand, the issue with the girl was developing into what would be a court case, so perhaps this made Geffen wary of dropping a ton of money for a video. But with a minimal budget, the guys went to Little Havana and Little Haiti with a filmmaker friend and recorded their video. It was a very grass roots shoot - everything was done on handheld cameras. But it was edited fantastically and actually turned out to be a great video, far better than their big budget video that was to follow.

Right after we finished the video shoot, our A&R rep gave us some unfortunate news. "Geffen is merging with MCA," they relayed. Damn. This was bad news. Really bad news. I knew that this meant we would get shelved. New acts rarely ever make the cut. Plus, with the stink of their recent troubles still clinging to them, things did not look good. Usually, when the parent company trims the fat, one of the first things to go are the new, unproven and untested bands. Never mind that Geffen just dropped $280,000 to record their album. Or the thousands that they spent on the video. I eventually got the news – we were indeed getting dropped. It was confirmed. The album *Tired of Laughing* was complete, mixed, and only a couple of weeks away from getting printed. The guys had worked really hard – I felt really bad for them. But I was also confident that we could get another label to sign them. It was a fantastic album. *Tired of Laughing* was much more mature than the demo we did. It still holds up to this day. It is a shame it got shelved. I put out a press release, which Geffen actually corroborated, which said that we had asked out of the Geffen contract. That was nice of them to corroborate, but it was totally not true.

Getting another deal did not take long at all. Aaron Jacoves, the A&R rep for Virgin Records, quickly snatched Young Turk up. Virgin was great. They were very low-pressure. However, they did not want to use the tracks from the newly recorded *Tired of Laughing*. They wanted some new material, as the scene was changing rapidly by this point. Grunge had just hit and hair metal had flatlined. Even thrash seemed to take a beating. Strangely, it was a great time for rock and pop-rock bands that existed outside of the hair metal genre. Artists like the Black Crowes, Lenny Kravitz and The Wallflowers were massive at this time.

Aaron wanted us to go back to Ardent, but we talked Virgin into letting us record it at Neon City. And then we could mix it in Los Angeles. We would save a ton of money by recording at Neon City. We did pre-production in New Orleans. A couple of days into pre-production, we were in a local restaurant and we asked the server to take a group picture. There was a large group of us, so they had us assemble in the courtyard for the picture. But the server was taking forever to take the picture, and we began wondering what was taking him so long. Finally, the manager came out and said, "No picture. You guys exposed yourselves. You are out of here. If you do not leave, I am going to call the police." It turned out that when the server began to take our picture, Rhett whipped his dick out. None of us had a clue that Rhett had his dick out. The owner kicked us out and the only thing that saved him was the fact that it was Mardi Gras, and everything was a bit crazy. It was these small complications that worried me. It was tough to leave them because you never knew what could happen. Trouble seemed to follow them everywhere. But I was a new father and Erin was only nine months old at the time. I did not want to be away from her all the time, so I would spend a week with them and a week at home. The week I was not there really worried me, because there was no one to pull them out of stupid situations. They were always getting into hijinks. Per diems saved them also. I knew if I left them with a weekly per diem, we would be in big trouble because they would spend it all on hookers and blow, and subsequently have nothing left after two days. They had to get a daily per diem, it was the only way. For the weeks when I was gone, I would take the money and hide it throughout the house we were renting. For instance, I would hide one per diem in the frozen peas in the very back of the freezer. The second day it was wrapped around the batteries inside the flashlight - I would use a different hiding spot each time. What I would do is call them each morning and tell them where to look for the per diem. Of course, they always tried to find them in advance - but I was pretty clever at hiding the money. It took some creativity. Once, I dumped out a big box of nails, put the money in the bottom of the box and put every nail back in the box. It was the wild dogs theory: if you put all the food in the bowl, the dog is going to eat all the food at one time and probably throw up and have nothing to eat for the rest of the week. But it worked. The house was still standing when I returned.

BMG invited us to a party at the RCA studios. It was a huge industry party. We were able to go to this beautiful, historic recording room where they had made all of the Frank Sinatra albums. It was very cool. I was talking to a couple of the executives when I realized I did not know where the guys in Young Turk were. I excused myself and began looking for them. I immediately found two of them in a vacant office with a female record executive. They were huddled together, giggling and whispering. Her blouse was undone, and the lady was groping them as they were her. I yanked them away. Two down, three to go. I resumed my search and found Rick making out with someone's wife - that someone happened to be the guitar player of Raging Slab. Another day in the world of Young Turk.

From there, we went to Carbondale to begin recording. We booked John Agnello to engineer the album. John came up from NYC. John had had a lengthy career as a successful engineer. He worked with some big names and worked in some big-time studios. Neon City was limited. As I mentioned before: we had vintage equipment. It worked great, but John needed more, so we had to get a few things for him, and he did the best he could with it - and in the end he was able to get a pretty good sound. The band had some very strong material and overall the sessions were great. This album was to be far more melodic than their previous efforts. After a couple of years together, we were pretty well in sync. They were easy to work with. They knew of my expectations, and I knew of their strengths and weaknesses. Once the session was wrapped up, we went to LA to mix the album. Nico Bolan did the mix. He was extremely talented and was a great guy. The boys and I had a great time in LA. While there, Katherine Turman (who then wrote for *Rip* magazine) interviewed the band and ended up hanging out with us for the remainder of our time there. We fell in love with Katherine and had a blast hanging out with her.

The mix came out great. The finished album, titled *NE $2^{nd}$ Ave*, is absolutely fantastic. It still holds up. I am very proud of it. After the album was recorded, they made a big-budget video for "The Saddest Song". Virgin dumped a ton of money into this video. This was the tail end of the MTV generation, and a video was part of the package. You had to have one. They paired Young Turk with a director who was pompous and egotistical. He was not interested in hearing any input from the band. The band absolutely hated his ideas. This was a disaster from the start. Rhett hated the director and wanted to kick his ass. Rhett came very close to punching the director multiple times. I had to separate them and run interference. Rhett was not one to shy away from punching someone. If I was not there, he absolutely would have. But somehow, they finished the video - you might even be able to find it on YouTube. They were right - it's not a very good video. It definitely did not help them, and it did not serve its purpose. Their first video was much better.

    Young Turk was famous for the amount of trouble they could find. I had a soda and candy machine in the studio and damned if there were not a couple of them who would continually break into the machines and steal the candy and soda. I ended up having to lock the lounge. Another time, I had just put fresh carpet in the control room. The next day I went in and saw Mike (the guitar player from Young Turk) talking to his girlfriend and putting his cigarette out on the new carpet. I was furious. I was probably most surprised when the local police chief brought them back to the studio late at night in a squad car. I thought, "Boy, they must have really done it now." But it turned out they were telling the chief about the studio, and he wanted to check it out for himself. He was an ardent musician. Having his support really helped us out.

    While Young Turk were preparing for their tour to support *NE 2$^{nd}$ Ave*, I flew to Miami to meet them. In the budget, I was able to include a tour bus. But I did not tell them about it. I wanted it to be a surprise. I arranged for the tour bus to show up at their rehearsal hall shortly after I had arrived. When they saw the bus, they were ecstatic. They were stoked because with earlier tours, they only had a cramped van. Not only did I get them a bus, I also hired an old boxer named Aguilar as their bodyguard. Not that they needed a bodyguard - they did not - but that was his official title, and his true role was to keep them out of trouble. He was incredibly tall, well over 6'4". He was an obvious heavyweight fighter, and he had a shaved head. He was badass. The boys had to listen to him, because if not, he could easily pick up two of them at the same time. It worked.

    In one aspect they were very lucky - to get signed by a major label twice. But on the other hand, they were not lucky. Because they did not take off. They most certainly had the talent. They had two really fantastic albums. They had the look. They had the attitude, but sometimes this business is all about luck. About being in the right place at the right time and in the right moment. They received some minor airplay, but nothing really stuck.

Nothing really happened with the album. It was a strange time musically. This was at the start of rap rock and nu-metal. Grunge peaked by this point. MTV began shifting away from videos. And they really did not fit into a particular category. They could have kept going. They could have weathered the storm and held out. But by this time, everyone was burnt out. Including myself. They had been at it for almost eight years. Erin was young, and personally, I felt like I was missing out on her childhood. They all stuck it out for a few more months but eventually, it fizzled out. I released them from their management contract. Everyone went their separate ways rather quietly and that was the end of Young Turk. But God, what a talented band. Those were some great years and great memories.

### Rick Diaz; *Young Turk*

*"I remember the first day I saw Carl behind the drums. Holy moly. I was very intimidated. I was a punk. I did not know anything. I did not even know what a click track was or anything of that sort. I did not how a proper recording was done - or even how drums were properly played. And Carl got behind that kit and he just went crazy. Everybody in the band sat there and basically said the same thing. They were in awe when they saw him play. Carl is one of those guys that plays really hard, and that's one of the things I like about him. Anyhow, I was 16 when I met Rhett, who was the singer. We started the band. He wanted to name it Young Turk. I actually never was very fond of the name, but he was very into Rod Stewart and things like that. And I think he actually named it because Young Turk means a bunch of young barbarians that went from town to town, pillaging and all that stuff. During that time, the glam thing was really happening. So, we started the band and then we made a little demo - when we were still in high school. We made an EP called 'Do You Know Where Your Daughters Are?' Rhett went to a music convention up in New York and there he met Carl, and he gave Carl the EP. And then Carl sent his assistant manager Gary who came and checked out the band. He liked the band, long story short. And then Carl decided that he wanted to manage the band and do something with the band and do a demo.*

*"We ended up going to Utica - we went a month prior to the actual date that we had with him to record, because that's how excited we were. So, we ended up being in Peekskill for a month. And actually, before that, I had a bit of an accident. I broke up a fight. So, my right hand and my left knee were pretty messed up. I have two screws in my knee, and my right hand was pretty mangled. But when I finally met Carl, I was not up to par because of the breaks and because of all the things that happened. And on top of it, I was younger, I was a punk, and I drank a lot and smoked a lot of weed and all that stuff. So, I was not as professional as Carl was at my age. The*

first time I met Carl, I got wasted at a bar that was across from Carl's studio in Utica, New York. And the first thing I did was puke in front of Carl. What did he do? Nothing. He looked at me like any normal human being would do. 'Look at this guy puking in front of me. What's wrong with him?' That was the first impression I gave him. Carl was telling Gary, 'Why the hell did you bring these guys up here? These guys are crazy.' We were a bit out of hand. We really drank a lot of beer. Carl was like, 'You guys are here to record, not party.' He really extracted what was most likely not able to be extracted, given the lack of musicianship that we had. Young Turk, in the beginning, did not lack songwriting ability, but we did lack that musicianship that was needed. Carl helped me a lot with drums and how to play with the click track and all of that stuff. So that first demo we did, he really extracted stuff from all of us that whatever we did not know we had.

"With that demo, he was able to get all kinds of people to come and see the band. Obviously, the band was rehearsing a lot more. There was more discipline. Carl really worked his ass off to get Young Turk a bunch of things. The first thing was a BMG publishing deal, which was a pretty decent one. With that money, we used it to bring in people from record companies from all over the place. We had all these people coming over and checking out the band. And it is funny because locally (Miami) we were not a big draw. We were the underdogs of the Miami scene. And slowly but surely when rumors started going out that we were showcasing, our crowds became bigger and bigger and bigger. So, by the time all these record companies were coming by, people were standing in line to check us out - they wanted to see why the record companies were so interested. We got a record contract. Michael Alago, who signed Metallica, was working at Geffen Records. He was a friend of Carl's and Carl got him to see the band - he fell in love with the band. He fell in love with a song called 'Love Me Like Suicide' and he signed the band to Geffen Records. Then we went on the road and that's when some shit hit the fan - which I'm sure you heard about. There was an instance where I was 20, some of the guys were 19 and this girl was like 16. She was backstage and she followed us to the hotel room and the band got in trouble because of that. The album that we recorded for Geffen was called Tired of Laughing. But we all decided that it is better just to go find another label. And the reason that happened was because Aaron Jacoves loved the band (A&R for Virgin Records). He decided to sign the band and the band did a whole new album in a completely new style.

"The Tired of Laughing album was more of a Guns N Roses type thing. Very hard. It was recorded in Memphis at Ardent Studios - where Zeppelin did Zeppelin 3. It was a great experience recording at Ardent Studios. And it was also a scary experience because it was during the time that the band was going through that whole thing and some of us were hiding out. I was doing my drum tracks going, 'Please do not let the cops come until I'm done with my drum tracks.' They could take me away, just let me finish my drum tracks. For the Virgin Deal, we began writing for NE $2^{nd}$ Ave. Which was more of a Rolling Stones, Faces or early Rod Stewart kind of thing. We recorded that at Carl's studio, which was cool. I always love the drum sound I got there. Then we did the mastering and engineering at the Record Plant in LA. And that was a lot of fun. We were in LA for a couple of months.

"As far as recording process and going on the road, all that stuff, it is expensive. All of that stuff is expensive. So, we did the album, and the album came out, and it did not do that good. And that's the story of Young Turk. Even after that, Carl tried. There was a lineup change. There were a couple of new guys we got, and Carl worked really hard to get us another deal, but we were a two-time band, and it never went anywhere. It had nothing to do with Carl or anything. It was like the old saying: you have to be in the right place at the right time at the right moment - all of that crap. Overall, it was great, and it was a fun experience. Carl is one of my great friends, and I love him to death. Years later, I brought another band to him called The Preachers. Unfortunately, these guys were a bunch of delinquents. When they stayed at Carl's studio, they stole a bunch of shit from Carl. After that, Carl never wanted to do anything with them. They stole stupid shit. Like, Carl had a Tony Iommi guitar pick - they stole that and some microphones. I was so embarrassed. And luckily, my wife and I stayed at Carl's house. So, I had nothing to do with any of that. Did they think he would not notice? Listen, in Young Turk, we did a lot of stuff that was very stupid, but that was the absolute stupidest thing to do. I mean, this was stealing the bread out of the hand that feeds you. It was ridiculous, man. That was one thing - Carl always helped me out. He helped me out on the last thing that I did, which was a few years ago, which was like a progressive rock type thing.

"So Young Turk was not an easy band to manage. Poor Carl had to read psychology books on how to deal with difficult people and all of that stuff. I think about it now that I'm older, and I think about all the things that should not have been. We should have been more professional. We should have partied less. We should have listened more to him. That's the bottom line. And we did not because we thought we knew it all. It is what it is, my friend. But again, I'm glad that I experienced it, and I'm glad that I was able to meet a great friend that's still a great friend of mine. We did a lot of gigs locally and we played a lot of festivals and things like that, but we never got to go to Europe or Canada or Mexico or overseas. We got to see a lot of the United States though. And we had a tour bus and the whole nine yards. That was another thing that Carl was able to do for us. He got us a really nice tour bus at a decent price. That was cool. We were able to tour, and it felt like we made it – but we really didn't. Now, we had a manager before Carl. It was during the first version of Young Turk. When Rhett and I were like 16. We were like the Muppet Babies. Rhett was so skinny. When he put on Spandex, they were baggy on him. The manager's name was Mr. Jefferson. 'You boys are stars'- that's how he talked. 'You is a star,' he would tell us. I used to do a drum solo and he used to love it.

"Mike was a big thing for the band. Michael Alexander joined the band after we met Carl. Carl said, 'You guys suck so much that you need another guitar player.' So, basically, he said, 'You guys can't do the four-piece thing, so you need another guitar player.' Mike was older than us. I would say almost ten years older than us. We were like 19 or whatever. And this guy was already 26 or something, maybe even older than that. Maybe 30. I'm not even sure. But he was older than us. But he wailed. He played guitar like Eric Clapton, Hendrix - super bluesy, super good. Carl also told me, 'If you do not get the hang of the click track, I am going to play on the demo.' And I told him, 'There's no way in hell you're playing on this. There's no way.' That pushed me to learn quickly.

"Monty, our guitar player, was a metal guitar player. He played all the Eddie Van Halen shit - all that stuff. Which is cool. I like it. But Michael (second guitarist) was a bluesy, freaking monster of a guitar player. I put him up there in the caliber of how Carl was as a musician. As good as Carl, maybe just the same caliber as guys like Richie Blackmore. If you ever hear NE 2$^{nd}$ Ave, or the Tired of Laughing album from Young Turk, listen to the guitars and you'll hear it. To make a long story short, we got him. He joined the band. And that changed the band completely. Completely. We went from a Motley Crue type thing to more of a bluesy Rolling Stone / Zeppelin thing that I really liked. So, Michael Alexander really changed the sound of the band a lot. There was another guy that changed the sound of the band a lot. His name was Eddie Oliva (brought in after Monty left). Eddie Oliva was a very young guy. He played on NE 2$^{nd}$ Ave. Great songwriter. Very influenced by the Stones, by that type of vibe. Rhett was writing songs with him a lot. So, the two guitar players after Monty really changed the sound of the band. And then finally we had Jeff Taylor, who was from Roxx Gang. I'm proud of the stuff what I did on Tired of Laughing and NE 2$^{nd}$ Ave. But that first demo that I did was not up to par as far as the drumming is concerned. But again, it got us the record deal, so it must have been something."

**Pat Kenyon;** *Engineer and Studio Manager for Neon City*
"There was another intern at Ardent Studios. She spent a lot of time hanging out with Young Turk. The band nicknamed her McNugget because

she was so small. She was probably 4'11". Real short. I know for a fact that she was fooling around with one or two of the band members. I remember they never really took her real seriously. And I remember her coming to Carl and asking, 'What advice do you have for me in the music business? How can I progress my career in the music business?' I remember Carl's words of advice to her very well, which was, 'If you want to be taken seriously, do not fool around with the band.' I think it kind of ended there.

"Near the studio was a strip joint called Super Dads. All the bands would go there. And I remember at one point, Young Turk took one of the rough mixes from NE $2^{nd}$ Ave and they had the strippers dancing to it. It was a very rough mix. They brought the cassette in and they handed it to the guy and they were like, 'We're a band and we're recording our album at the studio. Would you play this?' And they were like, 'Absolutely!' Of course, the strippers would wind up going home with the band or going back to the studio with the band – quite frequently. So, there were many parties that would happen. And I can remember one night, it was late. I will not say late, not for rock and roll, right? But it was about 11:00 PM and I was finishing up, just zeroing out the console, cleaning up, doing everything, like charting - doing the last little things. Rhett comes over, hands me a beer and he sits down and says, 'Hey we're having a bit of a party. You want to come over and hang out?' I finished up and headed over to the apartment that was attached to the studio. I walk in. Now, there were other bands and friends that would come up and hang out. Especially on weekends, right? I walk over and there are probably six naked women walking around. I know one of the band members (from another band) was there, no pants, just walking around with just his shirt on. No pants. I'm just like, 'What the hell is going on?' One of the girls, probably from the strip club, is all tatted up. She comes over and she bends over in front of me, and she is like, 'Do you like my new tattoo?' They always had women around them. With Young Turk, they would go out and were always getting into something - women, parties, trouble. They'd find all of these parties. They had long hair. They were bad boys. And girls surrounded the band members all the time, and the local guys did not like it. When it came time to record and do their work, they were good. But they knew how to party. There's no doubt about it. But those guys were so bad with money. When they were with us in the studio in Simpson, I was tasked with giving them their per diems every day. I could not give them the weekly per diem because they would spend it all in a day. Every day I had to dole out per diems and have them sign that they received it because it was cash. So, it was like, 'Okay, Billy, here's your per diem. Sign that you got it.' We would track it to make sure everybody got their money. I do not know how they would have survived without Carl, because they would have had nothing.

*"Aaron Jacoves was the A&R rep for Virgin Records. He came out a few times to the studio and really loved what was happening with the band. Virgin Records were pretty excited about the band. And then my understanding is Lenny Kravitz had his new album coming out, and Virgin sucked all of the wind out of Young Turk. Everything went over to Lenny Kravitz. So, the push that they were looking to do for Young Turk did not necessarily happen. It (NE 2$^{nd}$ Ave) did get some radio play. I remember hearing it on a couple of radio stations. But it did not really take off. There was no real push for it. And I think it just fizzled out. After that, I think there were some band member changes. And then they tried to do a few more demos, they tried to get signed, but it just fizzled - it just did not take off. And then it was the slow fade."*

**Rhett Perez;** *Young Turk, The 405's*
*"We came from the same school as bands like Nuclear Valdez, The Mavericks. Saigon Kick came out of here (Miami). It was an interesting time. We were a lot rougher than those bands and a lot less polished. We had some pretty good musicians. The music was just a lot less polished. That's what made it great. It is funny - we used to call Carl an old man. He was like 36 at the time. Now I look at look back, I'm 54 – fuck, I was a punk. I was 16 years old (when Young Turk started). We had made a horrible record called 'Do You Know Where Your Daughters Are?' And then all of a sudden, I found out about an event called the New Music Seminar in New York. I told my parents, 'Listen, I'm going to go to New York City to get the band signed.' My old man was kind enough to give me his American Express card – this was before there was even a strip on the back of it. Those were still the days that you ran it. And I took off by myself with 100 LP sized EPs. Those fucking two boxes weighed more than I did. I think I was 120 pounds soaking wet. So, I took off to New York City by myself with about $800. I met Carl there. I remember that moment well. I met Carl going down the escalator – he was there for the conference. And basically, I gave Carl an album, told him where we were from and whatever, and that was it. I gave him the album there, I believe. I think Carl was working with a band called Roxx Gang from Tampa that had gotten signed to Virgin Records. I met him the second time - he flew down just for a layover, down to Miami to meet me. I met him at the airport and that was about it. From that point on, I think they sent us a production deal and a management contract, and we signed up. From that point in time, we headed up to Utica to record. The management company was based out of Cortland. So, we decided to go to Cortland first. What we did not realize is that outside of Bear Mountain, there's another place called Cortland with a T at the end of it. It's spelled exactly like Cortland, but with a T: Cortlandt. Yep, we*

*ended up in the wrong fucking town. So, we rented a cabin there. And we were broke. We did not have a nickel between us. We had to get our girlfriends to come up and strip to hold us over. That's where we started writing songs for what became 'Train to Nowhere.' Earlier in the year, we had met some girls that had come down to Miami. They came to one of our shows and they lived up in New York. That's how we got to the cabin. At that point, 30 days felt like six months, too, because we had literally no money. We're living day to day in these crappy hotels that you rent by the hour. We stayed in a lot of shitty hotels.*

"*One of the great things that Carl did was he was able to garner a lot of interest for us. We had A&M records, Geffen, MCA, BMG music - all were interested. We kind of had a nice little buzz going. It was probably, I'd say, six months after our demo. We did several showcases, and A&M actually came to the plate first. Then all of a sudden, BMG had come down and MCA had come down. And then a gentleman by the name of Michael Alago, who signed Metallica, came down. He had much more flexibility because he had come from signing Metallica. He was basically at his first peak. One thing I could say about Michael Alago is he is out of his fucking mind completely. But the guy moved quickly, and he signed us. He saw the show and we had a deal in like three weeks. It was funny because when he came in, we were on stage. I remember vividly, Steve Stevens was at our show, Nico McBrain from Iron Maiden was there. It is a really small club, but we had like 200 people packed in there. And we saw a bunch of little helium balloons working their way through the crowd. And all of a sudden, the helium balloons worked their way to the front of the stage. That was Michael. I think a lot of our contemporaries down here in Miami never thought we had the talent. There was one guy from another band that actually started crying when we got signed. We basically just went balls out. We wrote songs that, for all intents and purposes, I think were all right. But through a lot of hard work and perseverance, I think we became better musicians between 'Train to Nowhere' and 'Tired of Laughing.' But that record was shelved. Some folks said that it was because we're in the same kind of genre space as Guns N Roses, and Guns N Roses were the kings of the mountain at the time. And then we were released, and eventually we ended up with Virgin, which to me, quite frankly, was probably the best record that Young Turk did as a whole. I think that's one of the things that Carl liked about the band - that we painted a lot of vivid imagery in the lyrics that detailed where we were at that time. And I forgot the name of the guy that engineered the record (NE $2^{nd}$ Ave). He was going through the middle of a divorce and needed a gig. I think the biggest artist that he had done was Dinosaur Jr. So, we were able to get him to mix, but he was just* a mess. A great guy and really good engineer. But again, he was going through a divorce.

"We had some very beautiful women in Carbondale that would come by and visit us. It was nice because being from Miami, we really hadn't traveled much. So, for us, being up in the mountains, seeing snow - for us it was fun. It was an adventure. We knew we were just stopping there for a little while and eventually moving on. For us, we were pretty popular there (Carbondale). For NE $2^{nd}$ Ave. we started from scratch. I do not know if we just wanted to start over or if we just loved writing. We were always writing when we were not on the road or not on stage. We had a pretty rigid rehearsal schedule. We rehearsed Monday through Friday. We were a crappy band with a really good attitude - until Mike joined the band. Rick had a really bad timing problem when we started the band. And Carl really helped him become a really good drummer. I mean, Rick was probably one of the best that I've ever worked with. And then Billy - he influenced so many bass players in Miami - everybody wanted to play like Billy because Billy did not play bass like a traditional bass player. We had very open spaces in our songs, which allowed Billy to almost tell a story with his bass playing. So, if you really look at it, it was almost like we had a lead bass in the songs. And Billy and Rick worked relentlessly. The only thing I think they worked harder at was partying and getting laid - but they became a really incredible rhythm section. We did something like 28 shows in 33 days for that tour. I ended up serving 90 days in county jail. So right when the record could have taken off, I ended up having to go to jail. And that pretty much just killed the album right there. You can get away with the bass player or drummer or guitar player not present but when it comes to the singer, the singer has to be there. Always.

"I think the industry had transitioned right when we had come out and all the Seattle music was starting to come out and we really did not have a place because we were not like the glam metal bands, and we were not really in the direction of the Seattle sound. I think the name had kind of become stagnant as I remember Carl coming back to me and basically saying, 'Look, I think we need to change the name of the band. I think we need to do something to freshen this thing up.' I was kind of burnt out. Young Turk was my first band. I started this when I was 15. After everything, at 22 or 23 years of age - all of those years were dog years. Between the drugs and drinking and fucking, partying and writing. We had enough material for another album - brand new material, but it was just tiring. I was tired. I think Rick and Billy wanted to keep going and they might have been right, but I was just burnt to shit, quite frankly. And then I met the woman who would become my wife. I've been with her for like 30 years, and now I have an eighteen-year-old daughter and I have a ten-year-old boy. And when you start looking at life and think about it, you think about how many things could have happened in your life. Would you trade it for anything else? Not a chance. So, with me, everything happened at the right time. We're all imperfect individuals, but I think in a lot of ways, the way we were as kids, Carl actually took a bunch of street kids and actually turned us into men. Not that our fathers didn't, but Carl was very much like a big brother. There is a certain work ethic that I still carry with me to this day and Carl was a major reason for that. I think everybody would admit that Carl made us the musicians that we ended up being and the men that we grew up into being. Now as for a reunion? We are all in our fifties at this point. And again, never say never. But the bottom line is I do not know who we'd be doing it for. Probably just for us. But it may be fun. Some of the guys I haven't seen in decades at this point."

### Michael Alexander; Young Turk

"I was rehearsing in a rehearsal warehouse in Hialeah, Florida, and there were these guys next door. They were rehearsing all the time, and a lot of stuff was going on in the room. I could see a lot of people going in and out. The singer used to come into my room every day and see me play – that singer was Rhett. So, he would sit there and listen and really not say much. But one day he walked in and invited me next door. He introduced me to the band and asked if I wanted to jam with them - and ultimately this led to me joining Young Turk. At that point, they were getting ready to do Train to Nowhere. They had a guitar player named Monte. Monte was good, but he was not able to cover the whole spectrum. They needed a second guitar player. He was more rock; I was more blues and Rolling Stones style stuff. So, they wanted to blend that. By the time I ended up in Hialeah, I had my own band going but I was always interested in those guys because there was always something going on in their room - like a big party. They attracted a lot of people, which obviously is a big thing in the business. They did that very well. So, when I jammed with them, I had a great time. There was a constant party going on. Plus, they were traveling, and they were doing well. So, I was in love with the whole thing. Train to Nowhere was 75% recorded when I joined the band. I added my guitar parts to Train to Nowhere, and that's how that happened. We learned to hang with each other in obliviated states of insanity. We got used to each other. And for some reason, when we got like that, we figured we should write. And we wrote all of the time. It was not like work. We were having fun doing it. We had that rehearsal warehouse in Hialeah, which was crazy. There were like ten other bands staying there and we had a great time hanging out there. So, from what I remember, we just hung out and we wrote. Rhett was always writing lyrics. I mean, he is an incredible lyric writer. It was hard for me to *keep up with him. He always had ideas. 'Give me something else. Give me something else,' he would say. Rhett was always pushing me, which was great. Now, I love Carl. Carl never did me wrong. I love the guy. In Tennessee, we were staying at a vacant all-girls school. We had these little bungalows. They (students) were on vacation, so we had the whole school to ourselves. We were staying in these little bungalows, and I remember walking through this mud, going to go see Carl in his bungalow. I walk in and I track mud all over his room. He is going, 'Jesus Christ, you're tracking in mud,' and while he is yelling at me, I look down and to my side, I see a stack of books on his windowsill. And the books are all about the same topic: 'How to Deal with Difficult People' and 'Dealing with the Mentally Insane'- shit like that. I knew he was reading those books because of us. Because we were out of control."*

"On recording Tired of Laughing: *"I remember that we were in Memphis, and everything was okay. We were really killing ourselves doing that album in Memphis, which was a dream come true - just to be at Ardent Recording Studio. I was in heaven. That is where Led Zeppelin was recorded. It felt like we made it! I loved it. But from what I remember, after recording, we were not doing well with Geffen. They had not dropped us. We did not quit. Rhett confronted them (Geffen) and said, 'You guys aren't really keeping up your end of the bargain. You got us on standstill. You're not pushing us.' Half a million dollars was spent on the album, and it was not coming out. If I remember correctly, Virgin Records stepped in and goes, 'Listen, we'll go back, we'll do another album, and we will put it out - and we will put you guys on the road.' Which they did. I'm very proud of the Geffen album. Somebody put it out. Now it is called Tired of Laughing: the Lost Geffen Tapes, finally it is selling somewhere, and it is a great album. When it comes to classic rock, I believe we really hit it. And the lyrics that Rhett came up with were incredible. Rick's drumming was amazing. So is Billy on bass. It was just a good combination, and everything clicked. It was a great album. For the video ('Death of a Salesman'), we had a friend that had a video company. He typically did advertising, commercials, and those kinds of things. He was nice enough to do it for us. And it is a pretty good video as far as I'm concerned, because the guy that did this is a real pro. So Tired of Laughing is a great album. Much different than Train to Nowhere, and I think a lot of that is my blues influence. It is very universal music. That's one thing I was very happy with about the band, that the sound was universal - anybody could get into the band. I hear a lot of Led Zeppelin, a lot of Lou Reed, and the writing - as opposed to Poison and all of the Cinderella type bands that came out in the '80s – was geared more towards the '70s. I think it worked."*

"Regarding NE 2$^{nd}$ Ave, "Carbondale had a lot of snow. The studio had a river in the back and a funeral parlor next door. So, I was ways paranoid to use the bathroom close to the funeral parlor side - because I pick up stuff like that. It was strange. There were literally dead bodies on the other side of the wall. In the rehearsal hall, there was a little bathroom, and right past that wall, I guess that was they were keeping all the caskets and the bodies.

"The vibe was very strange and very strong. I really hated going to the bathroom there and would not use that one at night. You could feel it. Carl would say, 'Well, I got a good price on the building.' It was on a nice street, and it had these neighborhood bars in the area. They all looked like they had been there a long time. Now that I think about it, it was great. But at that time, it was like, 'My God, we're stuck in the middle of nowhere.' Now I miss it. See, that's life for you. Now, we had gone on one small tour with the Geffen album. We only had a van for that tour, and it was very uncomfortable. We were practicing for our upcoming tour and when we went to the rehearsals, there was a big tour bus there. And I asked Carl, 'My God, whose bus is that?' He goes, 'I do not know. Let's go inside and find out. This is your bus by the way. No more van.' We had an album, we now had a bus, and we were working on a video - it was all pretty exciting.

"When we filmed our second video, the director was horrible, horrible, horrible. It just so happens the neighborhood where we filmed was one block away from where I grew up. My grandma lived there. Only one block away! So, I mentioned it, 'Hey, I grew up in this building. I remember the area; would you mind if we film a little bit of it?' He immediately gave me slack for my request. He did not communicate well with the band, let's put it that way. So that's the difference. We had a say in the first video. I love that first video. Once the second video came out, things started to get strange and weird and kind of disintegrate. I think that by the time the NE 2$^{nd}$ Ave album came out, the grunge thing started at that time. We were not a hair band, we were not a heavy metal band, and we were not a grunge band either. I do not think that was the main problem, but all the legal problems that we had - I believe that had something to do with it. Then some of the guys went to jail and that was it. It was supposed to be a rock band - it is supposed to be fun. A lot of guys got whaled on for no reason, literally. To make it through that would have been a miracle. Honestly, everybody was dented mentally. How do we put the puzzle back together after that? We were on tour with NE 2$^{nd}$ Ave and all of a sudden everything just stopped. Two guys were called back to Wisconsin to go to court. And that was it for the rest of the guys. Me and Eddie, the other guitar player, went home. Then Virgin dropped the whole thing and that was it. That was it, man. I had family at the time. My father was still alive. My grandmother was still alive. So, I went back to be with the family. What else can you do?

*Listen, I'm ready to make a comeback. I'm ready to get the band back together and make a comeback. I'm here in Miami playing blues and it is good and everything but forget about it. To get Young Turk back together again and get on the road would be great. I mean, the albums are already there."*

# Rockin' N Rollin' Again (Almost)

Once I sold Neon City, I dedicated all my newly acquired time to being a father. I did not give up on music, but the late '90s and the early 2000s were a strange time for the industry. MTV dropped the majority-video format. Music went digital, and the stores selling CDs and cassettes largely shut their doors. Many of the bands that had ruled the '80s had now taken on new vocalists: Motley Crue, Anthrax, Judas Priest and even Iron Maiden. Those bands were also doing a much different take on their foundational sound, as were the other giants, Metallica and Guns N Roses. What little of the genre that was left was almost unidentifiable from its previous version. The recording process changed completely as well. Everything went digital and it became possible for anyone to record at home with a minimal investment in software. Why spend a ton of money making your album in a studio when you can do it at home? So it just was not something I thought about. Erin was young and I wanted to be there for those years. Once you are in your 40s, you realize how fast time moves. You begin to understand that life moves quickly. I did not want to miss Erin's youth.

Locally, not many people knew of my heavy metal background. No one had heard of The Rods in Carbondale. I was ok with that. I kept my musical past relatively quiet. I really did not want to advertise it. You have to remember that I was the homeroom dad, so I kept it a secret - because who wants this heavy metal guy around their children, right? Of course, nowadays people would be cool with it, but back then, heavy metal guys still had an ill repute for drink, drugs, and women. A lot of times the kids would come to our house, or I would take them all to the movies, and I really did not want my past brought up. Carbondale was a very traditional town with old school values. At least back then it was. But one day I was doing some shopping in our local market when two guys approached me.

"Hey, are you Carl Canedy? Are you the drummer for The Rods?" I was shocked. I had lived here for years, and no one had known. Not a single person. It turns out I ran into the only two headbangers in Carbondale. These guys knew their stuff. And that was all it took. After that, the word spread very quickly. It was not long before the entire town knew.

Contrary to my earlier concerns, no one cared. They were all very cool with it. But it did open up some other doors.

The principal at Erin's elementary school was a friend of mine. After learning of my past, he insisted that I be music director for an upcoming play at the school. Erin had just joined the troop, so I agreed to. We did a play called *Candy Cane Lane,* and it went really well. I had a great time and it really made Erin happy that I was part of it. Right after, the director told me she was leaving. "I want you to take it over full-time," she said. "What do I know about children's theater?" was my reply. Her response, I remember clearly, was: "You have to take it over. There's nobody else."

By that point, Erin was very much musically inclined. One day, I walked into the piano room, and Dianne said, "Listen to this!" Dianne was playing intervals on the piano, and Erin, at only four and a half, was singing them! Which, if you do not know music, that's quite impressive for that age. She was nailing them! From there, I worked with her on her vibrato a little bit and she caught it right away. She would hold her note and then slowly add the vibrato – which she did perfectly. We tried to get her lessons as she was singing all the time, so a music director from the local Choral Society began giving her vocal lessons. His name was Dr. Barton, and he was absolutely fantastic. He was really good with her. She was young, but she listened. It is not easy to teach a five-year-old something as difficult as vocal technique. But Erin was easy to teach. She took voice lessons for many years. She eventually joined the Singer's Guild and from there it progressed to where she started doing community theater. So, through her involvement, I discovered theater.

I had a blast directing the Children's Theater. The kids were great. The parents were fantastic. The community was very receptive. A few months after I took it over, I combined the three schools in the area - much to the chagrin of a number of parents, because they wanted to keep it exclusive to the Carbondale area. But I felt it should be open to everybody - and so it was. As a result, we wound up with about 120 kids participating, and it grew way over my head. I had no clue how to handle it. I had other parents helping and I had a lot of support, but I do not think anyone can effectively coordinate 120 kids. We had no money, which was another challenge. The first play I wrote was called *50 Years of Rock and Roll.* The kids all lip synced. I had two MCs, a boy and a girl. It was multimedia - I edited a ton of videos and put them up on two large screen TVs that we rented. The kids had a great time. We had drums, microphones, guitars, and the entire setup on stage. In between there would be dialogue and there would be footage for each decade playing and so on. It was a ton of work, but it was kind of fun to do. I was involved with the Children's Theater for 11 years. It went so well that the Dietrich Theater's After School Players Program asked my friend Patti Dunning and myself to help.

I met Patti after she had reached out to me seeking info on starting a drama club at her school. Patti would quickly become a great friend, a business partner - and, eventually, the tour manager for The Rods. But we will get to that later. Now, my involvement with children's theater was pretty extensive, but none of that was by design. I had no clue when I started out, but experience is the best teacher and I learned through doing. With all of that experience under our belts, Patti and I started our own children's theater production company, and we took it a step further. We did school plays and even summer camp productions. It was a lot of fun. We did one for a summer camp that was '50s themed. We wrote these skits around the golden oldies. One of the moms made poodle skirts for the girls. The crowd went nuts. It was a huge success right out of the box. After the play, a number of the kids asked me, "Can we do this? We love this. Can we do this?"… and that led to The Pixie Chicks.

Some of the kids in the Children's Theater really wanted to sing instead of lip syncing. But we could not feasibly do that. With 120 kids, only a handful could sing, and it would not be fair to exclude the others. But Patti and I felt that there were a few in the group who had really good voices (and they expressed their desire to sing) and that it would be fun to start a group for them, so we started a girls' vocal group called The Pixie Chicks. Four girls, including Erin, made up the group. They did really, really well. I wrote some songs for them, and they appeared locally with Joe Snedeker on WNEP. Joe really helped launch the girls. He had them on a number of times, and it did them a huge favor. I wrote a song called "Your Name Goes Here Song", and they wound up performing it on *The Today Show*. Shortly after that appearance, we were in New York City for another event, and we visited *Good Morning America* as audience members. The producers recognized the girls from having been on *The Today Show,* so they asked them to sing live. So, in one month the girls were on both *The Today Show* and *Good Morning America.* That was a great experience and Dianne Sawyer was wonderful with the girls. She was very gracious and when the girls were going back in (she had them sing to the audience outside) she stopped and thanked me - which was really unnecessary, but it was Dianne Sawyer, so it was a cool moment. Robin Roberts was a different story. She was not rude, but she had a "better than you" vibe. I was talking to her and told her I really admired her as a journalist, but she just stared at me like I was an alien. It was very uncomfortable.

They went on to play at the Hershey Star Pavilion and many other places. I ended up writing a number of plays. *Little Elvis* was the one I am most proud of. Overall, it was a positive experience for the girls and for me. I learned a lot. Plus, Erin was with me through the entire experience. It makes it that much cooler that I got to do something with her that she really loved and enjoyed.

Erin was a natural when it came to theater and singing. She was five when she signed up with a talent agency to do some commercials. But I was not thrilled about it. And I think Erin eventually saw that it was not that great. It is a tough industry. I felt it was not in her best interest psychologically to be in that industry. It is an industry in which you are judged, and you have to be the right fit. It can be psychologically damaging to a child, and I did not want that for her. Erin stuck with music, and much later, got a degree in music. She is now a music teacher for a public school. She loves it and she is very happy. She works at a fantastic school and her students adore her. I am very proud of her. She is kind to her students, and she really does her best to tailor her teaching to each student. She tries to figure out ways to include everyone and recognizes that not everyone is going to be a musician, but that music is important, and they should explore it to whatever degree they choose.

On The Rods front, David and I still spoke regularly. By this time, he had also done a couple of solo projects: A'La Rock, and Feinstein. So David had his projects going on, but there was never any talk about The Rods doing anything until we did the Al Falso benefit. When Al passed, we were invited to participate in a benefit/tribute, which was a lot of fun. I really enjoyed playing with the guys again. Even after so many years apart, we fell right back in the groove. It was a great show. That was the spark. But right after that, David released the album *Third Wish* with his solo group Feinstein. It was a killer album - I really liked it. I know that when he was doing press for that album, a lot of interviewers were asking him what was up with The Rods. This was 2004, I believe. By that point, we had gone almost 16 years without playing together. Feinstein was invited to do the Wakken festival. In 2004, Wakken was one of the most anticipated European metal festivals. However, the deal was that if Feinstein played, The Rods had to play as well. They were really hoping to feature the return of The Rods. That show was not going to happen unless Gary and I went. I was in. I was willing to go for free if my travel expenses were paid. But at the same time, David was renegotiating publishing with a record label (name withheld so I do not get sued). They wanted The Rods' catalog, so this was all being pushed by the record company. The deal was: sell your publishing, go to Wakken (and Feinstein will get to go) - and maybe put out a new Rods album.

There was no way I was going to give up my publishing. It simply was not going to happen. David kept urging me to sell: "Come on…just do it." I was not falling for it. I do not think David was trying to deceive me - he would never do that. But I would never give up our publishing. So I refused. Which meant that Wakken was out for me. I did not want to sacrifice that opportunity for David (Feinstein playing Wakken), but it was not worth giving up the publishing and rights to our music. They were trying to get him to sell his publishing by using Wakken as the carrot. Our publishing was set up so that David and I both had to agree to any potential sale or use. Without an agreement, no sale could take place. Even though Gary did not have any publishing rights (he had not written any material), I figured Gary would understand the principle. I called Gary and told him that I was not relinquishing my publishing, and therefore I would not be at Wakken. I did not expect him to take my side, but I thought it was worth a shot. But Gary did not care - he decided he was going to Wakken. So that settled it. They were going to Wakken without me. The Rods playing without me was a tough pill to swallow, but I was not going to compromise my rights as a songwriter, and as an artist, to give it away to somebody (particularly for free), just because David did not recognize the value. And of course, Gary, I felt, sold me out because he could have just said "I'm not going" and that would have been the end of it. Instead, they went without me. Wakken is a huge deal, so I understand, but it certainly was not worth giving away our publishing for.

In the end, we kept the publishing, but Gary and David ended up playing three Rods songs with Nate Horton on drums. Nate is a great guy and a great drummer – but it was not The Rods. They billed it as "The Rods comeback" or some similar bullshit. It did not go over well because it was what it was. It was not the band, and ultimately it was damaging to the brand. We have not played Wakken since. Overall, it was very upsetting to me, and it was a tough, tough blow. It was very hurtful. There are so many things that I love about David. He is my brother. But he just did not get it at the time. He just wanted to play the gig - nothing else mattered to him at the time. He did not realize what would happen if we got rid of our publishing. But I was not giving in. And I had to hold my ground. I had to pay for an attorney. It was stressful. Years later we reissued The Rods' catalog and David got a big check - I think only then did he realize the value of holding on to our publishing. But that was years down the road and the Wakken incident certainly put a stop to any possible reunion for quite some time.

# Vengeance

David and I did not speak for a few months after Wakken. I was upset, but there were never any bouts of screaming or the slamming of doors. I do not think that was even possible. David is very non-confrontational, and we are both even-tempered people. David, I felt, should have recognized what I had hung on to all these years, which later allowed us to reissue all of our albums. Feinstein still went to Wakken. I saw a video of the show, and while they were all really great musicians, they were not a tight unit in my opinion. Some of the players were cutting him off. The bassist, Jeff Howell, was moving forward. Jeff was a great guy and a monster bass player (Jeff played with Foghat), but he was cutting in front of David. The band was called Feinstein, and here he was cutting David off. It was not a band - it was a bunch of side guys who were out for themselves. For the Rods portion of Wakken, it was a total disaster and a non-event. It was not good for the brand. And it did not move the needle. In fact, by all accounts, it was not a very good showing. That was kind of sad for me in a sense. It was exactly what I predicted. I was definitely glad I did not sign away my publishing. That is exactly what I told David when we spoke a few weeks later.

 I do not recall who broke the ice - who called who - but we had a phone conversation and we both laid out our frustrations. David and I voiced our concerns, and just like that, we were back to talking about The Rods. As a result of our phone call, we agreed that it was time for a new Rods album. This was 2004. A lot had changed since our last album, which was almost 20 years prior. I had been producing albums only a decade earlier, well into the mid-90s, but even production had changed vastly during that time. We came from an era in which you had to lay down your tracks in a studio. But by 2004, everyone could record their parts at home. Of course, we were all in the depths of our careers. David still had the restaurant. I had purchased a convenience store and had some rental properties. Gary had a career outside of music. Aside from the Al Falso benefit, we had not played together in some time. David and I slowly started writing songs and began laying out the foundation. I was not good with digital engineering, so I asked Shmoulik Avigal to help us out. Shmoulik helped me get the necessary components together. There was a massive learning curve. This was to benefit Shmoulik as well, as I agreed to do the drums for his solo record. We slowly began to lay down some tracks for what was intended to become *Vengeance*, only to scrap everything. We ended up recording what should have been our comeback album, but when it was all said and done, it was a disaster. It did not sound very good. The label wanted my drums mixed louder, so we went back to the drawing board and redid those parts. The label kept sending us back to fix specific parts and levels. Rightfully so - it was not up to our usual standards. With life happening, this took a year. There was a period of time where things were unsettled for the band - we were basically in a holding pattern. The original *Vengeance* was recorded and discarded. We wound up rewriting everything! We also had some technical issues. Back in the '80s, we would spend a few weeks writing, and then knock everything out in the studio in a matter of a few days. I do not think we ever spent more than a full month on a record. *Vengeance* took over a year. It was the new digital age, and we were living apart. There was distance. There were primary schedules to work around. We had families. We had careers that paid the bills. It was not like the old days when we would rehearse for a few days and then we'd go right into the studio and record it. That was simply not the case anymore. Remote recording is really great on one hand, but on the other hand, it has some negatives. Especially for The Rods, who were always a tight unit – and then we found ourselves separated by distance, time, and day-to-day life. That was a difficult adjustment. There are pluses and minuses to it, and we were definitely finding the minuses faster than we were finding the pluses.

On our second attempt, Shmoulik took my drum tracks and tried to correct them to the guitars – he moved them a bit too far and suddenly everything changed. I'm like, "What happened here? That's not what I played. Let's put that back." But they could not put it back because we were several generations away by that point. We could not get back to the original. I had to rerecord everything. Then we recorded at a studio in Cortland, New York. I did not get along with the engineer for that session. He was saying shit behind my back, and he was incredibly negative. Eventually I told David, "I do not want to work with this guy ever again. I do not want to be in his presence." So that was another delay. In the end, the engineer and I made up, and I have come to find him a good guy and a talented engineer, but at the time, I wanted nothing to do with him. We redid things so many times that we said, "Fuck it. Let's start from scratch." So that was our first and second attempt - both of them being failures. But we did learn from it. Nothing like learning the hard way, I suppose.

We were not ready to throw in the towel. Third time is a charm, right? I ended up putting my drums in my living room. I have a double living room with a high ceiling, which fortunately has some really great acoustics, so I had my Ludwig drums set up in the house. I did my drum tracks from the living room, and I demanded that no one touch the digital tracks, as that was what got us into trouble in the beginning of the project. That has been the way I record ever since. I tell everybody, "Here are my drum tracks. If you do not like it, do not move it. I will replay it." We spent a great deal of time writing, recording, rewriting, rerecording, and rerecording once again - but finally we were in a place where we were happy with the results.

David had been working with Ronnie James Dio for a few years prior. The details are his to share, so I will let him do that, but there was talk between David and Ronnie about a possible Elf reunion and potentially a new album. That would have been absolutely fantastic had that happened. During that period of time, Ronnie agreed to sing on a couple of tracks for our upcoming album. David felt, and I can never thank him enough for this, that my song "The Code" was perfect for Ronnie. Ronnie did two songs with us: "The Code", and one David wrote called "Metal Will Never Die". "Metal Will Never Die" David first sang to me while we were playing golf - I thought it was the coolest. David writes fantastic anthems. I loved the riff he intended to use. When we were recording, David played the part and knocked it out fast. And then it came time to do the guitar solo. He played the guitar solo and nailed it on the first take. It was fantastic. And then the computer crashed! So we kept it - it was meant to be. The solo was one and done. The sounds came together really quickly this time around. By that point we had the process down. The only thing left was for Ronnie to do his vocals. I was ecstatic that he would be doing one of my songs. David actually chose that song. That says a lot about David - that he was willing to pick one of my songs for Ronnie to sing. That meant a lot to me, and I can never thank David enough for that.

When it came time to record Ronnie's vocals, we set up at David's warehouse in Cortland. Now, David had always told me Ronnie was a one take guy. Even though David doesn't have a penchant for lying, I did not believe him. I have worked with so many great musicians and nobody is one take. Nobody. It is nearly impossible. In my experience, everybody has little pitchy things that need a few runs to hone. Well, David was absolutely right. Ronnie was one take - if he redid anything, it was to change a part or try a different idea. It was never because of performance. I was blown away by that. He was one of the greatest metal singers of all time and he was listening to my demo and wanting to tweak a melody – it was a huge honor. "Metal Will Never Die" was also on David's solo album, titled *Bitten by The Beast*. (On a side note, David has some really great solo albums. I love *One Night In The Jungle* and *Third Wish* especially. I highly recommend checking them out.) For the two songs featuring Ronnie, we had Shmoulik engineering, which was something I did not agree with. I really liked Shmoulik, but I did not feel he was the right fit. But we knew that Ronnie was not going to be open to having just anybody come in and engineer, and I think he was okay with Shmoulik because David was cool with him. There were some technical issues of course, things that David and I laugh about now, but at the time it was embarrassing. We were not prepared for the distortion caused by Ronnie's powerful voice. His voice was so powerful, and we did not see that coming. We were not used to working with that level of power. Brian New mixed the album, and thankfully, Brian was able to work on the distortion that occurred during the recording. Ronnie had come in on the tail end of *Vengeance*. By then, we had sorted out our issues with recording and we were on track – and finally we were getting things done. Sadly, Ronnie passed away right before the album was released. They were the last two songs he ever recorded. We had no clue that Ronnie was sick. I had no idea. I do not think David knew either. When he passed, it was a complete shock. It was very sad. It was tragic for everyone and especially tragic for David. He and Ronnie were so close, and they had quite a few projects lined up. Losing Dio was a huge loss for the metal community. Working with him for a couple of songs was truly a career highlight.

*Vengeance* was released on Niji Records. When Ronnie James Dio passed, his wife Wendy started Niji Records. The president of the company, Dean Schachtel, had been a good friend and a huge fan of Ronnie's. Dean had been a major label guy, and I am not sure if he fully understood an indie label approach. He spent a ton of money on things like these big foam fingers, like the ones you see at sporting events, though these were in the shape of the 'devil horns' that Ronnie liked to flash on stage. (The mano cornuto, or horned hand, also referred to by metal fans as 'devil horns' or 'metal horns', is actually an old-school Italian symbol of protection. For the Italian version, the hand faces downwards to send negative energy away.) The foam horns did not sell at all. We had to take this huge box on tour with us. It was full of foam metal horns and the poor road crew – they had to unload the box, and then set them up in the merch booth at every show. Of course, we did not sell a single foam hand. What metal guy wants to wear giant foam metal horns? Dean had come from a major label which had tons of money to spend on promotional gimmicks. Sadly, Dean passed away not long after the label began, and Wendy decided not to carry on with the record company.

*Vengeance* dropped on May 24th, 2011. It had been nearly a quarter of a century since our last release, so this was a big deal for us. At this point, metal, and especially old school metal, had made a resurgence. Thanks to the dedication and longevity of heavy metal fans in Europe, a plethora of metal-centric festivals had popped up, so the timing was right for an album and a tour. The reviews of *Vengeance*, overall, were quite good. Personally, it felt great being back on the scene. I missed playing live, and more importantly, I missed the fans. I also missed working with David. It was good to be back. I am pretty sure David and Gary felt the same. Once the album came out, Wendy Dio, who was Ronnie's wife and manager, offered us the opening slot on the Dio Disciples tour. The Dio Disciples, at that time, were Ronnie's longest surviving band members: Craig Goldy, Scott Warren and Simon Wright, paired with Toby Jepson and Tim "Ripper" Owens (Judas Priest), who alternated vocal duties. We were really excited about it, but at the end of the day, it was not much fun. We were on a bus for 31 days with the Disciples. We were not treated well by the road crew. The majority of the road crew treated us like shit. They had a tech, who was previously with Queensryche, who was an absolute asshole. While the shows went great and the fans responded well, the aura with the crew was very dark and negative. The guys in the band were cool. Simon, of course, is a great guy. Ripper Owens was fantastic. But the keyboard player, Scott Warren, was extremely arrogant. He was a side man, yet behaved like he was a total rock star. I really did not enjoy my time with him. We basically kept to ourselves.

Doro joined us on that tour for a few days. She is by far one of the nicest, most talented people in the genre. She has such an authentic and genuine vibe. The first time I saw her perform, I was like, "Holy shit! This is amazing!" The crowd went nuts. They adored her. After the show, she hopped on the bus with her backpack, got in her bunk, and hung out like the rest of us. I was expecting someone of Doro's stature to have a bit of an ego, but she is very down to earth.

Another frustrating part of the tour was that we had no PR. When we arrived at the shows, the press and the fans had not known that we were coming. We were a late addition, so we were seldom on the posters. Most of the press was done prior to us joining the tour. People were constantly going, "If we had only known you would be here, man. We had no idea!" But we showed up and we did well on the tour. We had a lot of fans, but it was more of a word-of-mouth thing. We played every night. We were getting better, and it was fun playing for an audience again. We were getting to be a tight unit. It was not a great experience on one level, but on another level, it was excellent.

We really liked being on the road again. *Vengeance* was doing well, and it was good to be back playing live. Erin was in college at this point and my properties did not require too much visitation – I think David and Gary were in a good place as well, so we decided to do some dates on our own. We booked some dates in Europe. Gary had a friend by the name of Veronica Freeman, and he asked us if we could take her along. Veronica was the vocalist for a band called Benedictum. Veronica is a powerhouse of a singer. We picked a few Dio songs and added them to the end of our set, and we would have Veronica come out and sing them. It was our version of a Dio tribute. Veronica has the perfect voice for Dio covers. The crowd absolutely loved it. She has a great stage presence. We eventually recorded "Smoke on The Horizon" with Veronica. Veronica was excellent and she was a great addition to the show.

Once we finished up the European tour, we did a few festivals and then went our separate ways. I'd had a blast and really wanted to keep up the momentum. I wanted to do another Rods album. David was constantly working on music, so it certainly seemed plausible. David is a pretty quiet and private person; he doesn't volunteer a lot of info. And I certainly did not want to pressure him. But I was pushing to do an album. As it turned out, he wound up making a solo album, *Bitten by the Beast* - which is a fantastic album. But that was a little bit of an irritation to me. Not that he did a solo album and not that we took time from The Rods, but that he was allowing me to believe that we were going to do a Rods album, when it was a solo album that he was working on. I did not know until the album was almost complete. I only found out because I walked into a restaurant and David was there with his wife. He told me about some music that he was working on, so I said, "Well, send me the tracks. I can lay down the drums." Then he said, "Well, Nate [Horton] is playing on it. I did not want it to be a Rods album and if you played on it would be." So that's how I found out that Nate was playing drums on it, and I was not going to be invited to play on it at all – and that it was strictly a solo album. I do not think he meant it maliciously. But he was not forthcoming, and he knew I was waiting to move forward. He did not want to confront me because I can be intense. Especially in those days. Today, that would be a different story. But at the time, he probably figured I would have called him out on it, and understandably, he did not want to deal with any possible drama. But whatever the reason, I would have preferred to have known that we were not going to do another album.

That led to another gap. We were on hiatus once again, but we were still playing dates on occasion. I respected his decision; however, I did not respect how it was unfolded to me - but that's how it goes. When you compare The Rods' issues to other bands who have been together for decades, we always have been in a good place. There never was animosity or hatred or bitterness. All things considered, of all these years together, I think we've come through it fairly well. I am certain David had his frustrations with me over the years – I am not always easy to deal with. Minor disagreements or disputes have happened, but David and I both see the big picture. We tend to get over arguments fairly quickly. At the end of the day, David is my friend and brother. I love what we built over the decades, and I love that we both strive to keep it going. Perhaps, deep down, my disappointment came from a place of fear – that The Rods would be a distant thought to David. I really did not want *Vengeance* to be our last album. I wanted to keep the train rolling. At the end of the day, musically, The Rods come first in my world.

Another way we made it this far was by eliminating some of the people in our camp who were trying to pull us apart. Surround yourself with good people, because it only takes a few mischievous people to destroy a band. We did exactly that right after the *Vengeance* tour. We had to get rid of our longtime tour manager, George Baroodie. George had a pretty severe drug habit and was always playing one of us against the other. George was an addict. He was trying to survive. That is what drug addicts do. They lie, they cheat, and they have to get money somehow - they do whatever they have to in order to get themselves well. I do not think George had a fun life, and that was all due to his addictions. So we temporarily stopped working with him. It took me a while to convince David that it was a real problem - and that we needed to cut him off for good. Eventually, George sent a Mafia-type guy after us to collect money. He was trying to extort money from us. He threatened to send someone to our houses unless we paid George what we allegedly owed him. We did not owe him anything. So that was a real problem. That was the nail in the coffin for George, as that incident finally convinced David that we needed a new tour manager. When you involve family members, and send a mafioso guy to my house, that's where it ends. Never again.

We hired a second tour manager named Gary Dallaire. Gary was my former partner in the early '90s. Gary was a hard-working guy, but he was not a diplomat. He often rubbed people up the wrong way. One day, after returning from a festival in Norway, Erin and Patti picked Gary and me up from the airport. On the way home, we stopped at Dunkin Donuts to get coffee. The people working behind the counter were taking their time and all of a sudden Gary started yelling, "Andale, andale... hurry it up!" I was like, "Holy fuck, what is that about?" I was shocked - and embarrassed that he would speak to people like that. Once we got home, my daughter pulled me to the side and had a serious talk with me. She said, "Dad, I do not understand. You typically avoid negative people in your life. You are a good person. Why would you associate with guys like that? His attitude reflects on you. It is not your attitude, is it, Dad?" A bit taken aback, I replied, "No, I would never treat anybody like that." And she drove it home by saying, "But Dad, it does reflect on you." I thought about it for a moment and concluded that she was right. Gary's actions certainly did reflect on myself and on the band. Guilty by association; or "you are the company you keep." I talked to David, and we agreed that Erin was right. That was when we ended our relationship with Gary Dallaire.

By this point, my friend Patti Dunning had accompanied us on a few trips. Patti was my partner for the Children's Theatre production company. Anytime we went to Europe, we usually had friends or family members accompanying us. Patti had stepped in multiple times to book flights, organize travel arrangements, and solve some unexpected dilemmas that popped up. She was a natural manager. She was a take-charge type of person, and she did not bog us down with petty problems. She was always a big help to us while on the road. So I threw her name in the hat as Gary Dallaire's replacement. David and Gary agreed to give her a shot. And it worked out well. She was excellent on all levels. Patti and David have a great relationship. They are both organized. They communicate well together, and they have a deep mutual respect. Bringing Patti on board worked out well. She is still our tour manager to this very day. She looks after the band and takes care of things. One time we had a show booked in Europe. As it was only one show, I did not think we would have enough money to take a crew. I said to David, "I am not sure if we have enough money to bring Patti." He said, "Well, remember when we were in Germany and suddenly flights were not happening and there was no way to get home? Remember how she stayed up all night and got us home the next day? So, there's your answer. We need to bring her." Patti has been great. If you have toxic people in your camp, cut them loose and do whatever it takes to fill the ranks with good people. It is amazing how much of a difference it makes.

After the *Vengeance* tour, life returned to normal. David released another solo album, titled *Clash of Armor*. I got my real estate license and became a realtor. For fun, I began playing in a local band. Gary was deep in his career. So, outside of the occasional festival, we were not doing anything. We knew another album was in the cards, but once again, we got busy with life. But I really missed playing metal. I missed writing, and I missed recording. I was not ready to hang it up. Maybe David had the right idea with the solo album thing? I really enjoyed those albums. He certainly seemed like he was having fun with it. Perhaps it was time I gave the solo album thing a shot?

**Veronica Freeman;** *Benedictum, The V*
*"I met Gary (Bordonaro) first. He was on one of my albums. I wanted to sing, and I wanted to go to Europe, but I did not have a full band at the time. But The Rods were touring. So, we came up with this thing that I would be a guest singer. I had a little bit of stuff going on, but not enough to go out on my own. So, I was blessed to be able to go on tour with them. It was a real blessing. I came out and sang some tunes – I think we did 'Mob Rules' and 'Heaven and Hell'. It was really, really cool. Carl was always the calm*

one. He was always chill. We did the thing in Cortland (Dio Days, which is the annual Dio tribute fest) and then we did some shows in New York and then Europe. That was pretty cool. I got to put on a corset and hop out there for a couple of songs - and that was golden. Life was golden. It was great."

**Patti Dunning;** *Rods Tour Manager*
"I was trying to get a children's drama club started in our local school district. My daughter kind of had that forte, and there were not a lot of outlets for her. So I was paying to have her take acting classes at a local theater. I had heard that the neighboring school district, which is a couple of miles away, had a children's theater. I called the school, and the principal gave me Carl's name. So I contacted him and asked him how he got his program started. In true Carl form, he said, 'Well, why don't you come down - we're doing a Christmas play right now.' He was recruiting me to help. He could not get anybody to volunteer for anything. I went down to help, and that is how we met. We quickly became friends. I became the stage manager for that production and a lot of future productions. From there, he had some ties with some local community theaters, so he had started his own private venture. He hired me at that point. From there, we became partners and did our own children's theater in some local churches.

"And then we did summer camps. And then we got hired by a town close by that has a theater, it is actually a cultural center which is called Dietrich Theater. It was a beautiful theater that they renovated, and they've made it the hub of the community. We did that for six years and it was quite successful. For one play, Carl came up with this idea of the girls doing a '50s and '60s review with poodle skirts and the whole nine yards. It was very well received, so that inspired the Pixie Chicks. The Pixie Chicks then became the whole entity. It was Carl's daughter, my daughter and there were two other girls who performed. There were four of them. And through the years, some came, some went, but my daughter and his daughter were the base. They were on Good Morning America. They were on The Today Show. They performed at Disney. They did county fairs and car shows up and down the East Coast. They were on local TV all the time. We did that for a few years. So, when they (Carl and David) asked me to be their tour manager, it was not a big transition to go from kids to a metal band. Honestly, it is kind of the same thing. I started doing merchandising and helping out, so I was going to all of the shows anyhow. Then it progressed from there to when they started to travel abroad. I was friends with everyone by that point. I was in the circle. And they were a very tight circle. So, to be a friend and be accepted into the group was really an honor. Honestly, I felt really honored to do that and that they would trust me to do it. But basically, I was just mothering them anyway. That's what a tour manager does. I always said it is like herding cats. It is funny to be around some of the other heavy metal bands - you're backstage and you are engulfed in a cloud of pot smoke. But they (The Rods) - all they want to do is have their tea and Danish. Usually, we set up. They do sound check and then they ask me to get them some tea and cookies. None of them drink and none of the guys have tattoos. When I am traveling, I like to drink, and I am the one with tattoos. It's kind of funny. The fans were just always so amazing. So almost everywhere we went, we had some local fan that would take us around. When we got into Europe there would be fans waiting at the airport. They would be waiting just to get autographs. I have pictures of us walking out of the airport with people coming with memorabilia that they want to sign. And it was crazy. I never understood what it was like till I was over there - how big they really were and how well loved they were. It is a little depressing to see here (USA) that they never got the following they deserve, or the credit, really. But what I saw in Europe was not limited to Europe, because we did South America. There is a whole new generation of young guys and kids that were at the shows. You could easily see three generations of followers."

*Ko Shibuya;* Super Fan

"I have lived in Japan all of my life. In December of 1981, I saw an article about The Rods in Music Life magazine. It introduced The Rods along with Y&T, Kix, and Billy Squier. They were grouped as 'the new US metal bands.' I was a metalhead so that article caught my interest. So, I took my bike and went to a record rental store to rent the Rods album for 200 yen. I was only a junior high school student and I could not afford to buy records, which cost 2,500 yen or so at the time. In Japan, we had rental shops, which were a more affordable option. I was very hungry for heavy music at that time. By that time, I had already heard many of the NWOBHM bands such as Iron Maiden, Saxon, and Def Leppard. But they were not enough for me. I wanted to listen to as many metal bands as possible. Once I heard The Rods, I became an instant fan.

"In the 2000s, I had wanted to see a Rods show for a long time, so I kept watching their official website and watching their tour schedule. I found out that they were scheduled to have a gig on September 13th in Auburn, NY. I sent Carl an email asking how to get a ticket. Carl answered, 'Come early and it will be no problem.' So, I flew all the way to the US. By that time, I had visited the USA several times, but I had only visited large cities. Never had I visited the countryside. When I got to the Syracuse airport, I found no public transportation to Auburn. So, I had to take a taxi to Auburn, which cost more than $200 - it was a huge expense for me! When I got to the venue, Mike, Carl's drum tech welcomed me. And then when I saw Carl,

*I felt like I was dreaming because my long-time favorite drummer was right before my eyes! I was able to see them at sound check. After that, I had the honor of having dinner with the band and crew. It was an Italian restaurant, but I do not remember what the dinner was like because I was so happy to see my heroes. The show was very exciting, of course. David pulled me up on stage and introduced me to the audience and said that I was a 'crazy guy from Japan.' He urged me to speak, but I had stage fright so I could not give a good speech. I felt very honored because The Rods were my heroes for a long time. I was very happy, and they all were very friendly and welcomed me fully. In November 2017, when they had some gigs in Tokyo, I saw them again. I remember we hung out around Tokyo and went to some heavy metal bars."*

## Canedy: Headbanger

David had made a couple of solo albums after the *Vengeance* tour. Time was quickly passing us by, and I kept thinking that David would want to do another Rods album. Eventually I figured it out after a couple of years - that there was no new Rods album coming. That was a bit disappointing to me because I had wanted to go right back in the studio and record another album after the *Vengeance* tour was over. David did not say much about it. At that point I thought, well maybe I will do my own solo album. People had suggested it in the past. I had never done a solo album before. I wrestled with the concept for a few months and then decided I would do a full album with songs that I had written – and as many archived songs as possible. Like David, I was always writing. Material was not in short supply. There were many songs that never made it onto a Rods album for one reason or another. So that became the impetus.

The Rods had a publishing deal with MCA in the early '80s, so the rights were not fully mine for the songs from the time frame of the first two albums. Everything else was fair game. I wanted to make sure they were 100% written by me. That means lyrics, melodies, the chorus, and the music – all fully written and arranged by me. Once that was decided, I started going through my catalog and looking through past material. Many songs were incomplete or were very rudimentary, so I had to do a lot of rearranging. I spent a few months tweaking everything and then laying down some initial demos. I wrote some new songs as well. Once the menu was in place, I went about finding some cooks for the kitchen.

I had played on John Hahn's album and thought he was super talented. When I asked John, he was 100% in. So that solved the problem of obtaining a primary guitarist. I also reached out to Chris Caffery, and he very kindly agreed to play a couple of solos. I asked David and he declined. He felt that (and perhaps he felt that way about his solo material) if he played on my solo album, it would make it more of a Rods thing. Which I can understand. I did want to include one Rods song and that was "The Code". I was disappointed with the sonic result of "The Code". Sound wise, I thought it could have been improved. Regarding *Vengeance*, we were in the dawn of digital recording. And sound wise, the album could have been better. So I thought, "Maybe I will rework it. I will keep Ronnie's vocals but rework the music." And so I reworked "The Code" and John Hahn did a great job on it. John played bass and of course the guitars, and I was extremely happy with the way it turned out. I have not exploited the song. And by "exploit" I mean I have not led any kind of promotion or push signifying that the Ronnie track is on there. It is on there because it was a highlight of my career as a songwriter. I've mentioned this before - I can never thank David enough for that opportunity. I will always be indebted to him for that. Once that was reworked, I set about finding bass players and vocalists for the remainder.

One of the highlights of the current recording method is that you can take your time and work on the album by bits and pieces. So it was a matter of finishing the tracks as schedules lined up from guest musicians. There was a local guy who had worked with Shmoulik named Nolan Ayres. Nolan is a great bass player. I thought Nolan was the right bass player for the project, so we used Nolan on a few songs. I would say, if I have a criticism of the album, it is that the mixing was very conservative. I felt that Nolan's bass should have been brought out way more than it was. Gary Chesick helped out with the arrangement and the key change on "Heat of the Night".

I was really stuck, and I needed a key change, and I was not sure how to make it work. We worked on it and Gary really came through. Gary Bordonaro played bass on "Ride Free or Die". Andy Hilfiger played bass on "My Life, My Way". That song was written for Jim Nunis and Billy Hilfiger, who both passed away a few years prior. I knew Jim was dying because he was going through some pretty intense treatments. When he was going through the treatments, he had told me that he had gotten a new tattoo, but he never told me what the new tattoo was. He only said, "I got a new tattoo and I love it!" I did not know whether he had gotten a tattoo of Popeye or Tasmanian Devil or some kind of Sanskrit. Some friends who were with Jim at the end told me that the moment he passed, his arm turned to reveal his tattoo, which said: My Life, My Way. And so that was the inspiration for writing the song "My Life, My Way". I thought of Billy and Jim when I was writing the lyrics to the song. Billy was a longtime friend and fellow musician.

Every time I went to New York City, Billy and I would hang out. He was a killer guitarist with a great tone. When Andy Hilfiger called me and told me of Billy's passing, it was absolutely heartbreaking. Everyone who knew Billy loved him. That's why I wanted Andy, who was Billy's brother, to play bass on the song. Plus, Andy was a great bass player.

For vocals, I reached out to Joe Comeau, who has an amazing set of pipes, and he quickly agreed to lay down some vocal tracks for "Cult of the Poisoned Mind" and "Crossfire". They came out great. For the other songs, "My Life, My Way", "Heat of the Night" and "Ride Free or Die", Mark Tornillo agreed to help me out. Mark Tornillo came to my house twice to do vocals. He drove from New Jersey to Pennsylvania. That was a huge act of kindness. He would not take a dime. Man, Mark is such a great guy and one hell of a singer. He absolutely killed it. Dave Porter did the vocals for "No One Walks Away". I really wanted Craig Gruber to play on some tracks. Craig Gruber and I had gone back and forth trying to arrange it. I had sent the tracks to his engineer in Florida, where Craig was also living. However, he was getting sicker and sicker, and I remember him telling me how his prostate cancer had spread. Ultimately, he was unable to play, and he passed shortly after. That was tough. I had known Craig for a long time, and he was always there to pitch in. On the song "Cult of the Poisoned Mind", my daughter Erin sang the harmonies and background vocals. She wrote the harmonies at the beginning. It was great to showcase her voice and to be able to work with her. *Headbanger* truly became a friends and family album.

 I was really struggling to do the drum tracks, which is not uncommon for some reason, especially as the years progressed. When I write a song, sometimes it is hard for me to come up with a drum groove for it, because I compose the track on guitar or piano. Then when I sit down to play, I am sometimes at a loss coming up with a cool groove. One night I was talking to Robb Reiner, and I said, "Robb, I'm really struggling to find a groove." And he said, "You're overthinking it. You just got to go sit down and play it and do not overthink it." Such simple words, but that was a powerful message. I was overthinking it. And I went up to my little studio room and I knocked it out and it turned out great. His advice was that of a sage – Robb gives some very wise wisdom. From that point on, I attacked all my songs with that same attitude. I will say that by producing it myself, of all the albums I've produced, I was the biggest asshole I had ever worked with. Pretty much, I was the most difficult. I was the biggest jerk. And that's because I tend to be a perfectionist, yet I can't always achieve perfection. So that creates a dilemma that is difficult to solve: I want it to be perfect, but I can't play it perfectly. I just keep basically banging my head against the wall and hoping for a different result. But the result is it is never going to be up to my expectation - it always falls short, which causes frustration on my part. Eventually I learned to go with it. I decided I would leave my tracks, warts and all - so if they were great, excellent. If there were little glitches, little things that maybe were not quite perfect, I would still go with it, as long as it felt right and it felt real.

 By doing the album, it seemed that it had brought the many pieces of my career together: the producing side, the drumming side, and the songwriting side. When I was doing interviews for what would become *Headbanger*, it seemed many interviewers were only familiar with me as a drummer and were unaware of my production history. And vice versa - some were only familiar with my production, but not my drumming. So this was a great way to introduce all facets. When I started, I began by making what I call 30-minute demos. I do not have a great voice, but I would lay down vocals. I laid down guitars and the bass tracks, as much as I could. Then I would add the drums. That is how I presented everything to the guest musicians. But since this was a solo effort, I left a couple of the demo tracks as bonus material on the album: "No One Walks Away" and "Cult of the Poisoned Mind". For those songs, I played every part and did the vocals. I added some of the demos to the album because a lot of times people will say, "Oh, I knew you wrote the song, but I did not know you played guitar." So, on those two songs, the listener could get an idea of what I typically had presented to Gary and David for all of those years. That was how I showcased a song.

*Headbanger* was released on October 14th, 2014. It was my first true solo album. It got some great reviews and the fans seemed to really enjoy it. I had a lot of fun making it. Now I know why David had made so many solo albums in the prior years – they are a great way to stretch your wings in-between the focal material. The Rods were still my (and David's) baby, but I knew that, based on this experience, I would definitely be doing another solo album. Unfortunately, as all the musicians were guest musicians, most lived far away and had other obligations, so playing some dates was out of the question. I really enjoyed performing so I was really itching to play some of the material live.

**Adam Bomb;** *Adam Bomb*

*"I believe Carl did something with a band called TKO (Brad Sinsel and Angels of Dresden). He did this cover of Motorhead's 'Ace of Spades'. And I was in TKO for a while - not at the dawn of the band, but at the resurgence of it, which kind of got us into the metal scene. But the singer and I did not get along too well. But I thought that was interesting. They were doing a tribute to Lemmy. So I checked it out. I was living in Pennsylvania at the time. I was teaching this guy how to play bass. There was nobody to play with. We found this local drummer and he sucked so bad. It was so destroying. Eventually we did a couple of gigs in the rural PA scene, which is not much. I had to quit. I just could not play with the drummer. So I started to look for drummers. I wanted to find a drummer that was suitable enough so that we could do some shows. It was just covers. Then I discovered Carl lives in Pennsylvania and he actually lived close to me. So I contacted him.*

*"We started talking and Carl agreed to come over and try and play with me and Rob (bass player), and I think he was pretty impressed by my guitar playing. It was probably good for him to find somebody that he could actually play with. Because the rock scene is pretty serious when you travel*

to Europe and stuff like that. We started rehearsing a lot and we did a couple of gigs and it sort of got me through a time in which I did not have much going on. I wanted to stick around the area, so it was sort of an off-and-on thing. Unfortunately, the way I work is a bit different than what Carl was used to, because I'm a bit more old school. Not that he wasn't, but it was kind of hard for me to just sit around and play covers of stuff I can do in my sleep. I sleep in rehearsals because that's not really how I work. I typically just show up at gigs. Also, I am a bit of a stoner – a full-fledged weed smoker. I reek of pot 24 hours a day. Unfortunately, Carl got annoyed by that. Carl saw things a little differently than I did. We certainly got along musically, and we went in and actually did some recording. I had some songs I wanted to do, plus I was getting into a bit of a Hendrix tangent. We went to record some demos. I was planning on going to Europe. But before I went, I wanted to do something to document the music we were making, even though it was only covers and stuff.

"We had a whole Hendrix set. It was really authentic to see Carl do 'Manic Depression' - it was quite an amazing thing. So I went into the studio with Carl, just him and me, and we laid the shit down. Then I laid down some bass to it and said, okay, tell Rob (bass player) he can come in and play on it when he wants. I did whatever I could. We went and nailed maybe 10 or 15 songs in the space of a couple of days. Then I was hooking up with this guy, Steve James, who was the bass player in a band called Dogs D'amour from England, and he was talking about doing some dates with me in Europe and putting something together. So I thought maybe a couple of songs I did with Carl I could use for that. We tried to use it (the original material) to get that band off the ground, but that band fell apart after one show, mainly because the guy could not tour. Carl was a bit upset with me when that came out. Well, he just put a lot of work into it and he thought I was using it for other purposes. And it was kind of a blind mistake I made. He just wanted to make sure that I included him.

"All I did was really put it out on YouTube. But I did manage to put out a little CD. I forget the name - I never really did anything with it. It was basically just some rough mixes of some quick studio time of unfinished work. Whatever sounded good enough to put on the CD, whatever I was listening to in the car when we were making it - that sounded good enough. Carl's one of the greatest drummers I've worked with, and he is also a very sensible person. He is great at real estate and stuff like that as well. He certainly helped me, even recently, with problems I've had in that area. I hope we get to play together again. We always talk about it and eventually we probably will, but it is just a matter of when I'm around and when he is not busy."

**Robb Reiner:** Anvil

"Anvil and The Rods started around the same time, though we were named Lips at the time. The Rods came to Toronto to play a famous dive bar called The Gas Works. Someone told us, 'Hey, man, this band from New York is coming up. They are a three-piece power trio.' It sounded enticing. So we went to watch them - Lips, myself, and maybe a couple of other guys. They played and it was amazing! We were all blown away. I thought Carl was a fucking amazing drummer. He had a style very similar to mine. It's how it came across at the time. I said, 'Holy fuck, this guy's got the same type of style. He's very good.' And the music was fucking great. It was hard American rock and roll with a tinge of metal. And we left The Gas Works very impressed. So I bought their first record. From that point on, I was a Rods fan, and I followed their musical career for a while. We (Anvil) never got to play with them until the 2000s, when we did a gig in New Jersey – it was TT Quick, Twisted Sister and Raven. Jonny Z organized it. They were raising money for hurricane relief. I think we ended up doing some dates in Europe with them as well. And that is how I got to really know Carl. Nowadays, Carl is a really good friend of mine. He's like my drumming buddy. He's a good fucking guy. I love Carl. We have a very similar type of style, so before I knew Carl well, I figured we had the same influences. I could hear it in his drumming. There were these little intricacies that I could hear. And when we talked, I was right. He loved fucking Buddy Rich and Ginger Baker and fucking Ian Pace and Cozy Powell. We have the same fucking list."

# Brotherhood of Metal

In 2018, Olly Han approached The Rods about making an album for SPV Records. Olly Han had tried to work with us several times, and for one reason or another, it never seemed to come to fruition. SPV made us a decent offer, to which we agreed. We found Olly to be a terrific A&R person. He left us alone – he let us do our thing and he simply said, "Just make a great Rods album." But the one thing he did recommend, which was really cool, was that we modernize the *Wild Dogs* album cover. He thought that it is an iconic cover, and it would be a good time to bring that back - restyled. We loved the idea. We gave it to the artist Eric Philipe and told him that we wanted a "metallicized version of the *Wild Dogs* cover." He nailed it and I think it turned out great. David and I absolutely loved it.

For the first time since our inception, we did not have a lot of songs written. David was writing some. I was busy at the time and found it difficult to sit down with a guitar and write. I was sending him lyrics from time to time, which is how things kind of are now. Getting enough material took us a few months. I recommended we record "The Devil Made Me Do It" from David's latest solo album, *Clash of Armor*. David was a prolific songwriter and his solo albums most certainly highlighted that. There were always a few songs from each album that I felt would be prime for a Rods album. Other songs, such as the title track, "1982" and "Louder than Loud" were great anthems that celebrated the longevity of The Rods and the metal scene. After a few months of writing, we thought there were some strong songs and SPV seemed happy with the demos. I recorded my drum tracks at my home studio. David and Gary did their parts at Lonnie Parks Barncastle studio. From writing to recording, it took us about eight months to complete. SPV never put any pressure on us whatsoever.

If you have made it this far, you have probably noticed Gary is the only member who has not provided commentary. It certainly was not for lack of trying. We told him that even if it was negative, or if he wanted to say the very worst things about me, we would still publish it. We would print it - unedited. I wanted to give him the chance to voice his side. I believe that there are multiple sides to a story. But it has been radio silence from his end, and I respect that. However, it would also not be fair to leave this part out and have the fans wondering what the hell happened. This was the last album we did with Gary. He had had enough and quit shortly after the album was released. He was not vested in The Rods to the point David and

I were. And that was ok. We did not expect the same level of dedication that David and I had. But I saw it early on. It was clear his heart was not in it. I do not think David saw it. David and Gary work well together. They are amazing on stage together. There is a long history of compatibility there. And that is not easy to find. Gary is a great showman. I said he does not care about The Rods because he makes it clear he doesn't. Maybe he did at one time. It started when we had a photo shoot and Gary showed up with a brown belt, dad jeans, and a pastel blue shirt - for a heavy metal photo shoot.

David had to buy him clothes. Not that he did not have the money, but Gary was unwilling to invest. This was when we were getting back together; we were sending some emails back and forth, trying to discuss grievances and trying to air out the dirty laundry. We were trying to get to a good place. When we got back together, we kind of accepted each other for the flaws and for the past indiscretions, whatever may have happened. I think in order to progress, we had to. Overall, I thought we were in a good place. We knew Gary was not into the brand; I knew he was just plodding along. He did not even want to record *Brotherhood*. He was bitter about the business, "because the business fucked me" as he proclaimed. I pointed out to him, "Gary, there is no business to fuck you." Meaning there is no singular person doing the fucking. It is not personal. It is the business. The business fucked itself. The business ate itself. You cannot take it personally. I asked, "Why do we do this? We do it for the fans. And we do it for the music.

When you first started, you did it because you loved to play and that is it. So, you must go back - take that step back to look at the real reason we do this. Why do you play music? You play because you love it. You cannot worry about the man fucking you." But Gary did the record reluctantly, and he was truly not that into it. He made no bones about it. It went up a notch during the recording of the album. David played the intro to *Brotherhood of Metal* and it had a lot of string noise and it was not sloppy per se, but it was just not right. I am a perfectionist, like David, so I recommended we redo it. This was on an email to David and Gary - we always relayed notes that way. Then Gary replied to me only and said, "David is old, deaf and can't play any better." So I sent his response to David. Because David has done everything for Gary. He bought Gary his stage clothes. A lot of times when we did shows, if they were not paying enough for Gary to leave work, David would pay him. And I only found this out after the fact, but David would pay him out of his own pocket to make it worth Gary's while to come and play the gigs. So I said to David, "Here's your buddy. I've been telling you all along. He does not care about the band, nor does he care about you." David finally realized that maybe what I'd been saying all along was kind of true. David is a loving guy. It bothered me that Gary would talk about him like that, as David never would have said such a thing to Gary.

I will take some responsibility for the next one, which in hindsight, I wish I had handled differently. The final straw came on the song "Smoke on the Horizon". I think that was the proverbial straw that broke the camel's back. While recording, Gary was singing on "Smoke on the Horizon". Gary has a great voice – he sang on "Ace in the Hole" from our first album. He was great at backup vocals as well. So we figured we would give him this song to sing on. And while not as strong as his earlier work, we felt he did a good job on it. In my opinion, it was good, but it was not great. And when I say great, I mean it was not stylized for The Rods. It did not fit our format. So I asked David to sing it, which he did, and then we listened to both, and it was clear that David's version was the better version – it was a better fit for The Rods. Neither of us knew what to say to Gary. We knew he might be upset, so we put that conversation off. I think that was a blindside to Gary, which was certainly not nice of us, and it was certainly cowardly of us. He found out when we had it mastered. He got the copy and said, "When were you going to tell me?" Sheepishly we said sorry. That was not a proud moment for us, but it was not my song, and I did not want to be the bad guy, even though I guess I was in some way, because I recommended David sing on it. I felt it was important to the brand to maintain our format. It is like saying, "Well, they should get a better singer in Motorhead" – there are plenty of vocalists that are better than Lemmy, but it would not work for the identity of Motorhead. You could even get Bruce Dickinson for Motorhead, but it would not be Motorhead. The Rods have a specific style. As David and I jokingly say, "If it has more than three chords and takes more than five minutes to learn, it is not a song for The Rods." Gary said he had nothing more to give and wrote us a polite letter telling us he was out. I feel terrible about the incident. We gave Gary almost a year to rethink it, and Gary wrote another nice letter. "Guys, I thought about it, I reconsidered, and I just I realized that I just do not have any more to give." He declined to come back. But David would not move on, and so we lost an entire year waiting for Gary to come back, which he was never going to do. I do not think Gary will be calling me anytime soon to make his commentary, but I would love that if he did. I know David has reached out. They had a good talk, David said. But I do not think he is looking to hang with anybody.

*Brotherhood of Metal* was released in June of 2019, and it got some great reviews. We did not tour to support the album. Without Gary, David was a bit hesitant to carry on. He had spent almost four decades sharing the stage with Gary. That chemistry is not easy to replace. I felt bad about him leaving and I felt bad for David. We waited a year and a half. We lost all that time waiting for Gary to come back. David was hoping Gary would change his mind. That was almost the end of The Rods. But I convinced David to at least try someone else out. If we wanted to continue, to do another album, that was our only option. I do not think either of us were prepared to throw in the towel. We had kept the machine running all of these years and we both felt we had plenty left to give. We both knew a local player named Freddy Villano. He had played on one of David's solo albums, so I knew David was comfortable with him. I had met him previously as well and I found him to be a genuinely great guy. We agreed to give him a shot. Initially, David was hesitant, but once we got Freddy in the band and we got a gig under our belts, it was clear that Freddy is a great addition.

Speaking of "brotherhood," I want to say a bit about David. It is not easy to find people that you can work closely with, create music with and still maintain a friendship with. For almost half of a century, David and I have had a true brotherhood. I still look up to David. I consider him a brother, a friend, and a partner, and I am thankful for him in every way possible. I firmly recall the many times I saw Elf play live. As mentioned, David was the guitarist for Elf. I used to see them regularly. They were amazing. They were massive. Elf was so big at the time; it was like going to a full-fledged concert. They were truly legendary. Even though (at that time), they were mostly a cover band, they were the biggest thing in the area. Initially, I did not really know the guys in Elf well. I knew them from the circuit, but we never talked with them much or hung out. But David knew of me, and obviously, I knew of David. So when David (and Joey DeMaio) invited me to join forces that day in 1979, my life forever changed.

While it did not work out with Manowar, David and I realized there was something special between the two of us. We worked well together. We wanted the same things musically. David and I just hit it off. After all these years, despite any disagreements, we never really argued or fought. I have always admired him. David is quite an interesting fellow. He has many talents outside of music. He was an avid outdoorsman in the early years. David built a cabin - by hand and by himself. All with trees that he cut down and processed by hand. That is not an easy task. I remember, close to our rehearsal hall, there was this small diner. David and I used to go there constantly after practice. David, at the time, had long, blown-out hair. And these old guys would come and sit with us. They would come and sit down and ask David for advice on fly fishing, trapping or hunting. They would ask him all these questions about tactics and ideal locations. These older fellas were meat-and-potatoes country boys. Real outdoorsmen. Yet they were turning to the young long-haired rocker for advice. We are talking 1979 or 1980, and when you are in the country, it is often, "That long hair shit doesn't go here, boy." You would think they would be giving somebody with long hair shit about it or dismissing them as a long-haired hippie. Instead, they showed him respect, asked questions, and sought his sage wisdom. David has that effect on people.

David and I share the same vision and we have worked hard to maintain that vision. I have nothing but respect for him. There are a lot of things that I admire him for. He has been a great bandmate all these years. And even to this day, we still work very well together. I cannot speak for him, but I believe and hope he sees that as well. Sure, we have disagreements. That is human nature. Have we been upset with each other at times? Certainly. But we see the big picture. Usually, we compromise. We both find the middle ground and one of us will defer to the other one. We usually work it out well. Musically, we are in sync, and I think we both realize what each other's strengths are. We have our roles that we have settled into over the years – it works for us and for The Rods. I trust him, he trusts me. I think that is the other thing - that we both have a common goal about the image and direction of the band and what the band should be. We live an hour and 15 minutes apart, so it is not as easy at times. I consider him a friend, and I believe he considers me a friend. We are also bandmates, but even without the band, we stayed in touch. Even when we were on hiatus, we were talking to each other. I am lucky to have met David on that fateful day in 1978. It has been a great ride and I am proud to call him a bandmate and friend.

**Freddy Villano:** *Widowmaker, The Rods*
*"My wife and I moved to upstate New York. I was what's called a 'trailing spouse.' It took me another year or two to fully extract myself from New York City. But I got up here and then started playing around with a lot of musicians from the area, some who are well known within certain circles outside of the local scene. Through that scene, I got to know Carl and Dave. I got to know Gary Bordonaro. I actually ended up interviewing Gary for a local magazine I wrote for. I interviewed Gary for that, and we became friends. Dave and I met through a mutual drummer friend who had played on a lot of Dave's solo records. Dave was doing another solo record, so I ended up playing on his album through that connection, which Carl ended up playing on as well. And then Carl and I did some gigs with another mutual friend of ours, and so everything seemed to kind of coalesce into this moment when Gary decided he wanted to retire. I had already made a record with Dave, I had already played live with Carl, and I was friends with Gary, so I kind of had his blessing as well. And so when Gary decided to retire from The Rods, there was already a comfort factor built in. It's just amazing to me how it has come full circle from that first concert when I was in 7th grade, watching The Rods, to actually being in the band. We have a*

*new Rods T shirt (with a logo on it that was taken off our backdrop) and I was putting it on one night to wear on stage. I asked my wife, 'How does this look?' And she said, 'Aren't those shirts for the fans?' I said, 'Well, I am a fan. I just ended up on the stage.' My first encounter with Carl involved communicating more through music than words. We hit it off instantly. We are working on a new Rods album, and I am probably biased because I am playing on it, but I am really pleased with how it sounds so far. The most surprising aspect is how inspired it sounds. We are recording remotely but it sounds like someone happened to capture a really fierce performance of the band playing together. That is an accomplishment I am really proud of."*

# Canedy: Warrior

Throughout the 2000s, I played with The Jeffery James Band as a way to keep my chops up. We played everything from soul to dance to rock. It was an extremely active band and there were always a lot of gigs. It definitely helped keep me from getting rusty. One of the guys in the band was a bass player by the name of Tony Garuba. Tony was in a band which had a heavy local following in the '90s by the name of Totally Lost Cause (TLC for short). They were contacted by Heaven and Hell Records, who wanted to rerelease their album. For promotion, they were scheduled to play a local TV show. They had been rehearsing with their drummer, but their drummer could not get off work and therefore could not make the appearance - and so they desperately needed a drummer. So they asked me if I would fill in for the TV show. It went very well, and it was a lot of fun. The drummer, due to his job, could not continue with the band, so at that point they approached me about working on some original material.

The guys were total pros and I quickly agreed. Charlie Russello, the guitarist, is absolutely amazing. Tony, of course, is a great bass player. And the singer, Michael Santarsiero, had a killer voice. They were all very talented. And that is how we started this project – what would eventually be the second release under 'Canedy'. We started writing material right away. This was not meant to be under Canedy. The intention was a side project, which we did not have a name for. We spent a couple of years writing. We would get together once a week and work on stuff, so it did not go fast at all. I am sure it was very frustrating for some of the guys, but it progressed, and all was going well. As we got closer to having a full album's worth of material, we figured it would make more sense to name the project something slightly marketable. That is when we decided to use Canedy. While that is the name of my solo effort, this was not a true solo album. This was a group effort. It was a band album. The other three had worked together for so many years that they were a tight unit. They were a well-oiled machine. So I tried to stay out of the mix until I had something to offer. Usually, Tony would bring in some lyrics and a bass line as a skeleton idea. He would bring in some clever stuff. Charlie would build a riff around it. And then Tony would work with Mike on a vocal idea, and I'd work on a groove. I knew Charlie was a great guitarist, but I did not know he was a shredder - which I discovered as time went on. More and more, I learned how talented he was by watching him orchestrate his guitar parts. Tony and Charlie are very tight, and they work so well together musically. Overall, it was a great experience working with them.

Getting the album recorded and mixed was no easy task. It took a couple of years. We all had careers and families, so we were rehearsing one day a week. And a lot of times, with the crappy Northeast weather, there would be many weeks when we could not get together. So it took a lot of time. Despite schedules and inclement weather, we were able to finish the record. I thought it came out extremely well. It was released by Sleazy Rider records. But of course, this was during Covid, and they really dropped the ball on promotion. We hired Chipster PR to run promotions for us, and they did a great job. But that was it. We got some killer reviews on the album. Overall, it was a lot of fun. We did a few gigs together. I always wanted to continue with those guys, but at this point it doesn't look like it is going to happen. Never say never though - it is always possible. We did four new songs and came up with a demo, which resulted in an offer from a label, but it was not much money, so we passed on it. At this point, it is a one off. But I am proud of that album, and I had a blast playing with Mike, Charlie and Tony. They are all super talented and genuinely good guys.

**Tony Garuba**; *Totally Lost Cause, Canedy*

"I auditioned for a seven-piece horn band, and the guy on the drums, his name was Carl. So, I auditioned, and I got the gig. I played with Carl in that wedding band for about ten years! We were doing a lot of resort gigs because they were the only ones that were open during the pandemic. And it was kind of weird playing for 40 or 50 people, but it is what it was. We were used to playing for hundreds. I think Carl was ready to step away from it – he was just doing it for the love of playing. I cannot speak for him, but it just seemed like that to me. Carl eventually left, and Canedy was formed almost by accident. I was in a band called TLC, and we had a reunion, and it went really well. And then we were asked to do a TV spot on an afternoon show, and the drummer suddenly had to work. So, I immediately thought of Carl because I was playing with him at the time. This is like seven years ago. And I gave him the two songs that we had to play. They were on one of our CDs. He came to the TV studio, and he knocked it out of the park. And the next time we were supposed to have TLC rehearsal, the drummer was sort of not into it. And I said, look, why don't we hook up with Carl? He had an album out. The first album was a bunch of different musicians. I said this album would be more cohesive. It would be us guys as a band and myself and the guitar player and the singer we all write, so it did not put so much pressure on Carl, because Carl writes a lot with The Rods, so he really did not have to shoulder that burden.

*"Playing with Carl has definitely made me more professional - or maybe just more attentive to detail. Carl really focuses on details and that helps, especially when you are with a live band. Recording is a whole different animal. You get to go back and pick your spots, but live, you must be on point. And playing with Carl has helped us. And I know I could speak for my guitarist that Carl has also helped him - because he mentioned that to me. That playing with Carl and Carl's attention to detail has made him play a lot tighter. Carl did not write much of the music, but he wrote all the drum parts, and that was sort of what we wanted. Like I said to him, 'Carl, you're a great drummer. Write great drum parts. Do not worry about the riffs.' I mean, the guitarist in our band is a GIT (now the 'Musicians Institute') graduate, and he has written two books. Our guitarist is a master musician. And I've always written, and Mike, our singer, has always written. Carl lent his recommendations, 'Hey, maybe we should do this twice.' We jammed a lot. Then a lot of times I would go up to Charlie's house and we would pick up on what we had jammed with Carl and Mike. And then we'd write some more and then we'd come down to the next rehearsal and let them hear it. I'd write some lyrics for Mike because I'm sort of the go-between. I write lyrics and music and Mike writes lyrics and Charlie writes music. So, I'm right in the middle. And so I'm doing a little of everything. Carl is the only drummer I've ever played with in my life that I could say it is not a chore. I think Carl really enjoys playing."*

**Mike Santarsiero:** *Totally Lost Cause/TLC, Canedy*

"Tony had been playing in a cover band – a party band that Carl played in as well. And when TLC decided to get back together, our drummer wasn't able to make the practice commitments. So we decided to move on. For Tony and Charlie, the obvious pick was Carl. I didn't know a whole lot about Carl, and I felt bad with Kevin's departure, but given the choices, I'd rather play and write music than not play and write music, so I went along for the ride - and my relationship with Carl, I feel, has probably been one of the more important ones and one of the more rewarding relationships I've had. When it came to writing and to the material for the Canedy album, it was a great experience. Charlie and Tony would get together. Charlie and Tony had been working together fairly steadily after TLC, after I left in 1996. Tony and Charlie are the primary riff writers of the group, and then Tony would have an idea for a song, what he thought the song should be about, and then I would say I was the primary lyricist. After we released our album, we didn't tour because of Covid, and then I got Covid. And when I got over it, I could not sing three notes. That was it. I thought I would never sing again. I thought it was over. But I had a 45-minute ride home from work every day in the car, so I would put on Journey and practice. We *didn't play for 15 months. The last eight months of those 15 months was me trying to get my voice back. So, I learned how to sing all over again on those rides home in the car, and I actually expanded my vocal range. Now my vocal range is now actually a couple notes higher than it was prior to Covid. I lost one or two notes on the lower end, but I picked up a couple notes on the higher – it was really strange."*

## Wild Dogs: 40 Years On

It was August 1981, and we were preparing to go into the studio and record what would later become *Wild Dogs*. To work out some of the new material, we were playing some dates with Foghat. It was around this time that I started having some strange premonitions. We would be in a restaurant, or in the dressing room post show, and everything would be fine. In fact, everything was great. We had a major label recording contract, and we were getting ready to go to England to record our second album. Life was good. But increasingly, something disagreeable would hit me – and it would hit rather suddenly. Out of nowhere, and quite instantaneously, I would get a sudden and severe chill. I would get extremely cold. And from nowhere this overwhelming feeling of doom and darkness would strike me. It was eerie. It was bizarre - and it was very scary. It was in those moments that I felt I was going to die before the album was done. It was not an anxiety attack. This was completely different. This feeling of death would come over me. And it did not happen once. It happened repeatedly.

We liked to goof on each other, so it became a joke with the band. They would laugh and say, "Don't worry - if you die, we'll take credit for all of your songs." That became a running joke with the guys. But it kept happening, week after week, month after month. In January, we were getting ready to go to England to record. We were getting some last-minute things together, rehearsing, and compiling equipment – we were set to ship off in less than two weeks. It was then that my cousin Anne called me. She said, "Carl, your mother's been diagnosed with lung cancer. She has a very short period to live." Of course, that was devastating to me. Here I am, soon to leave for England to record an album and then go on tour with Iron Maiden. It was everything we had been working towards. After years of paying our dues, we were finally seeing the fruits of our labor. But I was devastated. So I moved Mom out of her apartment in Elmira. I rented a house in Ithaca, and we moved Mom there. I was with her for a couple of weeks before I had to leave. The day I left, she was in the window waving to me as I got into the car. Because it had spread to her brain, one eye was closed. That parting view was the most heartbreaking experience of my life. But she was strong, and she was very kind, and she insisted that I go. I think she knew that she was not going to live long enough for me to get back - which was not what the doctors were telling her or me. Everyone said, "It is fine. Go, it will be fine. She will be here when you get back." And I was a fool. I should have realized that she would not be.

In 2022, some fans posted a "Wild Dogs 40th Anniversary" article celebrating 40 years since the debut of *Wild Dogs* - which was released on February 27th, 1982. I saw it and I did not think anything of it. And then it hit me – February 27th, 1982, is the day my mother passed. That blew me away. 40 years later, I figured it out. The premonition of "I'm going to die before the album is completed" was not about me – it was about my mother. She died the very day the album was released. Because I was on a plane on that day, and rushing to see Mom before she passed, I had no clue about the album release specifics. At the time, I would never concern myself with the release date of an album. It was not like it is now. Now you have a lead up, and you have pre-orders, and you have a release date that's posted everywhere and so on. In 1982, there was none of that. It just came out. After 40 years it hit me. Strange coincidence?

# Surprise!

As a young child, some of my extended family members treated me differently than the other kids. Some of them even went out of the way to do so. My cousin Gerard, who was a year or so older, was my idol. I followed him around constantly. His sister Rita clearly did not care for me. She would always call me a moron and repeatedly told me to "go back to Grandma's house." She made me feel like I was stupid and inferior, and that stuck with me for decades. That was something I have always had to shake off. Even though I know I am far from stupid, her remarks planted a seed in my young brain.

When I was four and a half, I was with Mom at my grandmother's house, and my Aunt Sophie and Uncle Al had stopped by to visit. I was standing with my mother when Aunt Sophie and Uncle Al were ready to leave. They were all so tall, which makes sense as I was quite small. They were saying goodbye when suddenly my Aunt Sophie looked down at me and said, in what seemed like a very stern voice, "You behave for your mother!" I was shocked. It seemed as if I had done something wrong. I didn't think I had, as I was just standing there with my mother. It really hurt me that she would scold me like that. What had I done wrong? What was wrong with me? What was I missing? Her words stung and stuck with me for many, many years. There was a feeling of 'something is wrong with this picture.' Many decades later, I would come to understand why people were so protective of my mother. I would also learn why they didn't want me to be a burden to her (more than they felt I already was). As I grew older, I realized that Aunt Sophie was a sweet lady. She and my Uncle Al were the 'eternally in love' couple. The lesson here is that children are vulnerable, and what you might consider good advice might actually be scarring to a child. It certainly was for me.

Even at that age, I noticed I was being treated differently and I really took it personally. Right before Mom passed, she asked me to make peace with the family. Which I did, but it was not easy.

More than 60 years later, it would all make sense.

In Elmira, during the '50s and '60s, Yunis was a big name in our somewhat small community. Tuffee Yunis owned and ran Yunis Realty with his brother. Yunis Realty seemed to own everything in Elmira in the '60s and '70s. They owned a great deal of important real estate, mainly business and commercial properties. Tuffee was somewhat of a local celebrity. He had been, at one time or another, president of the March of Dimes, the Jaycees, Elmira Heights Rotary Club, was on the Boy Scouts of America Sullivan Trail Council, and he was frequently the winner of some prestigious local award. But I had never met Tuffee or anyone from the Yunis family. The Yunis family was affluent. We were poor and we were from the other side of the tracks. I was a rock and roll guy, and I hung out with a different, less-affluent crowd.

    When I turned 66, as a birthday present, my daughter gave me a kit from Ancestory.com. Which I thought was a very cool present. I really did not know much about my ancestry beyond my mother's parents, who were Italian. I was excited to get back the results, but I really did not give it much thought. I read the directions, spit in the tube, and then sent if off in the mail. It came back a few weeks later. Well, the results were not what I expected. My mother was Italian, and my father, Lawrence Canedy, was Irish and Scottish, so that is what I assumed my heritage was, and that is what I had expected to come back. But that is not what came back. What came back insisted I was primarily Middle Eastern with a small amount of Italian ancestry. So I was really confused. I was like, "Okay, well, people can live in Italy and are considered Italians, but maybe their ancestry is not Italian." And that was my thought - that my mom's side had deep ties to the Middle East and had at one point emigrated to Italy. So I kind of blew it off.

    Not long after, I was contacted by someone by the name of Amy Yunis. Amy asked me if I knew of a 'Tuffee Yunis' - which I thought was a hysterical name. I told her I did not know him. Amy proceeded to tell me that, according to her ancestry report, we were a very close match. She did not say at what level, she only said "close". I assumed we were distant cousins. She kept insisting, in a rather kind manner, that we were close. She was very pleasant, but I thought it was a strange conversation and I dismissed it once it was through. But shortly after that I received an even stranger call from a gentleman by the name of Frank. Frank, who seemed like a great guy, came right out and said, "I know it is probably a shock to you, but it turns out that we are half-brothers!" He then told me that we both share the same biological father: Tuffee Yunis. "There is no way," I thought. My mother never dated. She was not the type. My mother lived a very quiet life when it came to dating. I had a father – who I had known. How could it be? Frank then told me that I had another half-brother named Brad. He told me the three of us were fathered by Tuffee pretty much around the same time. Frank was just a few months older than me. Brad was three years younger. This was very strange. I did not believe it. I begin to think that maybe Ancestory.com had messed up and sent me the wrong results. I kind of laughed it off. There is no possible way, right? But I did some more research. Frank had the same thought initially, and he had done some research as well. Well... it was true. It turns out that Tuffee had a family prior to Brad and Frank, and he had two children with that family. Then he remarried and had five children in his second marriage.

So, Brad, Frank and I were fathered while Tuffee was in his second marriage. He fathered ten children that we know of, but he did not have anything to do with Brad, Frank, or myself. None of us knew until we were in our 60s. Once I started researching, I found that my mother may have met him when she was managing a grocery store. At one point, my mother was going to purchase a store. And I remember this because I was 12 or so, and Mom was trying to take on this small grocery store. And then something happened and suddenly the deal was off. It turns out Tuffee and his brother had this huge falling out. It was actually reported in the paper. It was a huge fight – a physical fight. Because Mom was going to have a store, she obviously was in touch with Tuffee, who owned the retail space. But I had no knowledge of this growing up. Nothing at all. The further I investigated, the more the dots began to connect. By this point, everyone with answers had passed away - my mother, my father, and Tuffee (who passed away in 2001). Now, my cousin Peggy is ten years older than me, so I thought she might know something. I asked her if she knew anything about Tuffee Yunis, and she said, "I told my mother that if you ever asked me about Tuffee, I would tell you." She said, "Yes, I will tell you." She said that before her mother died, her mom told her that Tuffee was indeed my real father and that Lawrence, who was not my biological father, had adopted me and was raising me as his own. Tuffee Yunis was my real father!

Hearing that, a vast range of emotions flowed through me. Keep in mind I was 66. This was indeed a shock. And then I began to get a bit upset. In my youth, we struggled immensely. We never had money. Meanwhile, Tuffee was quite well off. I thought of my mom having to put a drum set on a payment plan. Of having to wear hand me downs. Of being teased because of my old clothes. Why did Tuffee not try to see Brad, Frank and me? Why did he not contribute financially at the very least? My brother Frank was an attorney, and quite sadly passed away as this book was nearing completion. Since the discovery, Frank and I had become very close, speaking multiple times a week. He will be missed. My other half-brother, Brad, is an accountant, and we speak from time to time. I do email with Amy on occasion. I'm sure it was a big shock to Tuffee's five children from his second marriage. Imagine finding out your father had sired multiple children with multiple women – two of them within a year - and then ignored them for the entirety of his life.

I thought about my father, Lawrence, and I realized that he was the one person in my youth who talked to me like a person, who looked me in the eyes and who seemed to value me as a person and seemed to care about my opinions. He never yelled at me, and he never spanked me. He took me on vacation. He was truly a great father. After finding out about Tuffee, I appreciated Lawrence even more. Here was this kid, who was not his blood, was not really his, and he treated me exactly like I was his. It made me realize how lucky I was to have him in my life. Now, I have a greater and deeper love and respect for him. At 66, finding out you had a different father sends you into this tailspin and you really begin to reevaluate your life. I questioned everything. And of course, once everything fell into place, I realized that's why I was treated so poorly by the rest of the family. Clearly, I was the bastard child, and many family members treated me as such. And I hated them for that – some of them were terrible to me. I now understand why, before my mother died, she begged me to make peace with the rest of the family. So one by one I went back and made peace with them, but it was not good.

**Frank:** *Brother*
*"I was adopted when I was a baby. Once I was an adult, my mother gave me my order of adoption, which had my birth name on it: John Joseph Cooper. It said "Elmira" on it. I had no idea where the hell that was, but I knew it was somewhere in upstate New York. I wanted to find out who my birth parents were for many reasons. After some inquiring, we got a letter from a New York family giving me all this information, but it did not identify who my father was. I only knew that my father worked in a supermarket. My birth mother was a social worker – a college graduate. After some investigating, it turns out she worked for the supermarket and there she met Tuffee Yunis. He had asked her to marry him. And then she told him that she's pregnant, and he told her that he is already married. And that was the last time she spoke to him. I was born in August 1952. Carl was born in January 1953. So, it is like a six-month difference. My son accessed a lot of stuff on the Internet through Ancestry.com and discovered a lot. There's another brother, Brad. I knew I was adopted. I knew I was a little different than my adopted parents. Carl and Brad were very upset because they never knew this. People treated them differently growing up. And it's a horrible thing.*

*"My mother did the best she could under the circumstances. Brad's mother did the best she could under the circumstances. Carl's mother did the best she could. It was not easy back then. We have a lot to be thankful for. We all have great kids. We each have one kid, and they're very successful, healthy, and lovely kids. So, on the one hand, we had parents*

that cared for us and we were able to have children. And I'm lucky. Carl's lucky, and he has a great talent and he's a really great guy, and I just want to hug him. I was the big family secret. I was 55, 56 when I found this out. I did not know about Carl and Brad until 10 or 11 years later. I went to the Yunis family first. I said, 'Listen, I'm coming upstate (which I didn't do that often). We're going to have lunch someplace; would you like to have lunch with us?' And John (Yunis) said, 'Well, not really.' So that was a little heartbreaking. I just wanted to find out what my father was like. Amy Yunis gave us a lot of information, however. Brad was the only one that knew Tuffee – but only a little bit. When he was young, he used to go to the supermarket with his mom and he would see him there. But he never knew that was his father. When his mom passed away, Brad told me he found a bunch of clippings about Tuffee with her personal items. And that is when someone mentioned to him that Tuffee was his father. So he did the DNA. That's what I was told. And it is a crazy situation for all of us – even the children from his marriage - it's not an easy thing to accept. This is a random set of events, and I guess it worked out well for all of us and our children. But it is something that you can feel. And I feel for both Brad and Carl, but especially Carl. The Irish family had nothing to do with him, and the Italians were not too nice to him. What did he do to deserve that? It was not his fault. You know what? He came through it really well, and he raised a beautiful daughter, and she has a lovely husband, so it worked out in the end. It's not something you're going to dwell on every day, but at times there's that poignant feeling, that if I had known about my brother, we could have got together when we were kids or teenagers or in our 20s or 30s. I missed all of that. Wow. I'm sure it had to be hard for Tuffee's other kids as well. Because imagine finding out that your father cheated on your mom not once, but three times? But I am glad to know Carl and we speak a lot. He is a great person, and I am proud to have him as my brother."

## Epilogue: Dear Diary; Seven Decades On

I turned 70 this year and it has been an interesting time to reflect. I recently produced a Christmas song for Adam and the Metal Hawks. It was one of the best sessions I have ever done. It was fun, it went quickly, and the guys were great to work with. I have many projects in the works. As I write this, the new Kelakos album is finally done, and we have titled it *Hurtling Towards Extinction*. It has a picture of us when we first got together, in front of the *Mayflower* in Massachusetts. Eric Philippe designed the cover. I am really proud of that album. It's a fun throwback to 1970s R&B funk. I am really proud of my style of drumming on that album, and it will see the light of day in December of 2023 on Deko Records. The new Rods album, *Rattle the Cage*, is in the works as well – and that will come out early 2024 on Massacre Records. Massacre released the title track in advance, and it has received some amazing responses. Overall, they have been some of the best responses The Rods have ever received. I also have a project going with John Hahn, Mike Santosiero (from Canedy) and hopefully Billy Sheehan. At this moment, we have completed seven songs, and they sound great! Tink Bennett just covered one of my original songs, "Southern Lady". It's on his album *Collaborations*.

At age 70, I find myself booking dates in Europe. The Rods have several dates booked in Europe, Australia and the States. And best of all, Madison Alexandra Hunter, my first grandchild, will be here before Christmas! I am in love with her already.

I have so much to be thankful for and so much to look forward to. So, 70 years on looks pretty good. I really can't complain about much. I reflect on things quite a bit. I'm grateful for the many people I have met in my life and for the many that I still consider friends. I love them all. It has been a wonderful ride. If it ends tomorrow, I will have no regrets. I'm still playing my drums. I still love playing my drums as much as I ever did. I can't say enough how thrilled I am to meet Madison Alexandra Hunter. Having my first grandchild is probably the greatest accomplishment – besides my daughter, Erin Alexandra Canedy. I want to thank Phillip "Doc" Harrington for helping me make this book a reality. He helped me to stay true to my story. God bless him for listening to my many hours of droning and repetitive babble while transcribing tirelessly. And an extra special thanks to Martin Popoff, Sarah Healey, and all of the friends and family members who provided commentary, photos, and support for this project.

Carl Canedy 2024

***Images above:*** *(L) The neighborhood kids. I am far left. Karen, my first friend, is next to me. (R) Me, somewhere around 3 years old.*

***Images above:*** *(L) Mom and me with my very first radio. (R) Dad and me.*

***Image above:*** *With Wadsworth Anthium. This was in the backyard at Jim Nunis' house. My cousin now lives in this house, so this is an iconic location for me.*

***Images above:*** *(L) With Wadsworth Anthium. (R) Lake Street, Elmira – I was 16 years old, and this room was my sanctuary.*

***Images above:*** *(L) This was during my first and last mescaline trip. (R) In NYC, high school years.*

***Images above:*** *(L) L-R; Myself, Peter Morticelli, David "Rock" Feinstein, and Gary Bordonaro, in front of the Shakespeare house. Unfortunately, he was not home at the time for us to get a picture with him. (R) The Rods with Sherry Cosmo*

***Image above:*** *The Rods backstage with Ritchie Blackmore*

***Image above:*** *Wild Dogs tour, circa 1982. Photo by David Plastik.*

***Image above:*** *In England for the recording of Wild Dogs. From the archives of Peter Morticelli*

*Image above:* (L)The Rods with Victoria Calandra (between David and me. (R) With Scott Ian (Anthrax) and Sherry Cosmo, sometime in the mid-80s.

*Images above:* (L) At the Breaking Sound Festival, 1984. (R) With James Hetfield of Metallica. .Photos by Joesph Carlucci.

*Images above:* (L) With Lars Ulrich of Metallica. (R) Breaking Sound Festival, 1984. Photos by Joseph Carlucci.

*Images Above:* (L)Arista Records promo shot. (R) L-R; Mike Lembo, Myself, Peter Morticelli, Gary Bordonaro, Warren Schatz, David "Rock" Feinstein and Tommy Nast.

*Image Above:* (L-R) Joey Belladonna, Tony Incigeri, myself, Dan Spitz, Jonny Zazula and Marsha Zazula, circa 1986.

*Images Above:* (L) Backstage at the Marquis. (R) England with David. Photos by Peter Morticelli

*Image above:* Combat Records signing. Pictured from L-R: Michael Toorock, Barry Kobrin, Alan White, The Rods and Walter O'Brien

*Image above:* With Alex Perialis and Attila at Pyramid Sound, circa 1986.

*Image above:* Jack Starr (Far Right) with Rhett Forrester (2nd Right), Myself and two female fans. Photo by Joseph Carlucci.

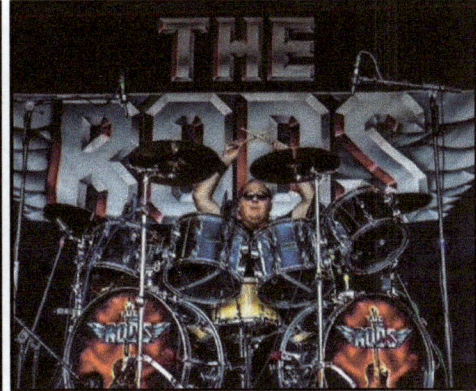

**Images Above:** *The Rods; Vengeance Promo Shot and Tour*

**Image Above:** *with my daughter, Erin, and Lips (Anvil). Photo by Brian Reavy.*

**Image Above:** *with the legendary Jonny Zazula.*

***Image Above:*** *(L) Rose Hall Live (R) The home office; my current sanctuary.*

***Image Above:*** *The Rods; David, Myself and Freddie.*

***Images Above:*** *Rock Until You Drop*

***Images Above:*** *With Alex Perialis; (L) Sometime in the mid-80s. (R) Revisiting in 2023.*

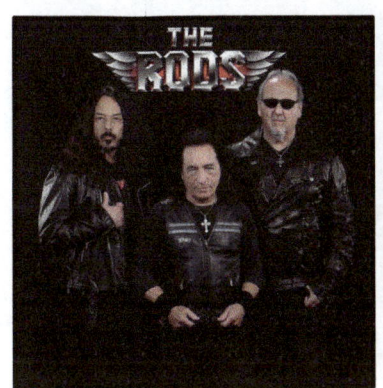

***Image Above:*** *(L) The Rods; Freddie, David, and myself. (R) David and I in the studio.*

***Images Above:*** *(L) 70 years on. (R) The Rods in 2023, still going strong! Photos by Jim Polkowski.*